AF505460

Liz Larner

*Don't put it
back like it was*

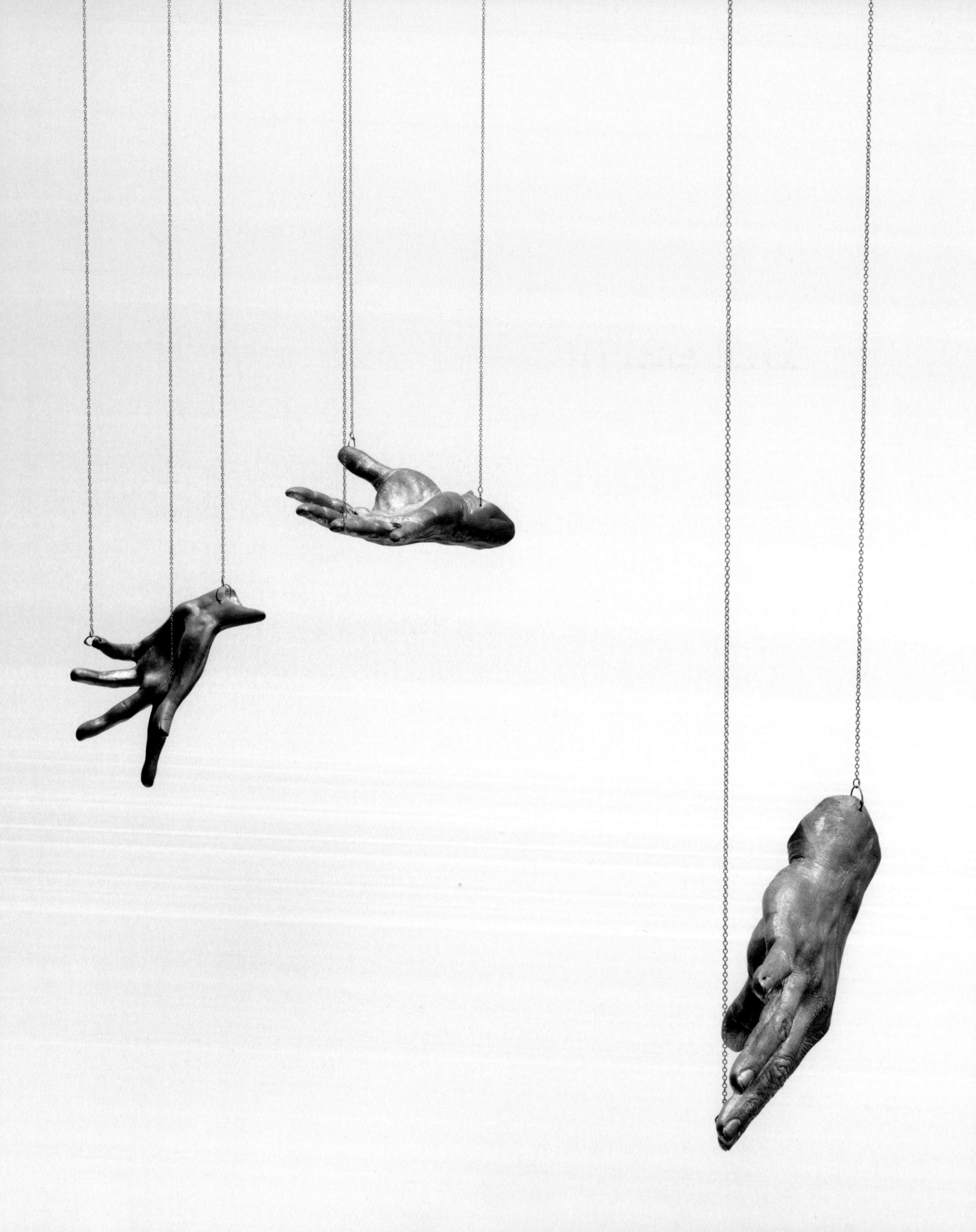

Liz Larner

Don't put it back like it was

SculptureCenter, New York

Walker Art Center, Minneapolis

Dancing Foxes Press, Brooklyn, New York

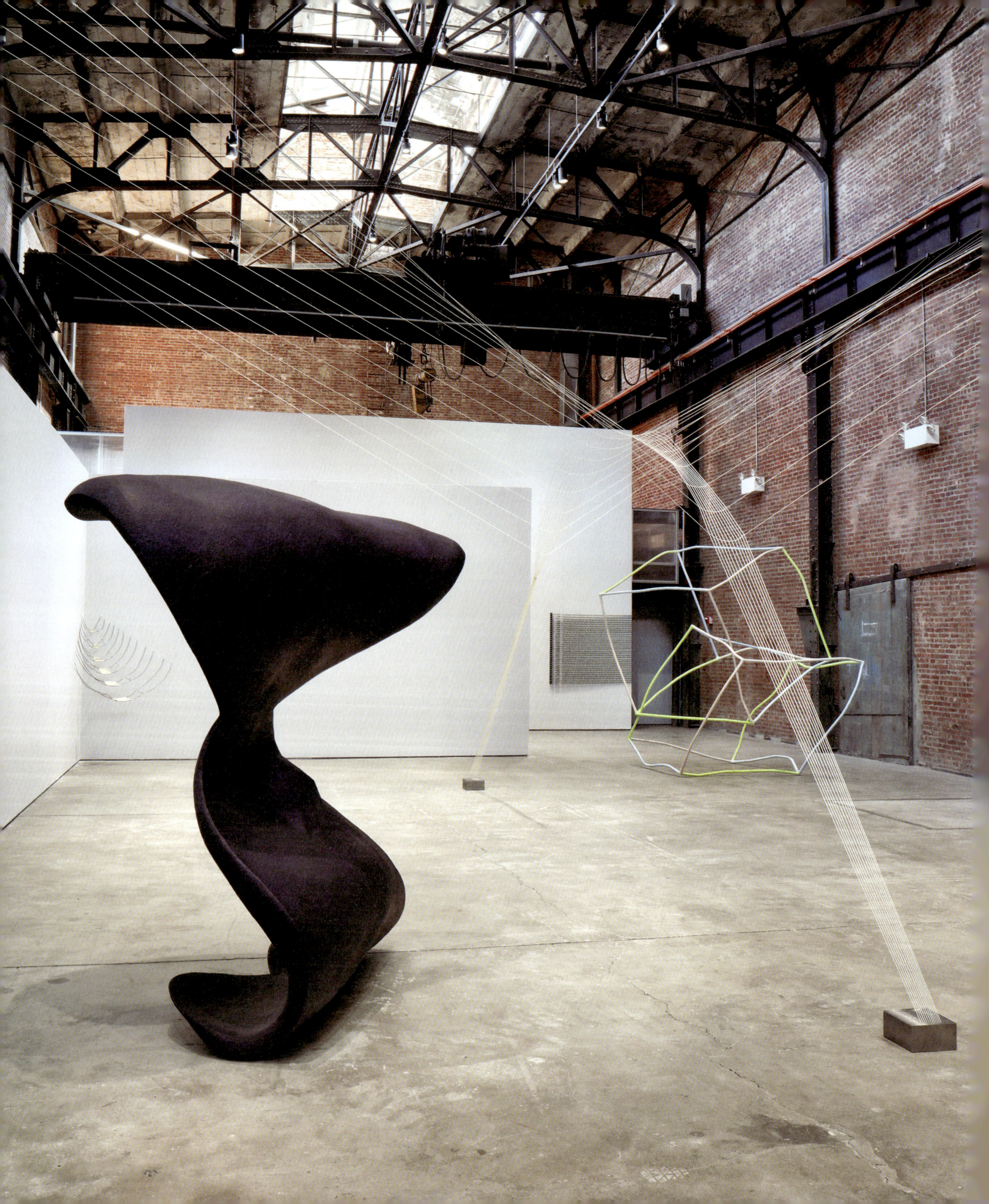

Contents

Foreword

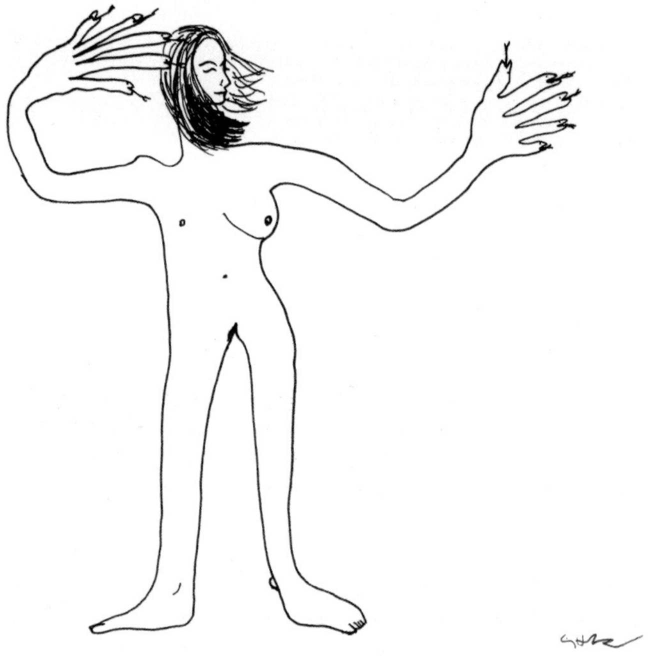

She Found Her Fingers on the Shores of the Lake of the Triple Goddess, 2020.
Ink on paper, 8 × 9 ³/₄ inches (20.3 × 24.8 cm)

Artworks often come with installation manuals, strict guidance from museum registrars, and conditions of supervision to see that they are correctly and safely installed. These metatexts ensure that a sculpture, for example, is exhibited consistently as it travels to venues around the world and as time moves away from the moment when it was first made. The typical directive is "put it back like it was."

Liz Larner's instruction to do the opposite (as codified in the title of this exhibition) requires us to shed our reliance on some of the frames and characterizations that have enshrined her expansive body of work within various trajectories of postwar sculpture—the long shadow of Minimalism, the endless "post" of Postminimalism, and the history of art making in Los Angeles, where the artist has worked for decades. Equally important, the title of the exhibition suggests that perhaps "the way it was" wasn't necessarily the best or only way. Larner acknowledges that we are not the same: our perspectives, our spaces, our societies are not the same, and our positions (and positionality) in space and time have everything to do with meaning.

Don't put it back like it was, Larner's largest survey exhibition since 2001, installs a selection of strikingly dissimilar works produced between 1987 and 2021, revealing the through lines of a larger sculptural project by putting things back together differently. Importantly, the exhibition repositions Larner's enduring formal and material concerns alongside her relationship to a rigorously developed feminist sculptural position. It offers an opportunity to view her work within today's expanded discourses around gender, embodiment, and posthumanism and to recalibrate our assessments of her hard-core disciplinary concerns with material, color, illusion, and installation. Larner affirms that sculpture's formal and material properties can extend our intimate, bodily understandings of the dynamics of power and perception that govern our larger social and political lives.

The works in the exhibition have been brought together from locations around the world. We want to extend our sincere gratitude to all of the lenders who have cared for these works over time and are sharing them with us now.

SculptureCenter is grateful to our board of trustees for its unflagging support of our mission. We thank the Girlfriend Fund, The Deborah Buck Foundation, Sarah Miller Meigs, and the Henry Moore Foundation for their generous leadership support, which made Liz Larner's exhibition in New York possible. We are grateful to those who provide leadership support for SculptureCenter's exhibitions and programs: Carol Bove, Jill and Peter Kraus, the Pollock-Krasner Foundation, Lee Elliott and Robert K. Elliott, Eleanor Heyman Propp, Jacques Louis Vidal, Miyoung Lee and Neil Simpkins, Robert Soros and Jamie Singer Soros, and Jane Hait and Justin Beal.

Allison Derusha, SculptureCenter's former director of advancement, and Joni Todd, its director of finance and administration, were instrumental in realizing this exhibition in New York. Christopher Aque, exhibition and program manager, and Kiersten Lukason, head installer, expertly organized and coordinated the exhibition's presentation at SculptureCenter. SculptureCenter's entire staff should be recognized for their important contributions to this and all SculptureCenter projects: Caitlin Furlong and Cheryl Chan of our advancement team; Olivia Harrison, Tucker Claxton, Ava Ferguson, Bella Masterson, Maddy Sinnock, and Molly Wasielewski of visitor services; and Danny Crump, whose efforts ensure that our facilities can meet the challenges of our most ambitious exhibition projects.

Many at the Walker Art Center have helped to realize this beautiful exhibition. Of special note, Siri Engberg, senior curator of visual arts, took the lead in coordinating the Walker's presentation, with immensely valuable assistance from Erin McNeil, program manager of curatorial affairs. They worked closely with the unflappable and keenly organized Jessica Rolland, senior associate registrar; Doc Czypinski, associate director of exhibition installation; and Jonathan Karen, lead technician, heading up our exhibition-installation team to plan for and install the diverse body of work in the show. We are also grateful to Sarah Lampen, manager of lifelong learning and accessibility, who worked with the artist and the team to identify ways to make the exhibition accessible to all. Many thanks also to our development team, who ensured we have the resources to realize this wonderful project; our content and communications department, which helps us connect the brilliant work to the lived experiences of our audiences; and to our visitor-experience team, which facilitated our audiences' meaningful interactions with the exhibition. Naomi Crocker, executive assistant, kept all aspects of the project moving and coordinated the project from the director's office.

We also offer our deepest thanks to the key funders who have provided generous financial support of the Walker's presentation of *Liz Larner: Don't put it back like it was*. We are grateful to Walker trustee Carlo Bronzini Vender; trustee John Christakos and his wife, Deborah; Sonia Regina De Alvares Otero Fernandes; trustee Donna Pohlad and her husband, Jim; Danniel Rangel; and trustee Susan White, and her husband Rob.

Together, we thank Galerie Max Hetzler, Berlin | Paris | London; The Modern Institute, Glasgow, Scotland; Regen Projects, Los Angeles; and the Girlfriend Fund, without which the production of this publication would not have been possible. Thank you to Karen Kelly and Barbara Schroeder of Dancing Foxes Press for their stewardship of this beautiful publication; to Lorraine Wild and Amy Fortunato for their expert design work; and to Connie Butler, Catherine Liu, and Ariana Reines for their new and revisited contributions to the discourse on Liz Larner's work.

We extend immense gratitude and thanks to Shaun Caley Regen for her more than thirty-year stewardship of Liz Larner's work, her unmatched knowledge of Larner's evolving practice, and her enthusiastic concern and care for this revelatory exhibition. We thank the team at Regen Projects for their diligence in supporting both exhibition preparations and this extensively illustrated publication.

Above all else, we are thankful to Liz Larner for her work and her extended conversation with SculptureCenter and the Walker Art Center. Her rigor, her restless intellect, and her inventiveness are endlessly inspiring, reminding us that now is always the time to look again. It has been an honor and a privilege to realize this exhibition and to reaffirm Larner's influential and important contributions to sculpture and to art.

Mary Ceruti
Executive Director
Walker Art Center, Minneapolis

Kyle Dancewicz
Interim Director
SculptureCenter, New York

Something about That Smile

CONNIE BUTLER

Smile, 1996–2005. Cast porcelain, 7 × 16 × 3 inches (17.8 × 40.6 × 7.6 cm)

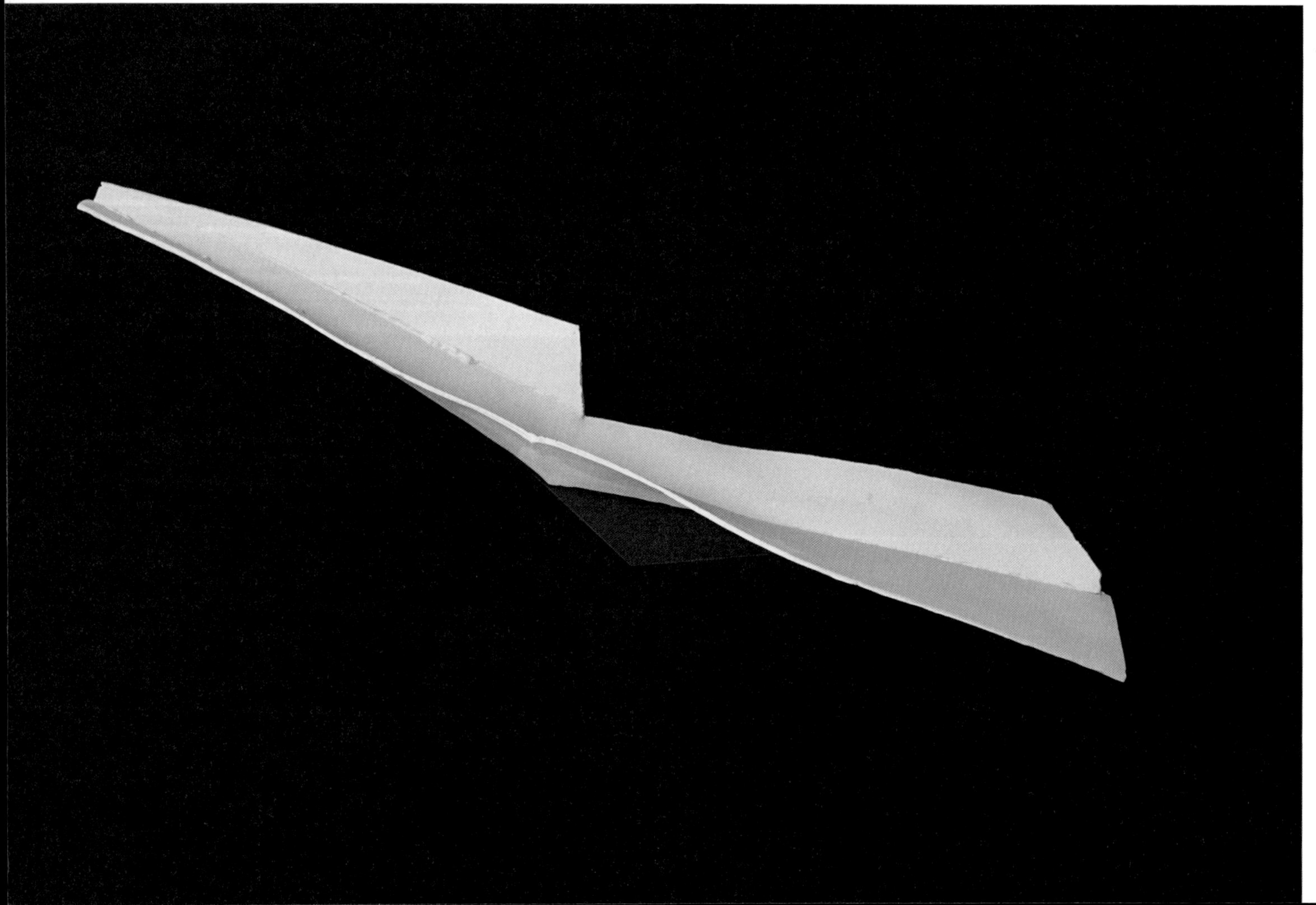

Among the most cryptic works Liz Larner has ever made are the porcelain winks and nods of a series called *smile*, which she began in 1996 and continued until 2011. With parenthetical subtitles, such as *fangs* or *abiding*, and shapes sometimes resembling a smirk, a sinister grimace, or an abstract, upturned glyph, these cartoonish matrices of irregular planes, fashioned from slip castings of foam-core models, arch into hollow forms. Because they are large, straining the limits of the porcelain, the firing had its way with the repetitive cases, and each sculpture took on a shape and a mind of its own. Strange thing, the solidification in precious material of something so fleeting as a smile. As a viewer, I must admit to not understanding these elusive works at the time. Each *smile* is an image without a body, an inside joke without an inside. Flesh into stone, or only teeth.

The artist, a person for whom a smile comes easily and frequently, has always wondered why: why she smiles when she smiles, and why so much. Where does this affliction come from? Women know about the problem of the too-easy smile. Larner's preoccupation with the smile developed just when, in the mid-1990s, the internet was beginning to impact our experience of sociality—our relationships to one another and to technology. Writing about organs, prostheses, and the self as other, feminist theorist Rosi Braidotti, a favorite of Larner's, describes the defining feature of this situation as "the degree of autonomy, mastery, and sophistication reached by technological devices that take 'life' and 'the living organisms' as object. The biotechnological gaze has penetrated into the very intimate structure of living matter, seeing the invisible, restructuring that which has no shape. . . . We are surrounded by multifunctional lidless eyes that are watching us, outside in and inside out; our technology has produced the vision of microscopic giants and intergalactic midgets, freezing time out of the picture, contracting space to a spasm."[1] Larner's ceramic glyph is made of material but is all image, a disembodied remnant of expression, friendly yet empty, perhaps a residual smirk that signals a deep questioning of the enterprise of object making and inhabiting a gender, full stop.

As a sculptural move, the *smile* series may have been disconcerting to Larner fans. Starting in the mid-1980s, she had created muscular, aggressively funny, and forcefully material works that punched hard at the hegemonic monumentality of modernist sculpture and questioned the very nature of built space along the way. Her wrapping of corners with chains and bashing of gallery walls with an absurdist sculpture-machine were seen as powerful and ecstatic, even celebratory—part of the feminist turn in conceptual sculpture of the early 1990s that included her peers Cady Noland, Mona Hatoum, Karen Kilimnik, Jac Leirner, Rita McBride, Jessica Stockholder, and Rosemarie Trockel.

The *smiles* are not only temperamentally distinct from her prior work but also more modest in scale, ranging from seven to twenty-one inches high and marking Larner's first foray into the seemingly delicate medium. They suggest a calculated retreat, the artist crafting an image rather than grappling with space by way of physical intervention. Retrospectively, this toggling between image and abstraction is almost always present in Larner's work. Rather than aggressively physical, the *smiles* are awkward, even tentatively constructed and crudely held together, as if turning flesh to stone were indeed an uneasy process. Encountered alone, they seem to have no connection to an image of a body, but grouped together, they become anthropomorphic.

Larner must have understood that the tension between subject and material, form and content, is what gives the *smiles* their charge. When she showed them in 2005 at Regen Projects in Los Angeles, she organized the white porcelain objects within a large black space created in one corner of the gallery by a dark painted shape across the floor, walls, and ceiling—a velvety black hole. Theatrical and phony, narrative yet a spatial dead end, *Her Diamond Deserts* (2004–5), a sculpture that included an aluminum armature covered in paper coated with India ink that curved from the rafters to the floor, completed the scene and kept the viewer at a distance. It was a disorienting and deeply humorous meeting of fictive and real space, of image and gesture.[2] Nested in the enveloping black of the India ink, the *smiles* were reminiscent of Beckett's disembodied mouth in his evocative and iconic video

1   Rosi Braidotti, "Organs Without Bodies," in *Nomadic Subjects: Embodiment and Sexual Difference in Contemporary Feminist Theory* (New York: Columbia University Press, 2011), 174–75.
2   Janelle Porter's essay "X Quantities" is the only place I have found writing on this installation. See *Liz Larner* (New York: Karma; Aspen, CO: Aspen Art Museum, 2016), 33.

Her Diamond Deserts, 2004–5 (detail), with *smiles*, 1996–2005, and *Guest*, 2005. Installation view, Regen Projects, Los Angeles, July 1–July 30, 2005

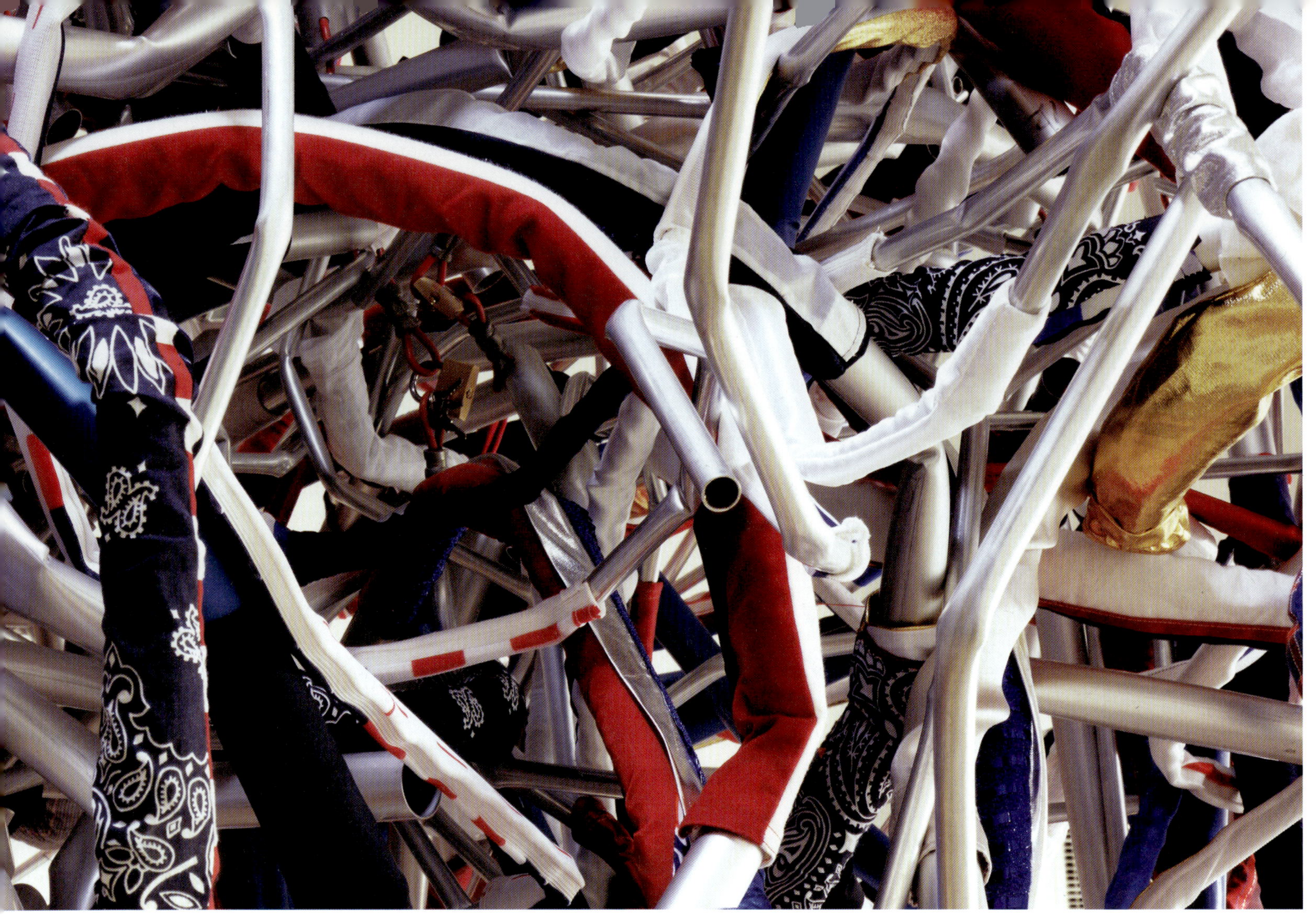

Not I (1973). Declaring its bodiliness, its anonymous humanity, the floating mouth is emblematic of our absurd and essential aloneness. Evocative of California's legendary deserts, Larner's title refers to "This Land Is Your Land," a folk song written by Woody Guthrie in 1940 that still strikes the Californian artist by surprise when the left coast on a map of the continent is mentioned. (She was one of the few women in a generation of Los Angeles artists to emerge into the international art context at a moment when this locale was viewed as somewhat provincial and even exotic.) Underscoring a nationalism that was obviously interesting to Larner at the time, the other element in the space was *RWBs* (2005), a sculpture made of a tangle of aluminum tubes dressed in red, white, and blue fabrics. The large cluster of twisted lines, held in place here and there by padlocks, alludes to military conquest and flag waving, the overflexed muscle of patriotism. Diamond deserts, Desert Storm, the desert of the Western imaginary, and the military-industrial complex (military rehearsal is routinely and covertly carried out in the desert cities of Southern California) are all blasted into this heap of shiny debris. Situated in this context, the *smiles* seem to signal the sense of deception embedded in America's description of itself to the world via so many military operations, branded as instruments of democracy and opportunity. The whole affair—the clump of red, white, and blue; the thick black paint; the black rubber flooring material Larner used to fabricate the structure; the metal ballast; the porcelain *smiles*; and the Americanness of *Her Diamond Deserts*'s landscape reference—constituted an homage, a surreal tableau of suggestive fragments intimating, perhaps, the illegibility of a place and of a smile.

Writing about the artist's work for her first survey exhibition at the Museum of Contemporary Art, Los Angeles, curator Russell Ferguson rightly suggests that Larner employs ambiguity in her work but not irony.[3] Her work is often funny in scale, linguistic reference, and even color choice, but it is never ironic. It has always been true, though seldom written in the context of art, that irony—a type of humor expressed through incongruity—is for the privileged. The verbal sleight of hand in which one's words express something very different from what they mean, it requires a certain distance of circumstance, a kind of emboldened presumption of a relationship to objective truth and its consequences. Art historically, one might say it has been a calling card for Conceptual and post-Conceptual artists, who have primarily and until quite recently been white men. It is interesting, for example, to ponder how the contribution of women artists to Conceptual art during the 1980s was subjectivity and narrative, but it rarely took the form of irony. Irony and first-generation Conceptual art seemed not to have room for the political or the personal until artists like Adrian Piper cleared space for the body and a direct address that conveyed a more complex subjectivity. Perhaps the everyday, the realm of women's work, just wasn't that funny or possible to get away from. Larner's work instead traffics in the uncanny, often suggesting humor through a shift in scale,

an indulgent dive into a rich color or texture, or by overtly presenting one thing in the place of another, completely unexpected object: asteroids on the floor; slabs of clay whose seams are split from weight and gravity; a smile that floats in space, disembodied and separated from its body.

Larner finished her BFA at CalArts in 1985. She mentions several artist teachers who were formative to her practice. John Baldessari's imprint is felt on Larner's early work, but more broadly he communicated permission to engage with humor amid conceptual rigor; Baldessari, along with others like Ed Ruscha and William Leavitt, can be credited with introducing humor into West Coast Conceptual art. His brand of Conceptualism was deeply involved with place and location, subjects that have always been in the background of Larner's work as well. Steeped in Michael Asher's legendary practicum, which essentially dismantled the notion of the studio and questioned the very making of objects, but also having attended CalArts during the years when Catherine Lord, as dean, attempted to overhaul the curriculum and the ethos of the fine arts program by introducing feminist and critical theory—a radical move that eventually led Lord to part ways with the school—Larner came of age as an artist by trying to rethink her commitment to materials and subject.[4] Another CalArts faculty member, whose conceptual approach to her photographic

3 Russell Ferguson, "Liz Larner," in *Liz Larner*
(Los Angeles: Museum of Contemporary Art, 2001), 19.
4 See Catherine Lord, *CalArts: Skeptical Belief(s)*
(Chicago: Renaissance Society; Newport Beach, CA:
Newport Harbor Art Museum, 1988).

Left (detail) and below *RWBs*, 2005

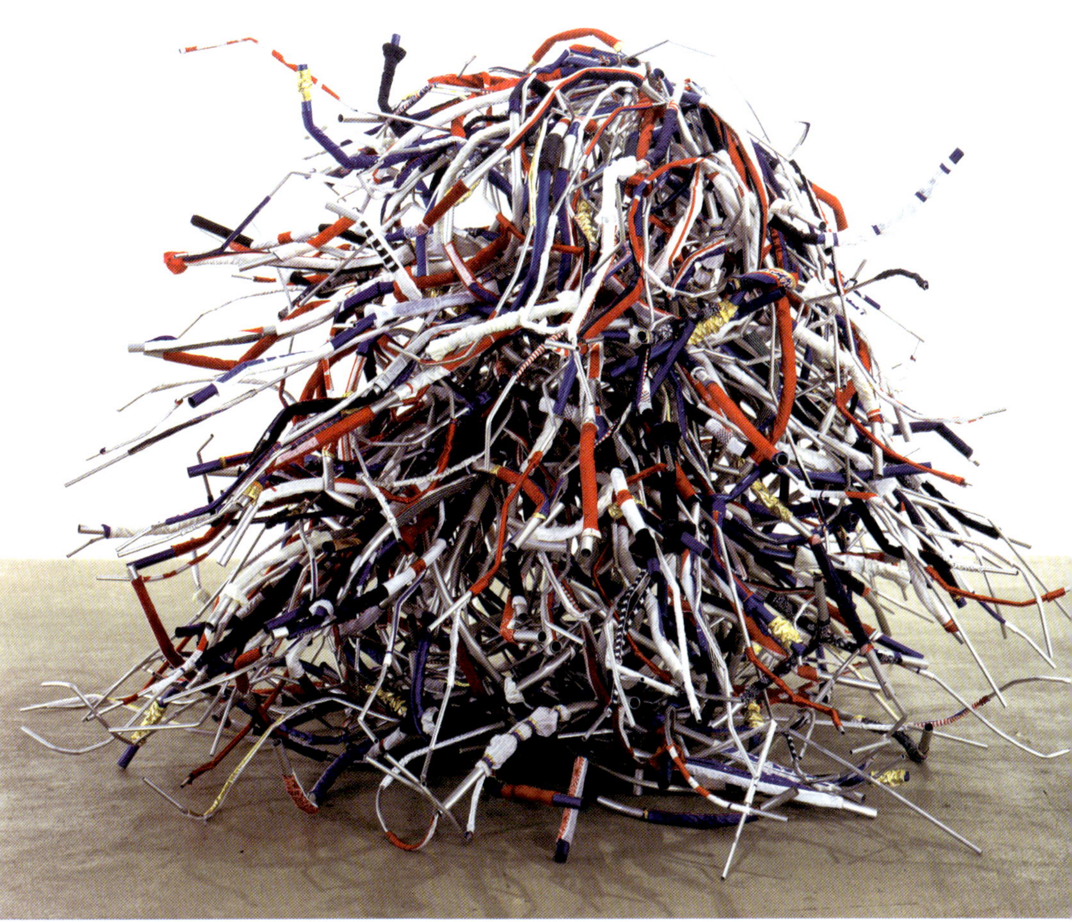

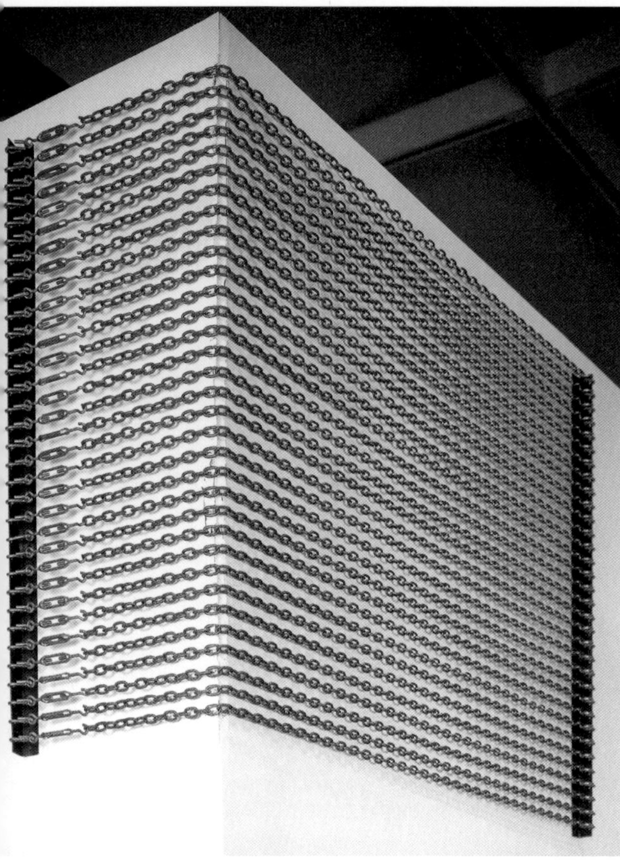

Wrapped Corner, 1991

bro-ey performances of the early 1980s now seem masturbatory and futile.[6] A symbolic dismantling of norms and received histories, *Corner Basher* was a celebration of force related as much to the legacy of CalArts and Los Angeles as to the postfeminist politics of the late 1980s. Like so many of us restricted by the constraints imposed on female identity by the broader culture and "fascist feminism" alike, Larner came out swinging.[7] *Corner Basher* is a low-tech machine for destruction, a ball and chain attached to a pole on wheels that, when activated by the gallery visitor, literally changes the shape of the wall by smashing a hole in it. The heir to a long history of destruction in art, *Corner Basher* is a manifesto, a gesture of resistance to constraint. While Larner has talked about her interest in modifying architectural space with this work, there is no getting around its aggression. Even if relegated to the corner by design, and even if Larner empowers the viewer to initiate the chaos, *Corner Basher* is both persistent and joyful in its desire to take down the wall as we know it.

Larner revels in the memory of her own desire to play in the same space as male sculptors, to repurpose their formal language against them by making something just as physically belligerent but that also manages to carry on the legacy of David Smith's totemic *Cubi* (1963–65) and Bruce Nauman's psychologically charged video corridors. *Corner Basher* and a small number of other kinetic works she made between 1988 and 1991 engaged with the psychological space of architecture and intervened in its contingencies. *Wrapped Corner* (1991) is another such work, this time static, in which metal chains are bound around a corner with a tension that defines the piece. The architecture and the sculpture are in a symbiotic relationship, as each seems to strengthen or delineate the other's form. If the chains are loosened, this dependency falters, and while the chains retain their contours, the wall shows scars. (Indeed, the corner supporting this work has been reinforced with metal to withstand the turnbuckles' tension.)

For me, what is worth revisiting in the writing on Larner's work is the default effort to locate it within a canonical history of sculpture by men. While of course Nauman is important for any artist of Larner's generation, and the relationship of her work to the body and performativity is certainly informed by his ideas and works (such as the great hour-long video *Slow Angle Walk [Beckett Walk]* of 1968, which documents, from the point of view of a camera turned sideways, the artist as he moves through a series of actions in his studio), Larner's voice was always her own. Her desire to turn a hegemonic history on its head precisely through a rebellious relationship to materials and the body can, alternatively, be knitted into a network of women artists who came of age at the same moment in both Europe and the United States. I am thinking here of McBride, Noland, and Meg Cranston, as

subjects was formative for Larner, was Judy Fiskin. Fiskin gave Larner the book *Let's Take Back Our Space* by Marianne Wex, one of four foundational texts the artist still refers to.[5] In the early 1970s, Wex amassed an archive of more than two thousand photographs of men and women in public space, a typology of body language according to gender, and concluded that women make themselves small and slender, while men arrange themselves to occupy maximum space. Even today, the photographic evidence is stark, and it made an impression on a young woman artist thinking about what it meant to put objects into the world.

Corner Basher (1988), Larner says with a smile, was a response to Asher and Baldessari, who, with Lord, Larner credits with turning her away from taking pictures. *Corner Basher* is in some sense the artist boxing her way out of a formal and material problem and finding her way to the production of space. But it also recalls the absurdist mechanical gestures of Mark Pauline and his Survival Research Laboratories, whose destructive and heavily

5   Marianne Wex, *Let's Take Back Our Space: "Female" and "Male" Body Language as a Result of Patriarchal Structures*, trans. Johanna Albert (Berlin: Frauenliteraturverlag Hermine Fees, 1979). In addition, Larner cites *Anti-Oedipus: Capitalism and Schizophrenia* by Gilles Deleuze and Felix Guattari; *The Dialectic of Sex* by Shulamith Firestone; and *Kindred* by Octavia E. Butler.

6   Liz Larner, conversation with the author, December 2019.

7   I take the term *fascist feminism* from Hannah Wilke's well-known work *Marxism and Art: Beware of Fascist-Feminism* (1977).

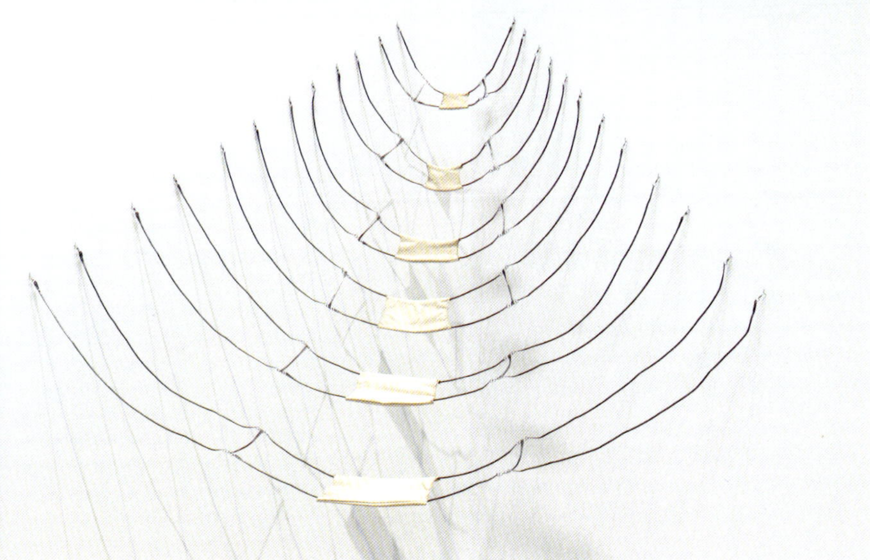

Too the Wall, 1990

well as of Trockel and Katharina Fritsch. A genealogy of the work of many women artists and makers often comes after the fact. Early experiences, teachers, and mentors weigh heavily in these accounts until we realize that much of their training took place in studio classes, galleries, and museums filled with works by men. Reflecting on her relationship to other women artists, Larner has said, "I'm not an overtly political artist in the usual sense, but I think the world has been made by men, and I think that it reflects that visually. Space has been built, carved, and thought through by men, and that's how we understand space, that's how we understand the world. I'm trying not to copy the forms of men."[8]

Not copying the legacy of form in modernist sculpture meant, for Larner, reassessing space itself through the lens of gender. Larner's works of the late 1980s and early 1990s, including *Rubber Divider* (1989), *Too the Wall* (1990), *Chained Form on the Diagonal Interrupted by Humans* (1990), *Wrapped Corner*, and *Forced Perspective (Reversed, Reflected, Extended)* (1992), were made as the field of human geography, and the critical architectural discourse within it, was emerging. This discipline mapped gender onto space and opened new ways of thinking about the power relationships embedded in built space. Theorized by such writers as Beatriz Colomina in her anthology *Sexuality and Space* (1992) and Joel Sanders in *Stud* (1996), architectural space was rethought as something to be disrupted and reauthorized.[9] By mapping space and exposing its contingencies and politics in relation to the body and sexuality, the field introduced ideas of class, queerness, and feminism into the language of architecture. Larner was clearly interested in these ideas, even if she didn't name them

as such. *Too the Wall* and *Wrapped Corner* were possible answers to the problem of the corner in sculpture. According to Larner, *Too The Wall* was about a female perspective in a world whose order has been set by men. In a play on the violence and implied resistance of the phrase "with our backs to the wall," the intense, muscular turnbuckles and steel brackets that grip perpendicular walls in *Wrapped Corner* counter *Too the Wall*'s delicate necklaces of steel, silver, and leather, which decorate a corner. A mix of expediency and nascent feminist rage dictated Larner's practical strategy for wrangling architecture.

From the beginning of her practice, the hybridity of Larner's objects spoke to a desire to make art that is ambiguous—or what Larner calls paradoxical.[10] Though that term was meant to describe the simultaneous violence and joy of *Corner Basher*, it is just as pertinent to her earliest photographs of the sculptures she would later show independently as *Cultures* (1987–). Photographed in odd and disorienting settings, such as poolside at the Tropicana Motel, these petri-dish experiments in form and

8 Larner, quoted in Ferguson, "Liz Larner," 44.

9 Beatriz Colomina, ed., *Sexuality and Space* (New York: Princeton Architectural Press, 1992); Joel Sanders, ed. *Stud: Architectures of Masculinity* (New York: Princeton Architectural Press, 1996).

10 Liz Larner, interview by Jane Dickson, *Bomb*, no. 96 (Summer 2006): 48.

13

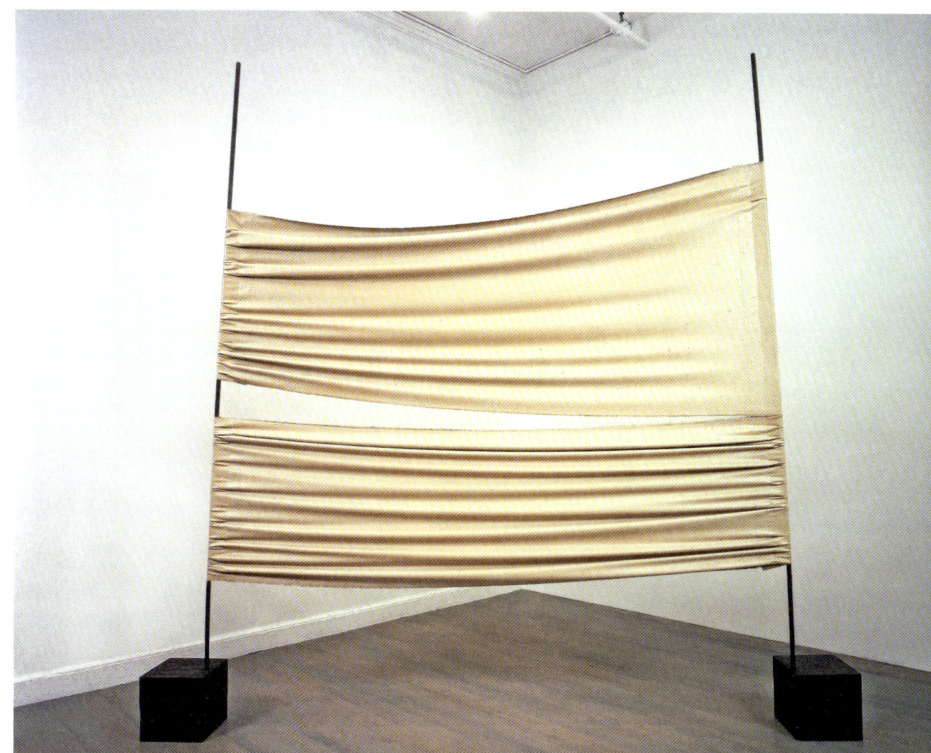

Rubber Divider, 1989

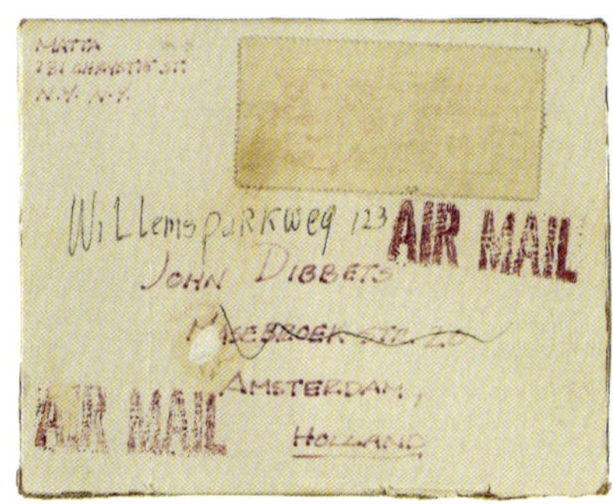

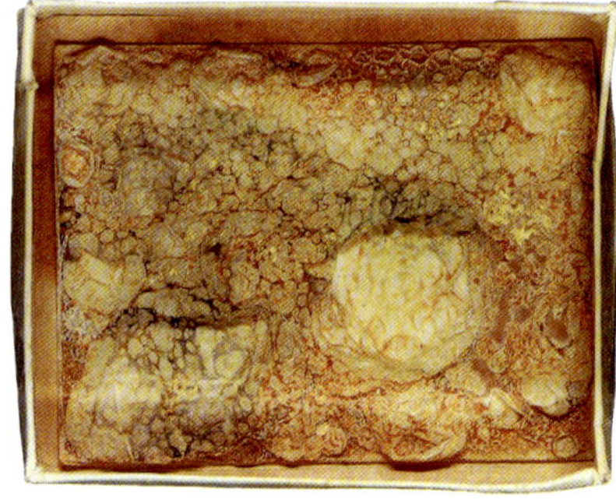

Gordon Matta-Clark, *Land of Milk and Honey*, 1969.
Agar, milk, and honey, 21 1/4 × 57 3/4 × 6 1/2 inches
(118 × 181 × 30 cm). Stedelijk Museum, Amsterdam

color never sat comfortably as the center of attention in a two-dimensional image. Though nominally photographic subjects, the *Cultures* soon became the first sculptural focus for Larner, even as she pushed the limits of their ephemeral properties and insisted on instability as an operating principle. She eventually began to articulate a sculptural base for them, to support their status as objects independent of the photographs. Each is made from three ingredients, two of which are organic substances, and one of which is a wild card. A random sampling includes *Orchid, Buttermilk, Penny* (1987); *Margo Leavin: 3 Breaths and an Inoculation* (1987); and *Whipped Cream, Heroin, and Salmon Eggs* (1987). Each title suggests a concoction of diaristic residue and everyday remnants. The works already point to Larner's interest in a disorienting mix of narrative and abstract content, as well as her fascination with the formal properties of materials. When she describes the process of mixing each culture, adding materials to the agar plate, she is as much alchemist as painter, talking about the "bloom" of the process, the moment at which each culture reaches its apex, its main event. In an interview with painter Jane Dickson, Larner says,

> I was intrigued with what something is perceived as and what it's called. The *Culture* pieces were involved with the doubling of a meaning, and the unraveling and remaking of that doubling in order to take it into other kinds of thinking. . . . I would color the agar red, yellow and blue. . . . The bacteria would be introduced to the medium in the dish, and it would ingest the nutrients suspended in the media and grow or culture; this produced colors called *blooms*. These are scientific terms. An endless generative back-and-forth between those different kinds of cultures was what I was after, but what I didn't anticipate initially was that death would eventually have to be part of it.[11]

The inevitability of death, of the transformation of her live culture into an object, evokes the work of Georges Bataille, whose concept of the *informe* or "formless"—which acknowledged the debased and abject—connects Larner's *Cultures* to the work of such artists as Gordon Matta-Clark, who likewise used agar in his work to initiate or hasten decay.[12] But the notion of death, of the full-stop moment when the materials have done what they will do and the element of transformation is brought to a halt by the alchemical logic of the culture itself, also introduces the very important ingredient of time. Larner's sculpture is not time based exactly, but the concepts of the performative and the live are at play in these early *Cultures* and the more overtly kinetic *Corner Basher,* as well as in the frozen-in-time *smiles* and her current ceramic work, in which time affects the final form. Mistakes and unexpected material happenstance are integral to the sculptural outcomes.

11   Ibid., 45.

12   Ferguson discusses this relationship to the *informe* at some length. See Ferguson, "Liz Larner," 26–27.

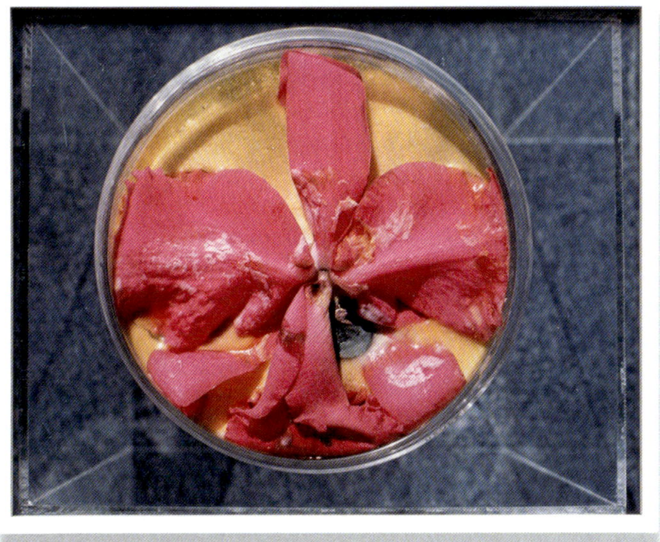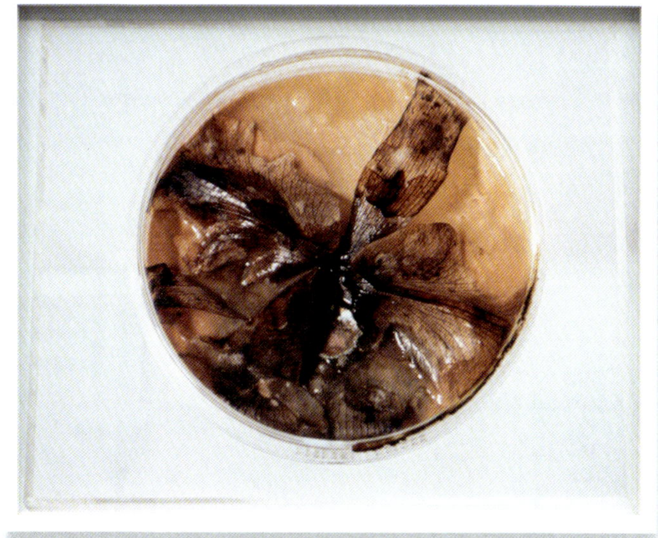

Orchid, Buttermilk, Penny, 1987. Cibachrome prints,
two parts: 16 × 20 1/4 inches (40.6 × 51.4 cm) each

Orchid, Buttermilk, Penny, 1987

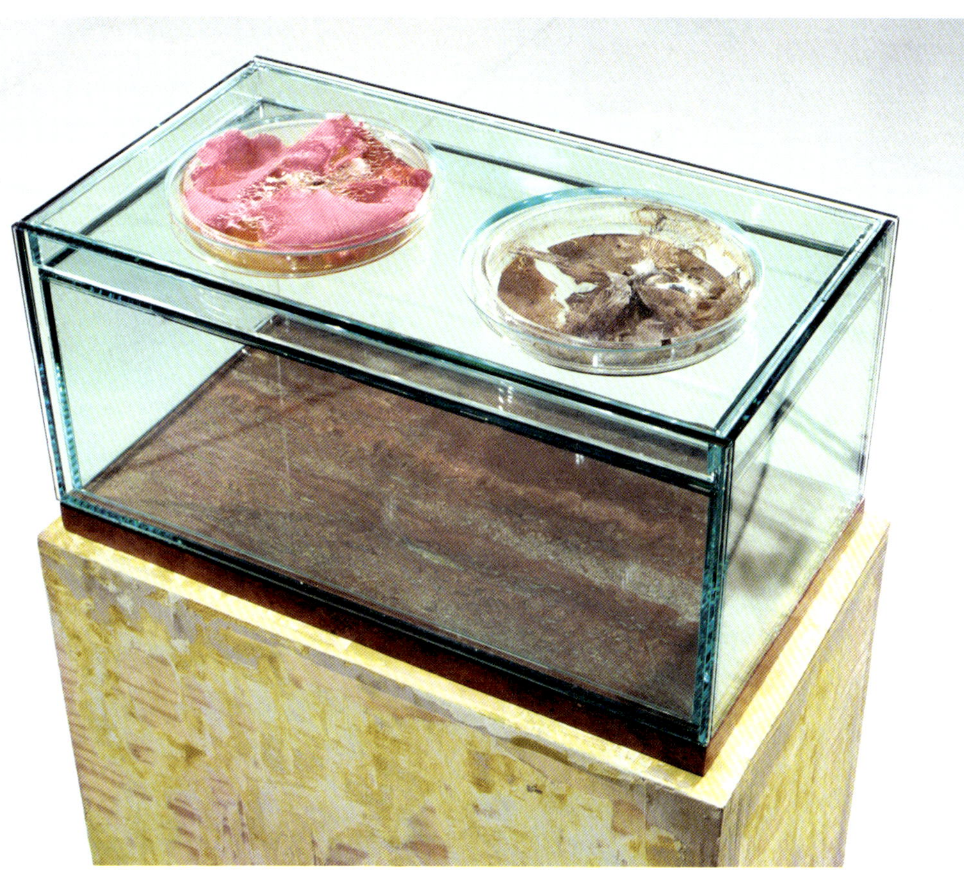

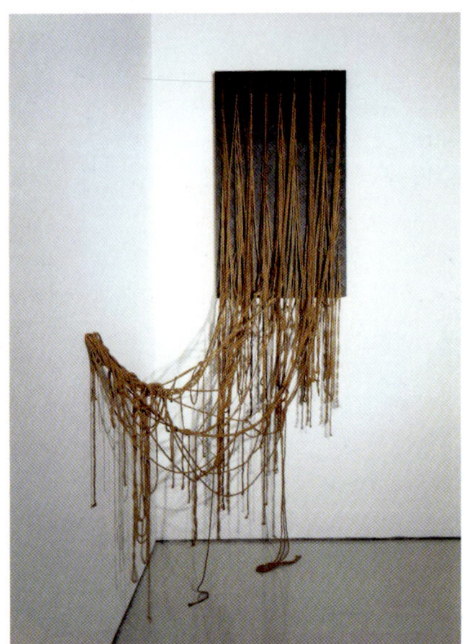

Eva Hesse, *Ennead*, 1966. Acrylic, papier-mâché, plastic, plywood, and string, approximately 96 × 39 × 17 inches (243.8 × 99.1 × 43.2 cm). Institute of Contemporary Art, Boston

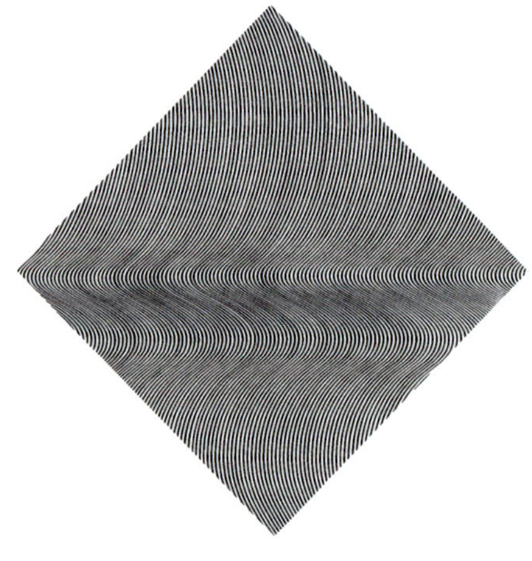

Bridget Riley, *Crest*, 1964. Emulsion on board, 65 $\frac{1}{3}$ × 65 $\frac{1}{3}$ inches (166 × 166 cm). British Council Collection

Larner's embrace of the *informe*, privileging of time, and cultivation of the unexpected are fundamentally feminist strategies. In Catherine Lord's assessment, a young student like Larner at CalArts would have inherited a polyglot legacy of stylistic persuasions: "The odd coexistence of painting, multi-media event, and feminism, go on to the loose alliance called 'conceptualism,' and then to more recent concerns with originality, appropriation, and the politics of representation."[13] The last on this list was adopted by the so-called Pictures Generation artists, who are perhaps the best known of Larner's peers at CalArts. But what this very lively pedagogical history meant for Larner was that finding her way out of photography toward an object-based practice would entail retaining not only photography's narrative impulse but also, perhaps, its roots in the alchemical. What began in the *Cultures* and extends into her ceramic works from 2010 to the present is an embrace of controlled chaos and process. In these early works, instead of the image *as* process, Larner shifted first to the image *of* process and then to the continued entropic evolution of organic material, color, and form, set in motion by the agar. Like photographic prints, whose emulsions change over time, these sculptures capture a moment and continue to evolve.

While it's too reductive to say that Larner's desire for an open-ended sculpture is a feminist impulse, it is true that her work has moved through formal and material shifts with a consistency and purpose that feel subversive. At moments, the work hovers at the edges of the *informe*, and yet it always resolutely and even joyously returns to objects that advance the modernist tradition of sculpture that is vertical, totemic, and even heroic in scale. Larner's work from 1989 into the early 1990s thinks through that of her formal mentors and reinvents the question of form and space, establishing a wide berth for her own practice. The beautiful *Bird in Space* (1989), an arc of nylon cords sewn together with silk and weighted with two stainless-steel blocks, is an homage to Constantin Brancusi's sculpture of the same name (1923–40), but Larner's iteration breaks free from the confinement of the lone sculptural base to occupy space in a way that can only be described as soaring and choreographic. *Lash Mat* (1989) and *No M, No D, Only S & B* (1990) draw on Eva Hesse's organic take on Minimalism but exaggerate her notions of embodiment, rendering them amusing and almost narrative. *Lash Mat* is a more-than-ten-foot strip of leather, flocked with false eyelashes, anchored high on the wall, and cascading down onto the floor. The artist has said that the work is an homage to three artists, Louise Nevelson, Bridget Riley, and Meret Oppenheim: "As Nevelson got older, she would wear multiple false eyelashes; the pattern that I used to lay the eyelashes on to the column was inspired by Riley's painting *Crest* (1964). And of course, when it comes to hair and art, it's

13　Catherine Lord, "History and History," in *CalArts Skeptical Belief(s)*, 6–7.

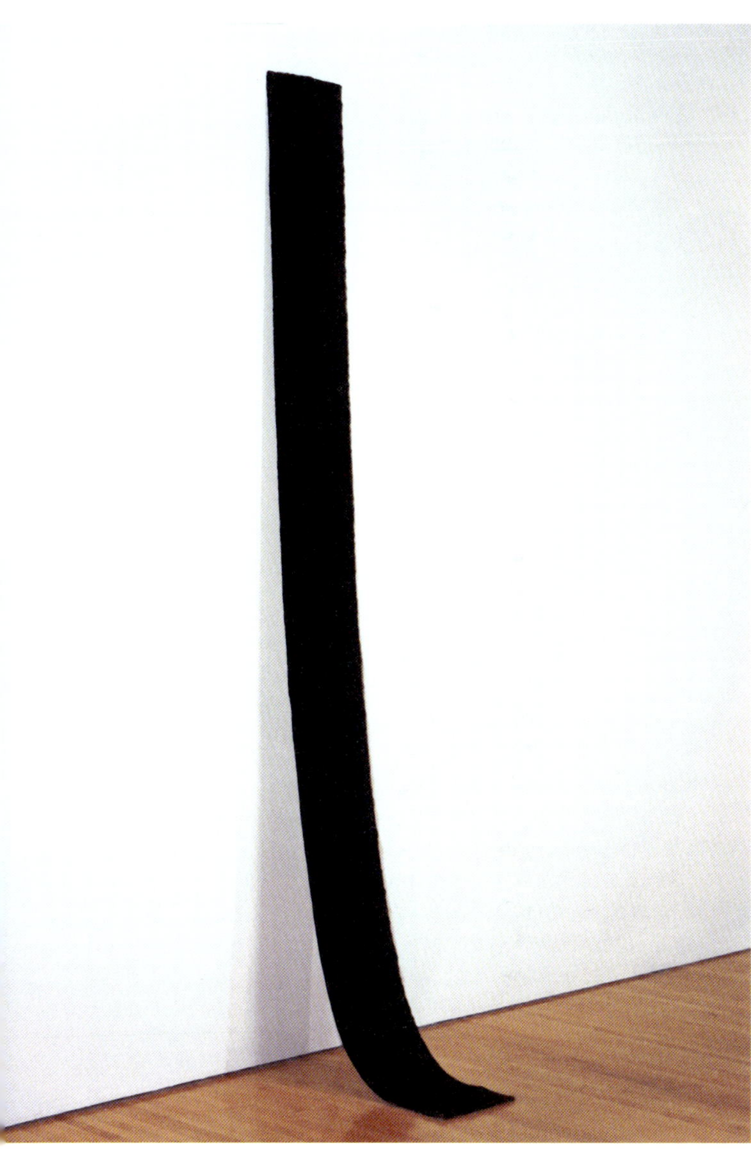

Lash Mat, 1989

hard to not think of Oppenheim's famous fur teacup, *Object (Le Déjeuner en fourrure)* from 1936."[14] Like her ceramic *smiles*, this arched brow of a sculpture is a gesture of embedded indignation at feminine excess and accoutrements. The materially related *No M, No D, Only S & B* proposes an alternative family with no parents, only sisters and brothers, suggested by the limp pairs of reddish brown leather pouches containing sand, resembling abandoned boxing gloves, collapsed in a heap on the ground. This work and its suggestive title point to a new configuration of bodies that eschews the vertical in favor of something like an embryonic network of form. The seeds of this idea lie within Hesse's work, specifically pieces such as the iconic *Hang Up* or *Ennead* (both 1966), which have been read by feminist art historian Griselda Pollock as effusively material, as the body overflowing and insistently abundant.[15]

Extending this notion of a porous and networked body into her ongoing critique of the contingencies of sculpture and architectural space, Larner made *Verwoben (Head ,Torso, Foot)*, a work initially installed at Galerie Peter Pakesch, Vienna, in 1989. This loosely configured collection of woven structures made of

14 Liz Larner, interview by Heidi Zuckerman, *Liz Larner* (Aspen, CO: Aspen Art Museum, 2016), 161.
15 Griselda Pollock has written about Hesse extensively. See her discussion of *Hang Up* in *Encountering Eva Hesse*, ed. Griselda Pollock and Vanessa Corby (New York: Prestel, 2006), 37–46.

No M, No D, Only S & B, 1990

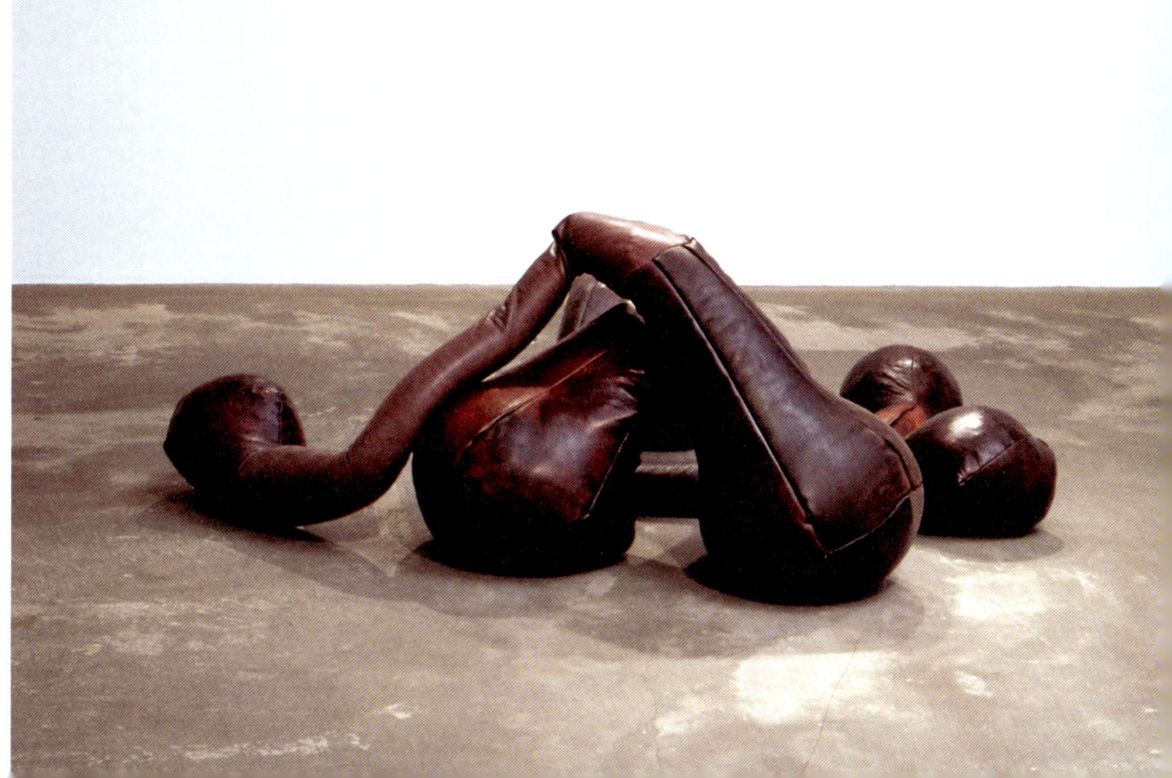

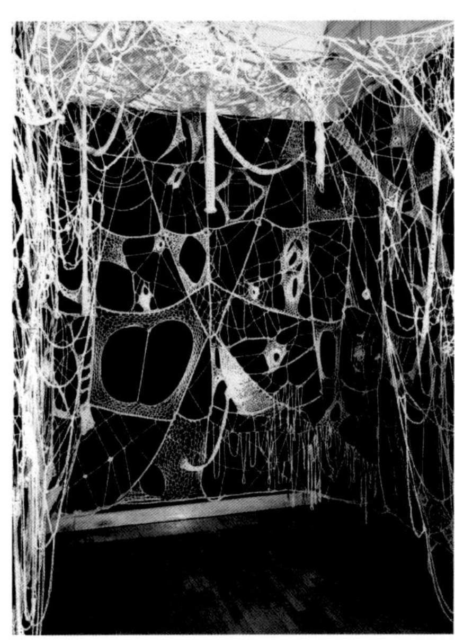

Faith Wilding, *Crocheted Environment (Womb Room)*,
1972/1995. Woolworth's Sweetheart
acrylic yarn and sisal rope, 108 × 108 × 108 inches
(274.3 × 274.3 × 274.3 cm) (variable)

strips of fabric, plastic fiber, metal, rope, ribbon, wire, and fur crisscrossed the gallery space; each part of the elegantly strung-out body was tautly attached to the walls and floor by long extensions of material hovering in the space between head and toe. Despite their functioning to orchestrate the viewer's movement, Larner's partitions are attenuated and fractured, handmade and provisional. Reconsidered today, the work clearly nods to feminist histories of craft and weaving and celebrates the intersections of those histories with camp and kitsch, but it also looks and feels strikingly contemporary; it embodies precarity and yet asserts its materiality with muscular force. "Head" is the most figurative and referential part of the work, made of clippings from international newspapers (dated October–December 1989)—of figures from Mao Tse-tung to Patty Hearst, Alfred E. Newman to Desmond Tutu. Hung highest in the room, this preinternet gathering of luminaries formed a floating brain trust of cultural memory. "Torso" was made from a collection of unbleached painting linen, wrapping papers, Viennese fabrics, and clear plastic strips and is reminiscent of Miriam Schapiro's fabric works and Faith Wilding's *Womb Room* (1972), initially titled *Crocheted Environment*, created for the feminist art space Womanhouse. Like Wilding's work, Larner's installation both seduced and repelled, firmly keeping the viewer out while celebrating the space by fervently and colorfully occupying it. Larner's decision to anchor the gut of the sculpture with such an obviously feminist nod is key to understanding the push and pull of her relationship to her roots as an artist.[16] Even if, by the early 1990s, CalArts had infamously and carelessly disposed of the bulk of the archive of the Feminist Art Program, the legacy of that educational experiment has a long reach, which is only now beginning to be understood. The foundational, once rendered invisible, rises again and again.

Works like *Verwoben* situated Larner among female peers whose work was then collected in the 1991 exhibition *Plastic Fantastic Lover (Object A)* at Blum Helman Warehouse. Initiated by artist Mary Weatherford and curated by Catherine Liu, the exhibition attempted to establish an international cohort of women artists of Weatherford's generation whose sculptural practices were somehow independent of a "master" style. Larner's contribution was a work called *Irontwig Butterfly* (1991), and her catalogue page contains only a small but famous photograph of a dancer in arabesque on a cliff high above the Grand Canyon accompanied by the words LOVE and SPACE. Included in the exhibition were artists such as Polly Apfelbaum, Angela Bulloch, Sylvie Fleury, Aki Fujiyoshi, Rebecca Horn, Annette Messager, Beverly Semmes, Jessica Stockholder, Rosemarie Trockel, Andrea Zittel, and Weatherford. This attempt at a genealogy of contemporary sculpture was also a gathering of women artists

16 Despite the connections of this work to that of Wilding, Larner claims that Wilding's is a "little too into the horror and pain of being a woman for me. . . . I'm more [concerned] about how the enslavement and subservience of women has been a byproduct of the limits of reproduction and women have been used as means to the power of men through the children they bear and their free labor." Liz Larner, note to the author, March 10, 2021.

whose practices are feminist in their rejection of conventional (masculine) histories of form. Larner's own legacy might be seen today in the temporal, spatial moves of Nairy Baghramian or the collected trash sculptures of Ser Serpas, a young artist who finds form in the ephemeral only to recirculate her materials into the world after they are shown, staging encounters across time with the forms of our cultural refuse.

Larner's radical moves within her oeuvre range from the abstract gesture of *Wrapped Corner* to the bodily referentiality of *Hands* (1993), a series of hanging, hollow cast-pewter hands. As she describes it, the latter was a project of redefining the nude by breaking down the body and the work of art to their most essential element (art making at its most elementary and clichéd involves the hands, which symbolically stand for the human body).[17] By extracting the hands and committing them to sculpture's time-honored process (casting) and material (pewter), the artist reinserted the figure and the figurative into her work. *Hands* might also be read as a retrospective nod to her persistence with the craft of making, even in the wake of her strong, one might say academic, conceptual training under the likes of Asher and Baldessari. What was most jarring during Larner's early career were these dramatic shifts from bold uses of found materials, repurposed to disrupt architectural space and challenge its constraints, to delicate gestures that asserted her interest in the tropes of and sculptural reliance on the female body in its subjugated form. In retrospect, both represented merely different approaches to the same set of concerns.

Larner's early chapter culminates in a work that was her most ambitious up to that point. A group of three corridor pieces from 1991 brought together all her concerns: color and form, the body from inside and out, the suspension of mass and weight in space, and sculpture that both is freestanding and consumes the architecture around it. Shown first as a group at Regen Projects in Los Angeles and then broken apart into individual works, *Corridor Yellow/Purple*, *Corridor Red/Green*, and *Corridor Orange/Blue* are immensely satisfying. Each piece consists of two roughly parallel elements, either floor based or suspended from the ceiling by thin cords or cables, some anchored by counterweights on the floor; all are several feet long and materially unique: *Yellow/Purple* is dyed leather and painted metal; *Orange/Blue* is fabric and painted metal and wood; and *Red/Green* is painted metal and wood, fabric, and dyed leather. The freestanding elements are bulkier, heavy and jagged. Operating on the level of Pop object, the corridors are graphic, their colors delineating

17   Liz Larner, conversation with the author, December 2019.

Verwoben (Head, Torso, Foot), 1989. Installation view, Galerie Max Hetzler, Berlin, September 14–October 27, 2018

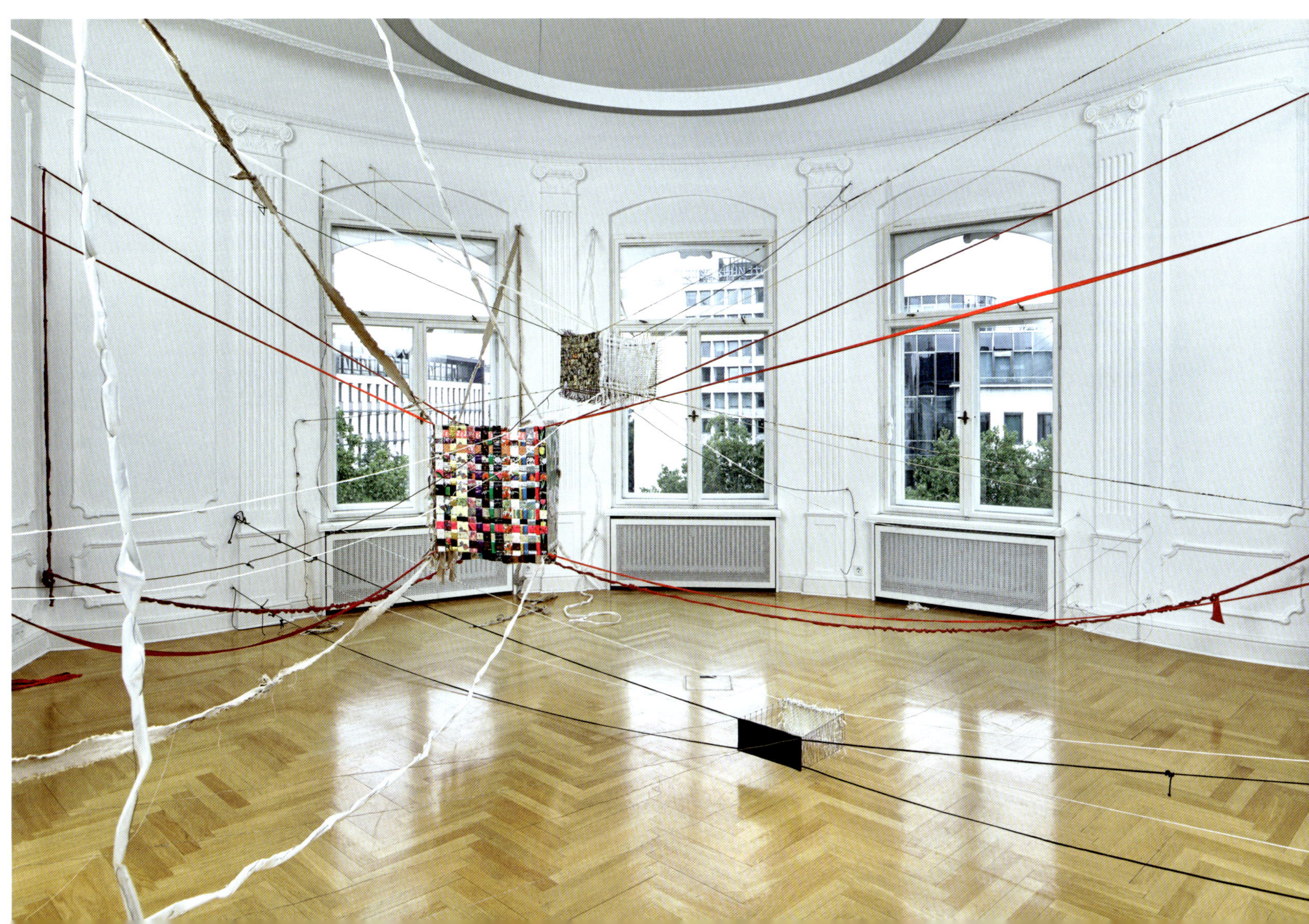

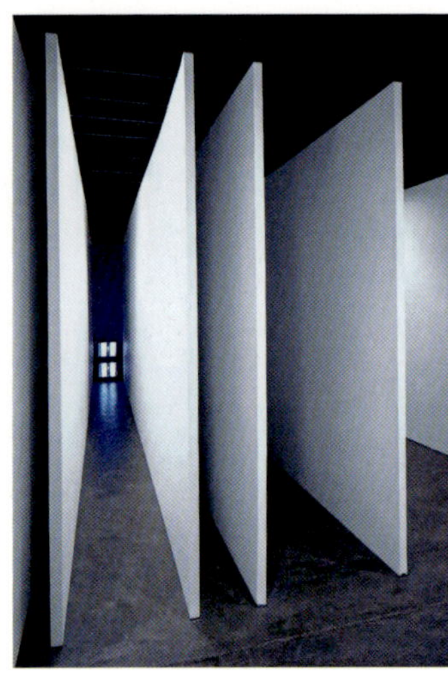

Bruce Nauman, *Corridor Installation (Nick Wilder Installation),*
1970. Wood wallboards, water-based paint, three video
cameras, scanner, frame, five monitors, video recorder,
video player, video (black-and-white, silent, indefinite duration),
dimensions variable

beginnings and ends, their scale an invitation to engage. They also
function as partitions seemingly modeled on vertebrae—elements
of an organism's anchoring system—inscribing porous spaces for
a human body to move through.

While reminiscent of Nauman's video corridors, Larner's
renditions rip open the sterile whiteness of those austere,
psychological spaces. These are not the psychological spaces of
Richard Serra's threatening curves of dark corten steel; they
cultivate something very different and stop short of monumentality for its own sake. Though awesome in scale and balance, they
beckon a viewer to inhabit them. Citing the influence of Bridget
Riley, and specifically the retinal problem of not being able to
focus when looking at a Riley painting, Larner has said that the
corridors "came from a two-dimensional idea namely that there
is a vibration—a visual buzz—between opposite colors and so
I wanted to make a three-dimensional space with that idea."[18]
Larner's bold wielding of color has much in common with the
work of artists such as Mary Heilmann, Semmes, and Stockholder;
the contemporaneous installations of the latter, for example,
immersed the viewer in expansive tableaus of deep, saturated
color.[19] Larner's bold pairings of primary and secondary colors

18   Liz Larner, "Wonderful Pussycat," interview by
Peter Noever, in *Liz Larner: I thought I saw a pussycat*
(Vienna: MAK, Museum of Applied Arts, 1998), n.p.

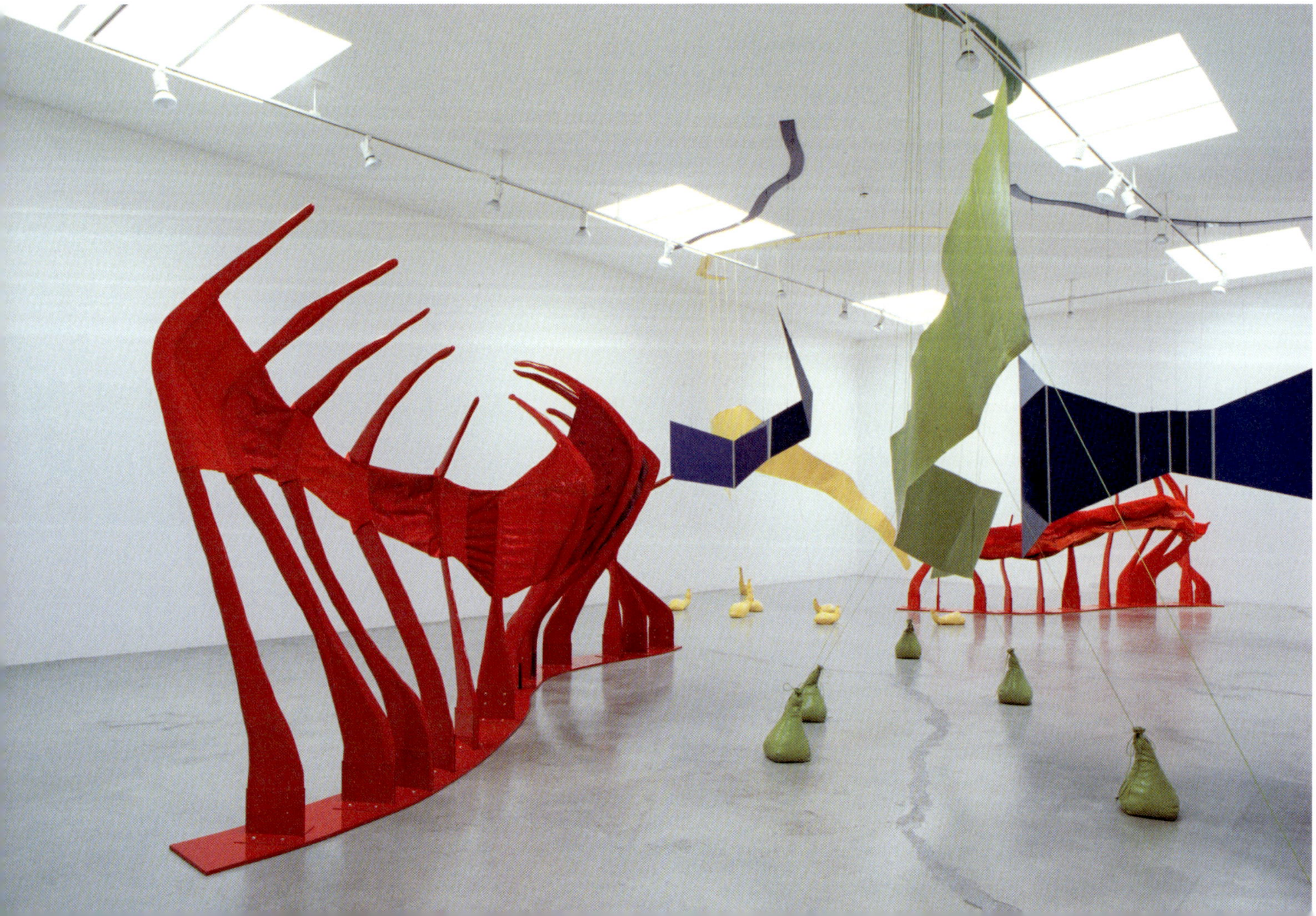

are mobilized through provocative material clashes. Made of leather, fabrics of high and low grades of decoration and texture, car paint, stainless steel, and wood, the red component of *Corridor Red/Green* combines slick, glossy car paint and lowbrow sequined fabric, tautly stretched between its curved, graphically awkward riblike forms, to constitute an unsettling, erotic, supine figurative structure. While Larner pushes the fluidity of cut steel as far as it can go, she embraces the slight clunkiness of her dips and arcs. Like her *Cultures*—which are in some sense a commentary on the history of action painting, yielding automatic compositions of constantly changing colors—her corridors celebrate the revelatory movement of color and form in space.

Indeed, as is true of Stockholder's space-eating installations of the early to mid-1990s, such as *Your Skin in This Weather Bourne Eye-Threads and Swollen Perfume* (1995), Larner's exuberant corridors evoke the monstrous—as in the attraction and repulsion of the female body, its terror and excesses. (A tattoo flash she designed in 1992 is simply the word MOTHER in blocky Helvetica.) Braidotti has written about the implications of this concept: "The woman's body can change shape in pregnancy and childbearing; it is therefore capable of defeating the notion of fixed *bodily form*, of visible, recognizable, clear, and distinct shapes as that which marks the contour of the body. She is morphologically dubious. . . . Woman as a sign of difference is monstrous. . . . The female body shares with the monster the privilege of bringing out a unique blend of *fascination and horror*."[20] Here again we are reminded of Braidotti's notion of organs without a body, the body "redefined as libidinal surface, field of forces, screen of imaginary projections, site of constitution of identity."[21]

Switching gears again away from her seemingly more rigorous investigations of color and form, Larner returned to fragments of nature in *Park* (1996), produced in response to a call to make a temporary work for *The Garage Project*, a show at the MAK Center artist residency at the Mackey Apartments in Los Angeles. The installation consisted of a forty-foot-long agave tree resting horizontally in space, propped up by a cement column acting as a de facto pedestal without which the tree was merely a tree. It has since been realized in three more iterations for different exhibitions and has been written about as an homage to a long line of artists, such as Robert Smithson and Joseph Beuys, who have used dead and live trees to address issues of site or social sculpture. Given its conception as a piece for the garage space of a building designed by Rudolph Schindler, *Park* reads as a love letter to California's history of modernist design and indoor-outdoor accommodations of light and space.

19 See Connie Butler, "Terrible Beauty and the Enormity of Space," *Art and Text*, no. 46 (September 1993): 60–65.
20 Braidotti, "Organs Without Bodies," 80–81.
21 Ibid., 178.

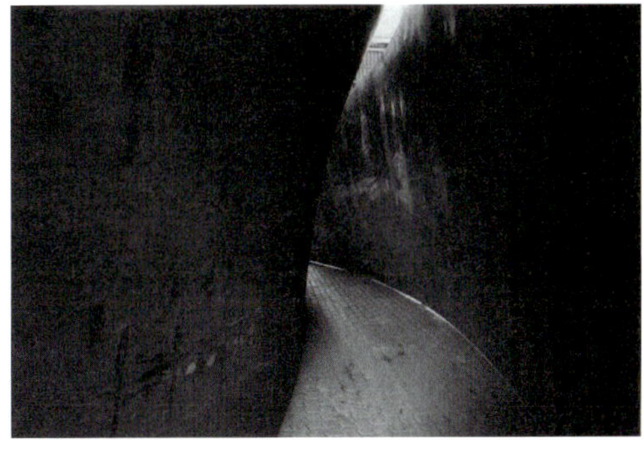

Richard Serra, *Betwixt the Torus and the Sphere*, 2001 (detail). Weatherproof steel, three spherical sections, three torus sections, 142 × 450 × 319 inches (360.7 × 1143 × 810.3 cm)

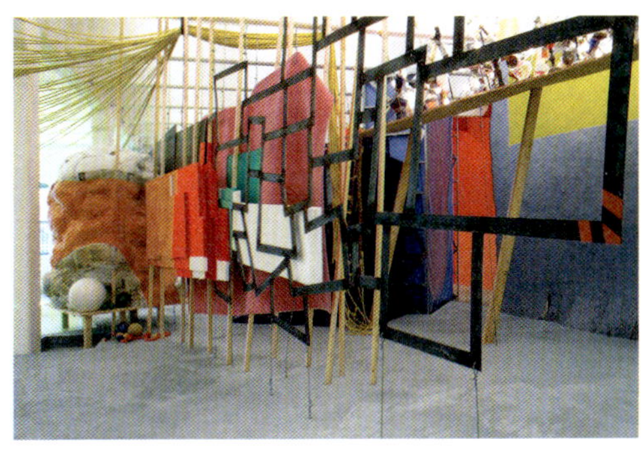

Jessica Stockholder, *Your Skin in This Weather Bourne Eye-Threads and Swollen Perfume*, 1995. Installation view, Dia Center for the Arts, New York , October 5, 1995–June 23, 1996

Opposite page *Corridor Red/Green, Corridor Yellow/Purple, Corridor Orange/Blue*, 1991. Installation view, Stuart Regen Gallery, Los Angeles, January 15–February 12, 1991

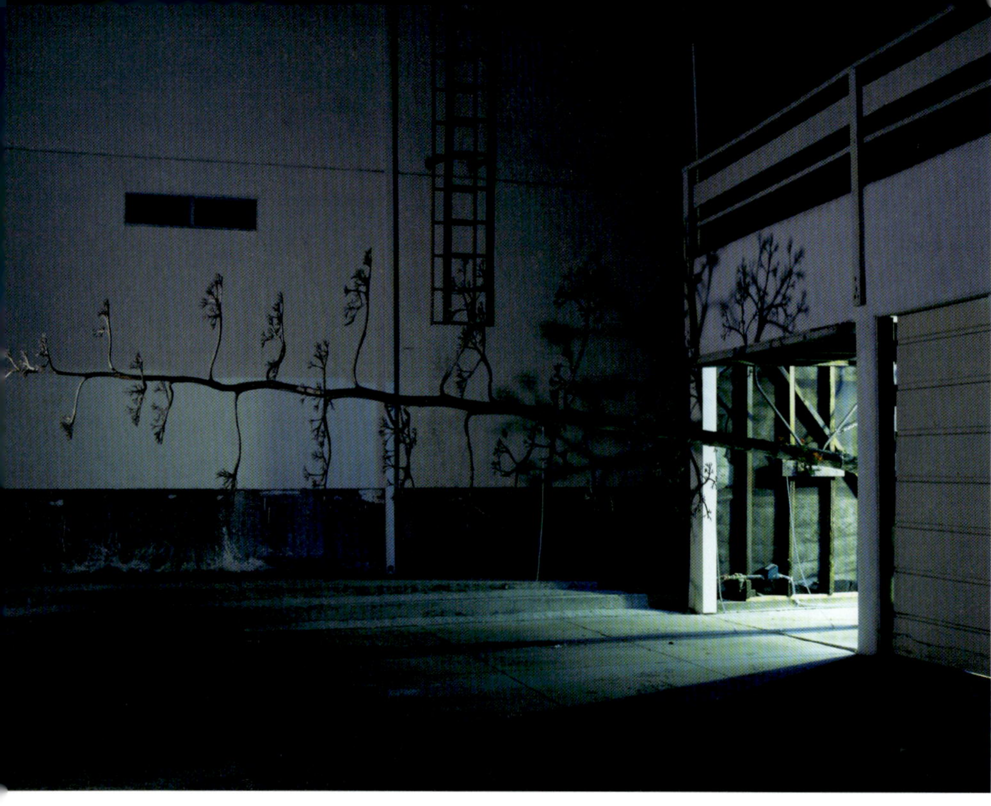

Park, 1996. Agave Americana, concrete and plant material, 40 feet (12.2m). Installation view, The Mackey Apartments—MAK Center for Art and Architecture, Los Angeles, April 13–August 14, 1996

The issue of place has always been important to Larner; this fascination with location is at times more obvious than at others. When *Park* was produced, in the mid-1990s, Larner's generation of Los Angeles artists was being packaged and circulated in the European context as something exotic, their work as new forms of art from the Far West frontier. The Baudrillardian version of the West circulated by Hollywood— vast expanses of desert populated only by bikers and roadside diners—also had something to do with the chutzpah of a work like *Park*, which is essentially nature as found object, a simulacrum. Hailing from Sacramento, the capital of California, but having chosen to settle in a wilder, less gentrified part of the state, Larner is captivated by the uniqueness of the Californian identity, sharing Joan Didion's "recognition of a sort of California spell."[22] One source for Larner's thinking about place—and an influence on *Her Diamond Deserts*—was Didion's book-length essay *Where I Was From*, in which she writes, "Such calls to dwell upon the place and its meaning (and, if the meaning proved intractable, to reinvent the place) had been general in California since the first American settlement, the very remoteness of which was sufficiently extreme to raise questions about why one was there, why one had come there, what the voyage would ultimately mean."[23] It is this slippage in language, the migration of meaning

from placeness to memory, from history to feeling, that Larner takes from Didion. But *Park* is also about fecundity in the face of entropy, the generation of something from a dormant subject. Larner's tree itself functions as a base, a petri dish from which other plants could grow. A nasturtium, for example, with its glorious burst of orange and yellow, was seeded in the dead trunk. What Larner constructs is more than the sum of its parts. Since *Park* can be remade at any time for multiple contexts and exhibitions, its meaning seems to evolve exponentially across time. In its ability to morph and replicate, it too is a monstrous object. It is both dead and alive—undead, even—creating multiplicity out of singularity.

Larner's work after 1997 and into the 2000s shifted dramatically through the use of new technologies and materials that allowed her to exploit another of modernist sculpture's long traditions: drawing in space as a way to generate volume. While Larner doesn't make many drawings, she does use line to describe form both on paper and in space. *I thought I saw a pussycat* and *2 as 3 and Some, Too* (both 1997–98) are works of intersecting volumes suggested through color and line that retain the visual effect of having been "drafted" in digital form. Though *2 as 3 and Some, Too* was made without the use of computer modeling, it creates a mirage of form from the negative space of nested, wobbly

22 Porter, "X Quantities," 33.

23 Joan Didion, *Where I Was From* (New York: Knopf, 2003), 28.

frames of cubes; the title emphasizes that the work is a three-dimensional riddle. Suggesting a collapsed or soft Tony Smith, the sculpture is made even more elusive by its color, which is applied to the metal form via thin sheets of paper imbued with watercolor, that most transient of mediums. The color technically sits on top of the metal but seems to also describe its shapes; color and form are equal and as one. These networked sculptures remind me of the German-Venezuelan artist Gego, whose drawings without paper, made between the mid-1970s and 1980s, are suspended nests and webs of line that inhabit space provisionally. Writing about these works, art historian Briony Fer asks what sculpture becomes when it contains "nothing but air": "It shows us what is left of the art object when you have taken away precisely that which conventionally defined or supported it: whether mass from sculpture or ground from drawing."[24]

Many of Larner's sculptures of these years occupy corners. Intrigued by the areas of architecture that are structural but ambiguous, she has said of the corner, "People have dealt with the wall, or the floor, but where two walls meet is a really beautiful, poetic space. Where two axes arrive and touch each other should not be dead space; it should be one of the most powerful spaces. I like moving things into the corners and sometimes trying to change the shape of the corner."[25] Whereas her early corner

sculptures sought to mask or alter the corner physically through bashing or binding, these clusters of form collaborate with the corner, nest in it, relish its interstitiality. As one critic noted, rather than congealing, these nested forms almost always seem to be coming apart, much like her earlier woven works, which also gained traction from their own precarity.[26]

It is this persistent pursuit of a sculpture that is formally stable but inherently precarious in its methodology and production of meaning that characterizes Larner's move fully into ceramics in 2009 after the conclusion of her *smile* series. The slab sculptures, as she calls them, are part of a long line of ceramic practices that embrace the wrong, the accident, and the counterintuitive in California's great history of radical ceramic artists (Claire Falkenstein, John Mason, Peter Voulkos, and Ken Price, who was an early teacher of Larner's, come to mind). Larner's numerous wall-hung slab works produced between 2009 and 2011 were all roughly the same horizontal format, measuring about twenty by thirty-five inches, with a central, vertical rupture that sometimes broke through the structure of the thick clay. Their blobby organicism and rough untreated edges contribute to the weird sum of entropic parts that make these finished objects. Returning full circle to many of the ideas about painting that she had mulled in the petri-dish cultures, she has said that these ceramic sculptures

24 Briony Fer, "Gego: Line as Object [Henry Moore Institute, Leeds, UK]," *Artforum* 53, no. 4 (December 2014): 274; https://www.artforum.com/print/201410/briony-fer-49137.

25 Larner, quoted in Ferguson, "Liz Larner," 92.

26 Jan Tumlir writes, "Likewise, her 'woven' works always seem rather to be coming apart, as though they were paintings caught in a process of unraveling, and with the addition of a few shards of cut mirror underneath. . . . The result is something like sculpture made from a shattering of pictorial space." See "On Liz Larner's 'I thought I saw a pussycat . . . I did! I did!,'" in *Liz Larner: I thought I saw a pussycat*, n.p.

2 as 3 and Some, Too, 1997–98

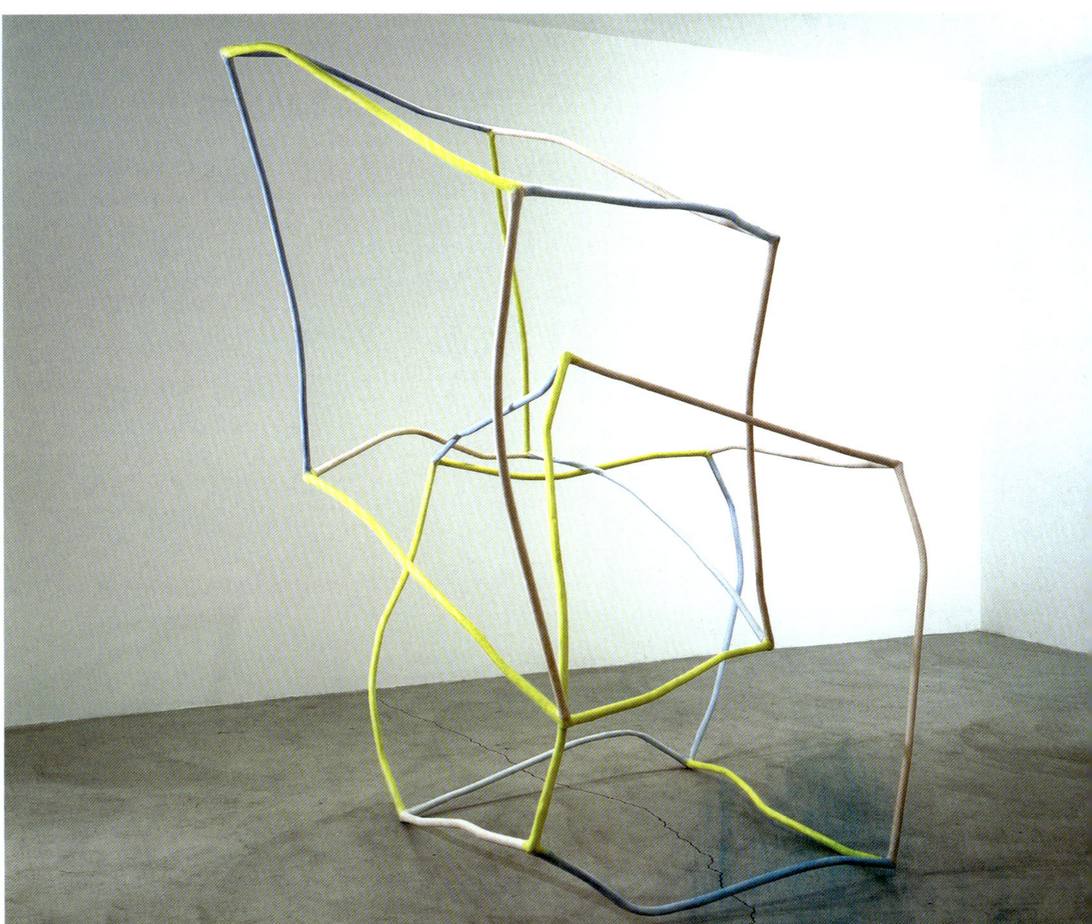

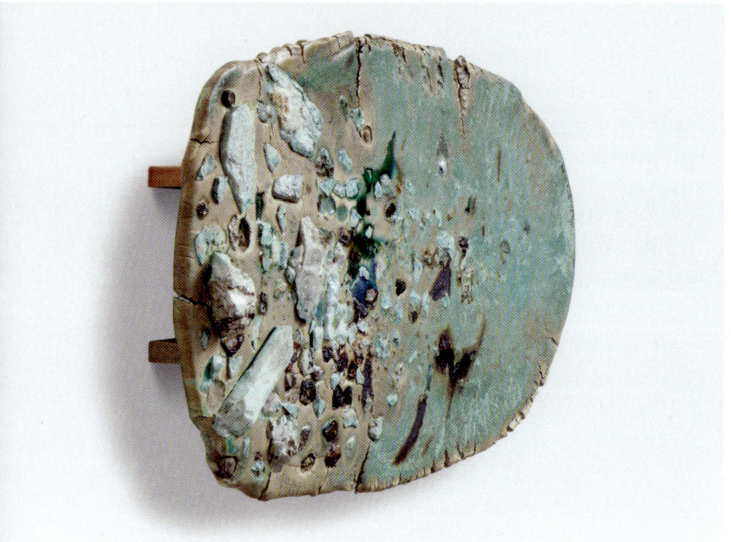

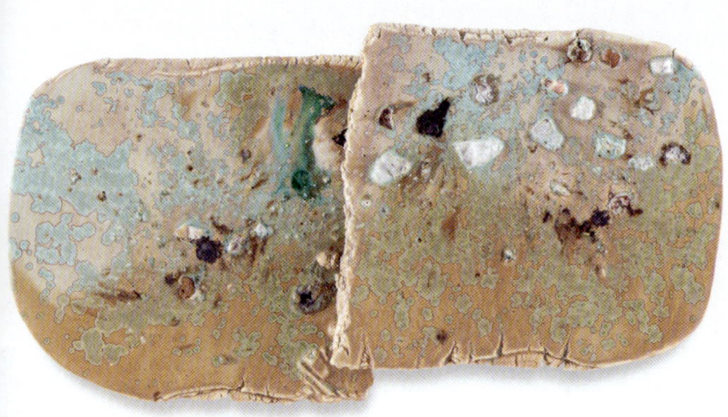

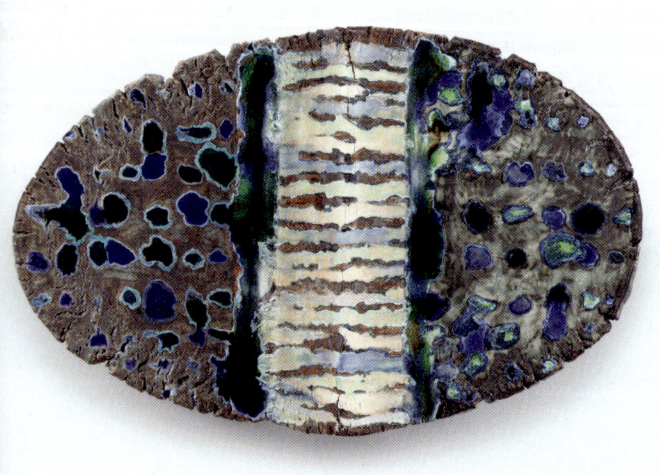

are about relinquishing control. The willful hanging on the wall of things that start flat and want to be flatbed sculptures—in the Leo Steinberg sense of a tilt from painting's vertical orientation to a horizontal one—is one perversion that Larner embraces. Starting in 2013, she adopted geologic terms as the titles for these serial works: *subduction, mantle, inflexion, calefaction*. Again playing with science, Larner turned her experiments and freestyle innovations into lasting and evolving works of great beauty.

What is clear is that Larner isn't much concerned whether this work is ceramic or sculpture or something in between. Though classes with Ken Price at the University of Southern California in the late 1990s triggered new ideas about polychromy and organic forms, Larner continued to evade style and liberally, even indulgently, embrace visual pleasure in these very sensuous works, which come closer to painting than any others she has made. The gorgeous *V (planchette)* (2013), a sculpture more than eight feet tall and made not of ceramic but of aluminum covered with paper painted with egg tempera, is a sexy wave, a dancelike curve, that is also about the movement of abstract painting. It's a deep purple, like the color found in many of her ceramic *inflexions*, and it threatens to take over the room if left to its own devices. Larner's 2019 exhibition at Regen Projects, *As Below, So Above*, extended this push and pull of ceramics, sculpture, and suggestive narration to a new level of complexity. Mixing illusion and reality, the personal and the individual, with nods to the Anthropocene, ceramic sculptures hovered on the floor like icebergs adrift on a sea of concrete.

Her preoccupation with the Anthropocene provided the structure for her most recent show, executed and realized as the COVID-19 pandemic seemed to be receding in spring 2021. Titled *As Stars and Seas Entwine*, the exhibition centered on *Meerschaum Drift* (2020–21), evoking sea-foam and comprising, uncomfortably, many linear feet of plastic waste collected over three years, painted with acrylic (plastic) paint and strung together to form a shimmering necklace of discarded single-use materials that will essentially never disappear. (*Meerschaum*, German for "sea-foam," is a soft white clay that can be found in certain parts of the Black Sea.) This large floor installation shared the space with a dispersed group of ceramic asteroids. She roots her landscape of form in both the terrible reality of such things as the Great Pacific Garbage Patch, located somewhere between California and Hawaii, if not in our imaginary of the climate apocalypse, and images from the dystopian science fiction of Octavia E. Butler's *Adulthood Rites* (1988), from which Larner quotes in the press release for the show: "Plastics ... were used in furniture, clothing, containers, appliances, just about everything. Sometimes the poisons leached into food or water and caused cancer, and sometimes there was a fire and plastics burned and gassed people to death.... The only place that has enough of it to be a real danger is right here."[27]

27   Octavia E. Butler, *Adulthood Rites* (New York: Warner Books, 1988), 143. See also the press release for *As Stars and Seas Entwine*, Regen Projects, Los Angeles, March 27–May 22, 2021, https://www.regenprojects .com/exhibitions/liz-larner9/press-release.

Top to bottom
viii (calefaction), 2015 (three-quarter view). Ceramic, glaze, stones, minerals, 21 $^5/_8$ × 37 $^1/_2$ × 7 $^5/_8$ inches (54.9 × 95.3 × 19.4 cm)
calefaction subduction, 2015. Ceramic, glaze, stones, minerals, 19 $^1/_4$ × 36 $^3/_4$ × 8 $^1/_4$ inches (48.9 × 93.3 × 21 cm)
passage (Ravenna), 2021. Fired ceramic, glaze, glass, oil paint. 27 × 44 × 9 $^1/_2$ inches (68.6 × 111.8 × 24.1 cm)

Like Larner's early *Cultures* and the paradoxically titled *Park*, *Meerschaum Drift* is a tectonic structure that takes material that is not exactly alive and renders it differently, reanimating it and giving it new use value as sculpture. If the Anthropocene names an epoch in which human activity has inexorably shaped and changed the Earth and all its natural patterns, the practice of sculpture is itself analogous to the anthropogenic production of matter and form. A necklace of waste, a landscape of accumulation presumably used and gathered by the artist in her studio, is disquieting in its mass. How can one body generate something so massive? What is the difference between the materials we discard and the materials we intentionally aggregate to make art? The meaning of Larner's *Meerschaum* doubles back on itself like the soft persistence of the sea's edge, which generates and delivers beauty to us as much as it delivers our refuse. The transformation of human detritus is an old trope in sculpture, and Larner embraces this very simple device, daring us to feel visual pleasure in the face of something as awful as plastic, rendered seductive through her canny application of glaze and metaphor. The asteroids function as a chorus, punctuating the artificial sea-foam as if watching over it or organizing its beautiful, treacherous ebb and flow. The asteroids hark back to Vija Celmins's tromp l'oeil rocks, obsessively painted to look real, standing valiantly against their natural counterparts. This conversation with nature is an age-old move in sculpture. In Larner's hands, the matter of sea and stars tangles exquisitely, harnessing our space for just a moment to suggest an embrace of a future in which we account for what we make.

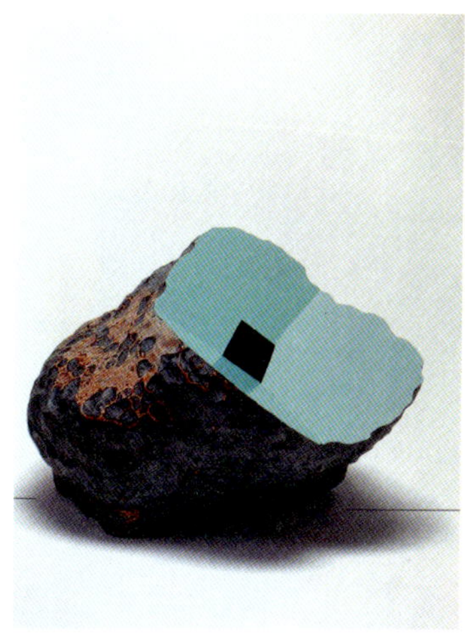

Ken Price, *Pastel*, 1988. Fired and painted clay, 12 $\frac{1}{2}$ × 17 × 17 inches (31.7 × 43.2 × 43.2 cm)

V (planchette), 2013 (detail)

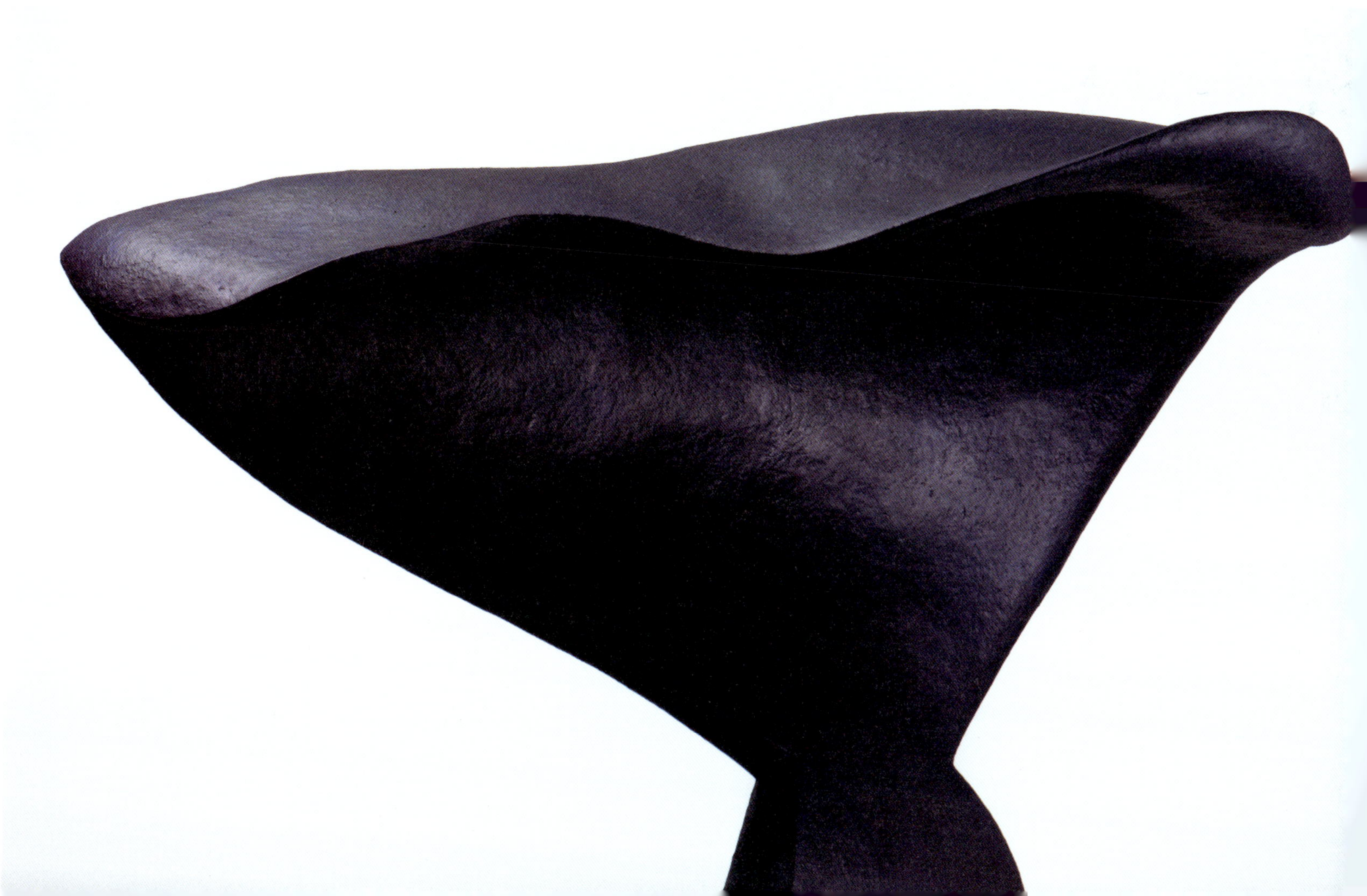

Mary Ceruti and Liz Larner in Conversation

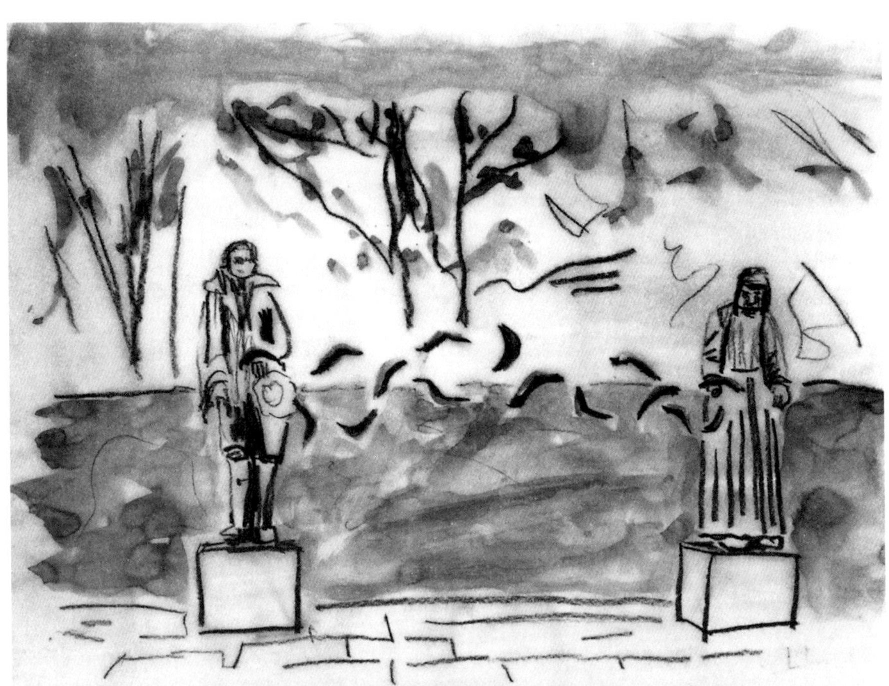

Sketch for *Other Hands Give Back*, 1993, an unrealized sculpture
for Sonsbeek 93, 1993. Graphite, charcoal, and watercolor on paper

MARY CERUTI   In talking about ceramics and minerals, you have said that you learned early on that a basic principle and lesson of geology is that rocks fall down. Gravity is also the most elementary factor of sculpture. Your work always acknowledges that reality, whether by emphasizing horizontality and a relationship to the floor or by using tension to suspend something.

LIZ LARNER   Sculpture is still about gravity and all the things that means, but it's also about a lot more now because of what we're doing with materials and resources, how we use them, and where and when. I call my work sculpture and think of myself as a sculptor. When I started out, I broke things down simply for myself: what a thing *is*, what a thing is *called*, and what it *feels* like and consequently means to someone. What you think about in relation to your experience of it, how your experience of it inflects your thoughts, and how your thoughts about it inflect your experience.

MC   You mean the bodily experience?

LL   I mean the body as a sensing subject. Sculpture is the art of embodied experience. That is what attracts me to it. It's one of the reasons that I moved away from photography. One needs a body to experience sculpture. It requires the somatic, the physical—what we all innately have to deal with all the time, outside of maybe sleeping and dreaming. Sculpture allows for all the senses to be engaged, since it is experienced in time and space. It can trigger certain sensations through materials, forms, and color in complex ways, and time and movement allow for a kind of eventuality. At one point, you have the direct, immediate experience of the work, and then, at another point, you've moved on to another place, but you remember what you experienced.

MC   Can you say a little bit about how you imagine the viewer's experience of your work?

LL   The word *viewer* kind of presupposes eyes. There is a blindness to all our other senses in the term *viewer*. Maurice Merleau-Ponty understood seeing to be the carrier term for all perception, but this idea itself points to the blindness inherent in hierarchy.[1] I like to think of the viewer as more of a *sensor*, a being using every sense to understand an object. The viewer of sculpture moves— must move—to experience the work of art. In any case, much is overlooked in the ease of this term but is also contained in it, unspoken, needed and still there, like the silent *e*.

1   See Elizabeth Grosz, *Volatile Bodies: Toward a Corporeal Feminism* (Bloomington: Indiana University Press, 1994).

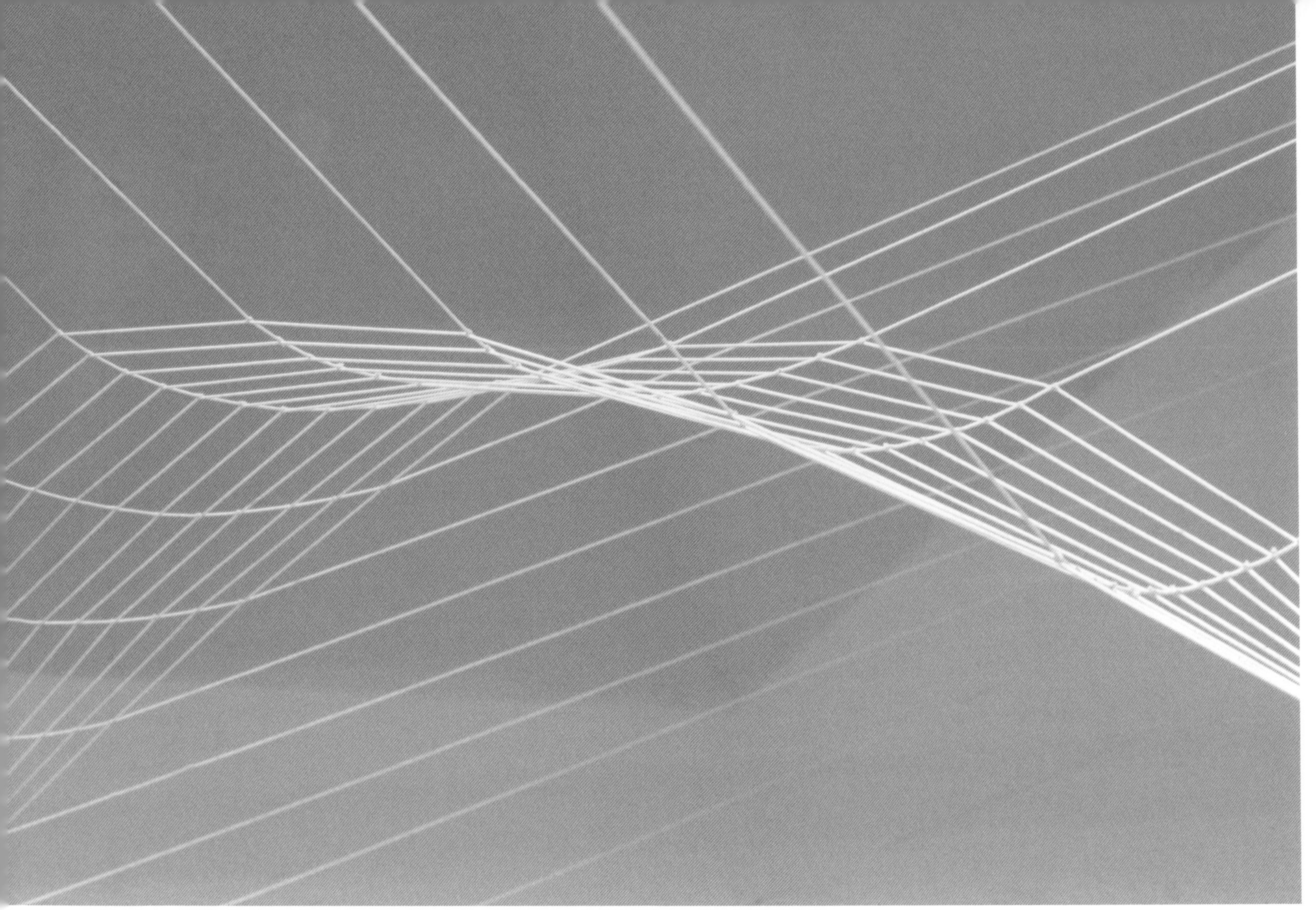

Bird in Space, 1989 (detail)

Viewer is also an interesting term because it's a singular way of saying one and many at the same time. It could mean an individual or any number of people, maybe even animals, plants, insects, or minerals. I like to think of the viewer's experience as an encounter, which accounts for the preciseness of any one life-form or thing being in a particular place at a certain moment in time. The floor encounters the sculpture at SculptureCenter at 3 p.m. on January 21, 2021, for example. Also, different bodies with varying ways of moving encounter sculptures. I get a lot of pleasure and a settling sense when I attend to the specificity called for when installing a sculpture or several sculptures in a particular place in time and space.

MC   As we have worked on the plan for the installation of the exhibition at SculptureCenter in New York and at the Walker Art Center in Minneapolis, we have had some interesting conversations about accessibility—about how different bodies might encounter the works.

LL   I hope much of what I make is flexible enough to adapt to various viewers or visitors, spaces, contexts, times, and environments. Adaptation is something that I've allowed for in my sculpture since the beginning. I like the indeterminacy of an object in relation to different spaces. When we talked about installing *Verwoben (Head, Torso, Foot)* [1989] at the Walker with accessibility in mind, I realized that adding a ramp over the lines of *Foot* could be an important adaptation. When we looked at it in the space, that idea wouldn't function for the concerns of the exhibition team, so all viewers will see it from two sides. We decided to make the access the same for everyone. For *Bird in Space* [1989], I will add or subtract nylon cord, depending on the space in which it is installed. The blocks that hold the cord

to the floor can be adjusted to change the arc depending on the site, too. At SculptureCenter, we needed to add cord to the lines that extend to the wall. The cords that attach to the wall, or what can be seen as the wingspan, are wider because of the width between the walls. This work can assume different proportions depending on the space it is installed in. In the early 1990s, art critic and historian Kirby Gookin wrote a short essay that focused on this unfixed aspect of some of my sculpture.[2]

MC   To your point about the work's relationship to architecture: *Verwoben* shares with *Bird in Space* and *Chain Perspective Reflected* [1990] that multipoint attachment.

LL   *Bird in Space* is almost invisible at times and really obvious at others. *Wrapped Corner* [1991] needs the corner to support it, and it exerts great strain on the corner. I made *Guest* [2004] so that it can be anywhere, and the linkage doesn't bind. It can be rolled up, laid flat, pushed together. It can reside on the wall, floor, table, corner, shelf, drawer, worn, be held in hands . . . pretty much anywhere, in multiple configurations.

MC   Emerging from the physical requirements of installation, the relationship of these works to architecture registers certain social, cultural, and bodily conditions. *Verwoben*, to me, suggests a networked body or body parts isolated and connected. It is not a figurative piece in the traditional sense, but the title tells us to think of it as a figure or as body parts. I think of this work and others from that time period—the late 1980s and early 1990s—in those terms because that was when many of us began to engage with computers, an engagement that came along with the idea that there is a network that doesn't originate from a single place but has nodes.

2   Kirby Gookin, "Dimensions Variable: Liz Larner,"
Parkett, no. 36 (1993): 119–23.

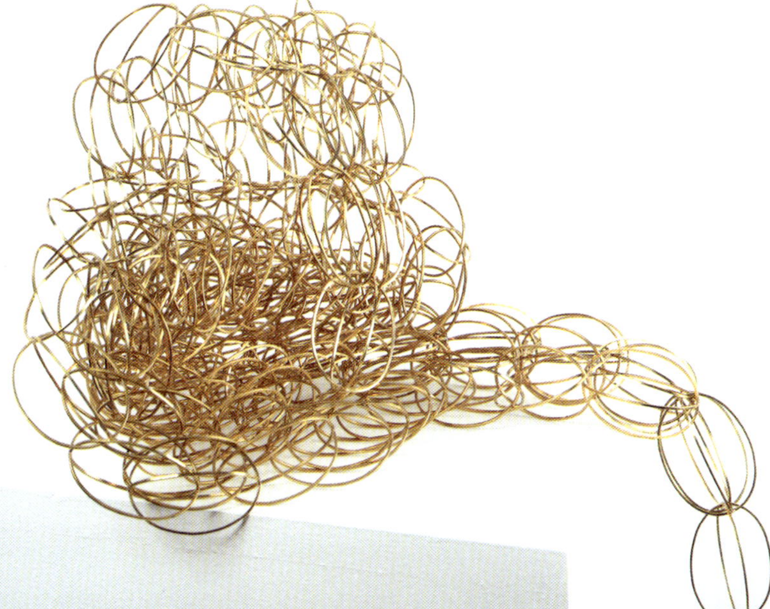

          Guest, 2004

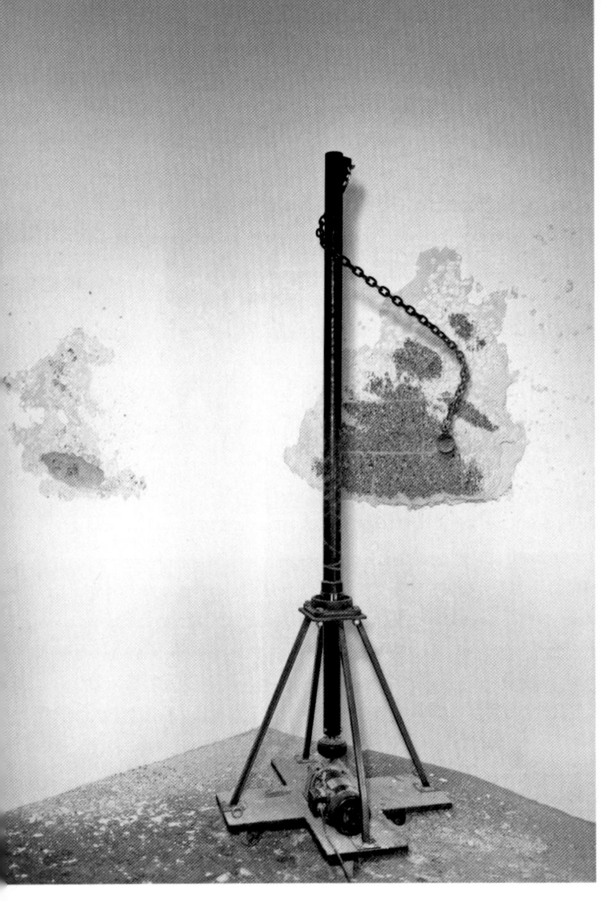

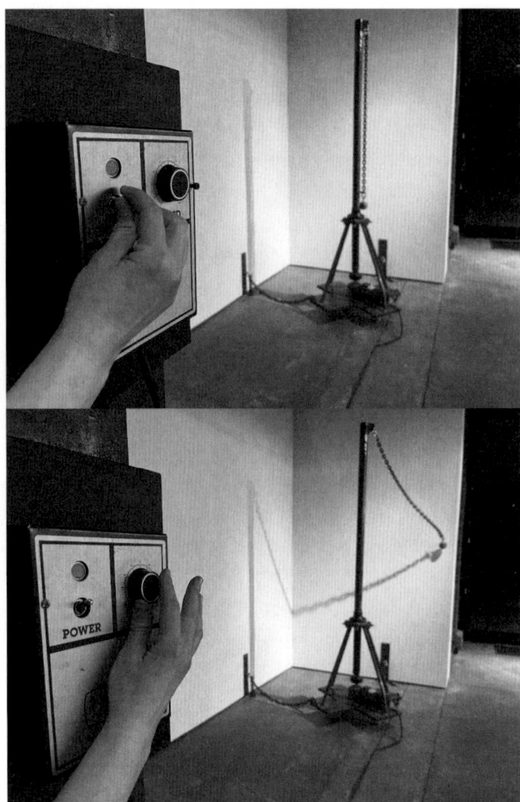

Corner Basher, 1988

This leads me to think about how consciously you deal with the relationship between machines and the body. In even blunter terms, *Corner Basher* [1988] might be seen as a primitive robot, or a prosthetic extension of the body. Around the time you made it, you also had proposals for self-destructing machines.

LL   Your take is an interesting one. Yes, I was thinking about this around the time I made *Verwoben* and *Corner Basher*. The title *Verwoben (Head, Torso, Foot)* gives you a hint as to this diffused, almost prosthetic figurative endeavor. And then the materials: *Foot* has to do with shoes. *Head* includes some images of heads from newspapers from the last months of 1989 on one woven panel. But it is also a figurative piece in the way one encounters it. It's very figurative, in terms of what the viewer's body does. There's a performative aspect, as some viewers negotiate the space and others observe them. A movement must be made to get over or under the extensions that support the densest parts of the weavings and attach to the architecture of the space that *Verwoben* occupies. This movement is for all bodies.

I was considering the different ways of putting an object in a particular place in space, and that led me to understanding that each space needs to be separately considered, whether it is a white cube, an unusual and materially rich space like SculptureCenter, or a garage at an apartment designed by Rudolph Schindler in Mid-City, Los Angeles. Its adaptability to different spaces is part of the piece. So far, *Verwoben* depends on the room it is in to support it.

The sculpture I made right after *Verwoben* was *Come Together* [1989], a combination of materials that form a nexus. The central part is a large, intricate knot, and lines—of tape measures, phone cords, human hair, ribbon, rope, lace, wire, TV antennae cable . . . —that attach to the surrounding walls and seem as though they come *from* the walls, ceiling, and floor. For me, the lines of support of *Verwoben* unfurl from the weavings toward the wall. Both sculptures are network assemblages. Anthropologist Anna Lowenhaupt Tsing says that "to learn about an assemblage, one unravels its knots."[3] We're in a time, where things come together, become assemblages, entanglements, collisions . . .

3 Anna Lowenhaupt Tsing, *The Mushroom at the End of the World: On the Possibility of Life in Capitalist Ruins* (Princeton, NJ: Princeton University Press, 2015), 83.

MC   Works like *Reticule* [1999], made up of identical intersecting parts, generate variable forms and rely on color to produce a specific optical effect. I know you think a lot about color, and, of course, most pigments come from mineral or biological sources. I wonder if we could talk about color in a similar way to how one might talk about other materials.

LL   Can color work in a different way when it is doing something besides reinforcing form? Something that enables ideas detached from dominant assumptions to come forward? The open-cube steel sculpture *2 as 3 and Some, Too* [1997–98], covered in paper and painted with watercolor, clearly shows how color can alter one's perception of a form by creating shifting three-dimensional spaces while not canceling out the form. Because the color does not follow the form, the work seems to move as you move around it. *Untitled* [2000], a paper-covered stainless-steel-cube wall piece, does this in a different but related way. Color changes one's initial assessment of the size and width of the cast-polyurethane piece *Reticule*. The red against the blue gray makes the sculpture appear thinner than it is found to be once one moves around it.

In that case, your movement is what tells you how big it is, not your eyes.

The ceramic wall-slab pieces allow me to work with color and form more freely and more often; these idiosyncratic explorations, where I might work with a pigment or glaze or material for a few pieces but always in different ways, have become an extensive part of my process. I hope the ways I use color, form, and materials encourage a shudder or a shake-up of perception.

MC   Well, now that you have brought up ceramics, let's talk about your ceramic slab pieces.

LL   Ceramic has an incommensurable quality of being both delicate and tough. It's a hard material that can appear soft, a material that can last for millennia but is also fragile. Most everything in one way or another comes from the earth, but clay is formed near the surface, in soils and sediments, and retains its close relation to the mineral world, or so it seems. Water is essential for clay formation.

Reticule, 1999

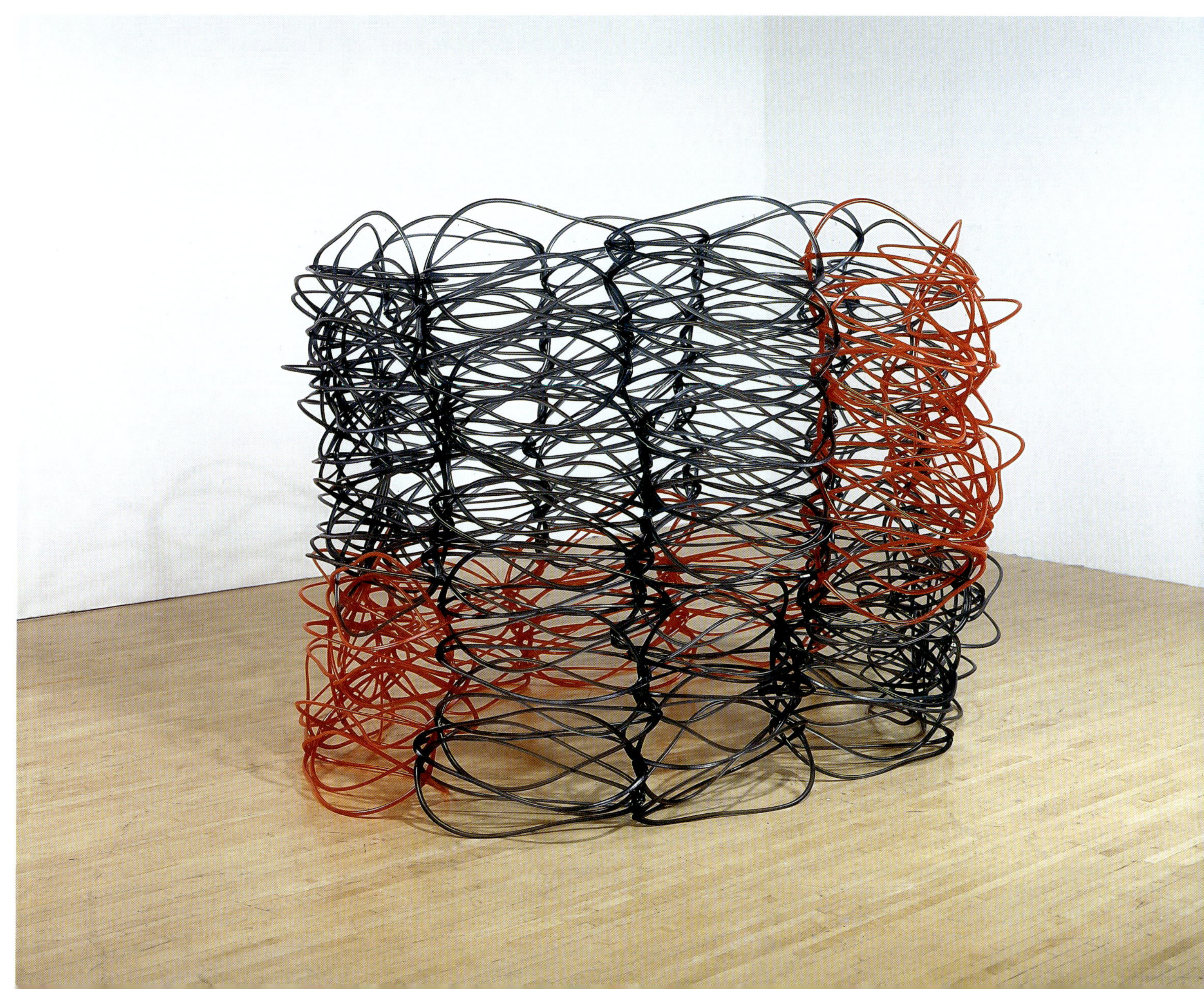

MC Humans have a very visceral response to clay and its elemental and alchemical characteristics. With your slab works, I keep coming back to the idea of the micro and the macro. Likewise, your *calefactions*, which have minerals embedded in them, seem to bounce between cosmic and microscopic scales, depending on how you're looking at them. Is that making sense to you?

LL So much sense. The material and forms of the wall ceramics inflect the visual experience of them; the color also does this. As you say, in the *calefactions*, what looks like something far away—in the cosmos or night sky from Earth, or islands in a sea or land masses from space—shifts back to the close-up views of bits of mineral, stones, clay, and earth. I hope the micro and macro views conflate and the viewer has cause to consider them together.

MC We have talked in other contexts about whether clay is a renewable resource.

LL A lot of what is left to us from ancient cultures is cuneiforms, symbols, and words written on clay tablets, not paper, because paper is biodegradable. The ancient history of humans is preserved on these tablets, ceramic jars, trinkets, and sculptures. Fired ceramic objects often last even longer than stone objects. We have profound attachments to things that endure and allow us to have a sense of ourselves over historical time. The idea of immortality is tied up with value, which is probably owing in part to this desire to know our past.

MC That is an interesting entry point to talk about *Firestone* [2019], an almost-life-size abstracted figure. It weaves together many different threads that have run through your work over the years, and one of them has to do with the materiality of ceramics.

LL *Firestone* is a supine form, an odalisque, but the material is durational and tough. Reclining without seeming vulnerable.

MC If I remember correctly, the germ of this piece came while you were working on *Public Jewel* [2015], a public sculpture commissioned by the US government for the plaza of the Byron G. Rogers Federal Building and US courthouse in Denver, which is when you started to get into minerals. Am I remembering that correctly?

LL You are. I wanted to use minerals and stones from Colorado for that sculpture. I was describing what I wanted to do to Karen Hillenburg, and she suggested I talk to jewelry designer Suzanne Felsen. Suzanne told me about the Tucson Gem and Mineral Show, which is the largest gem-and-mineral show in the United States, so I went to it in 2010. People come from all over the world to attend, buy, sell, discuss, and study. I found my way to geologist Ed Raines, who works with the collection at the Colorado School of Mines. I also visited a show about minerals found in Arizona that included examples of the same minerals from all over the world. I loved the form of a particularly beautiful hematite specimen. It was kind of elongated and low and reminded me of

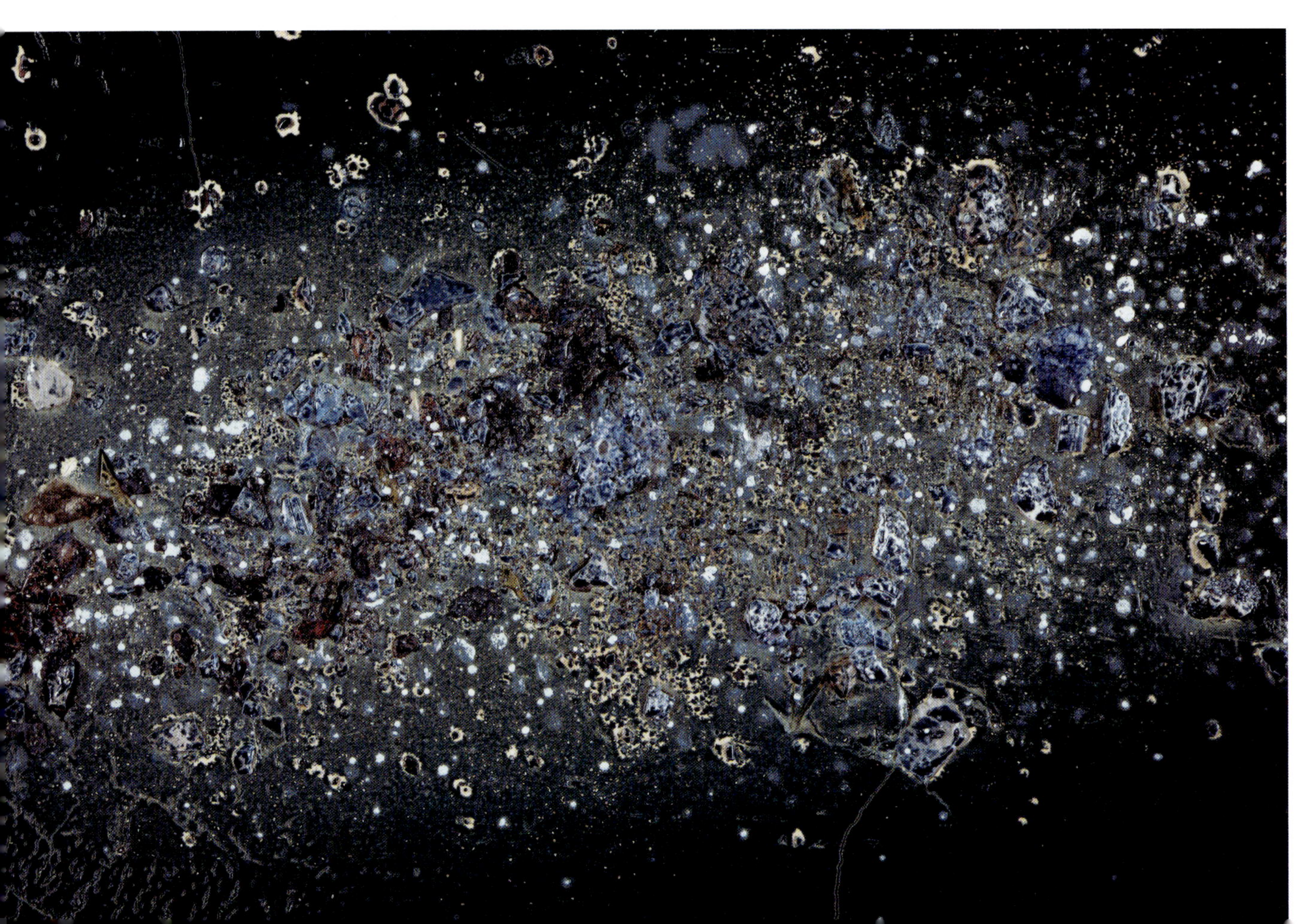

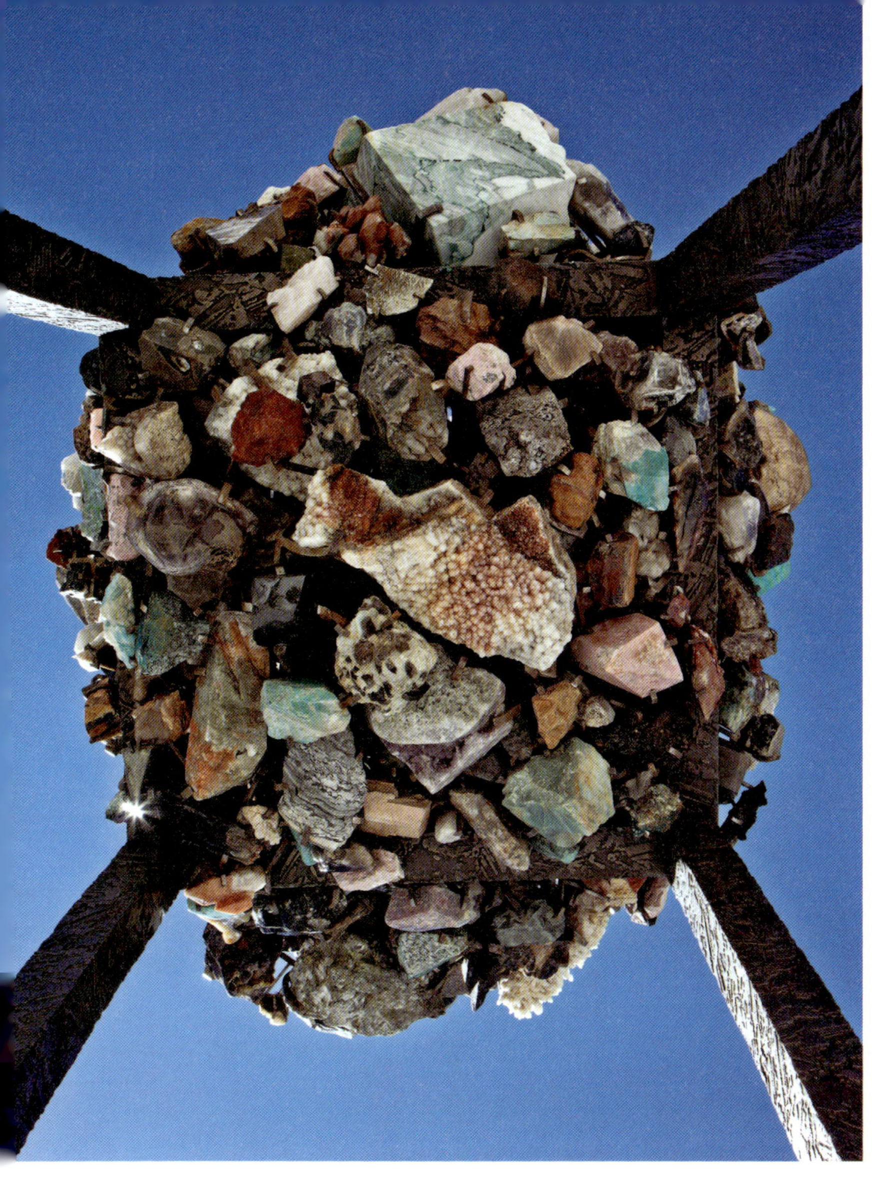

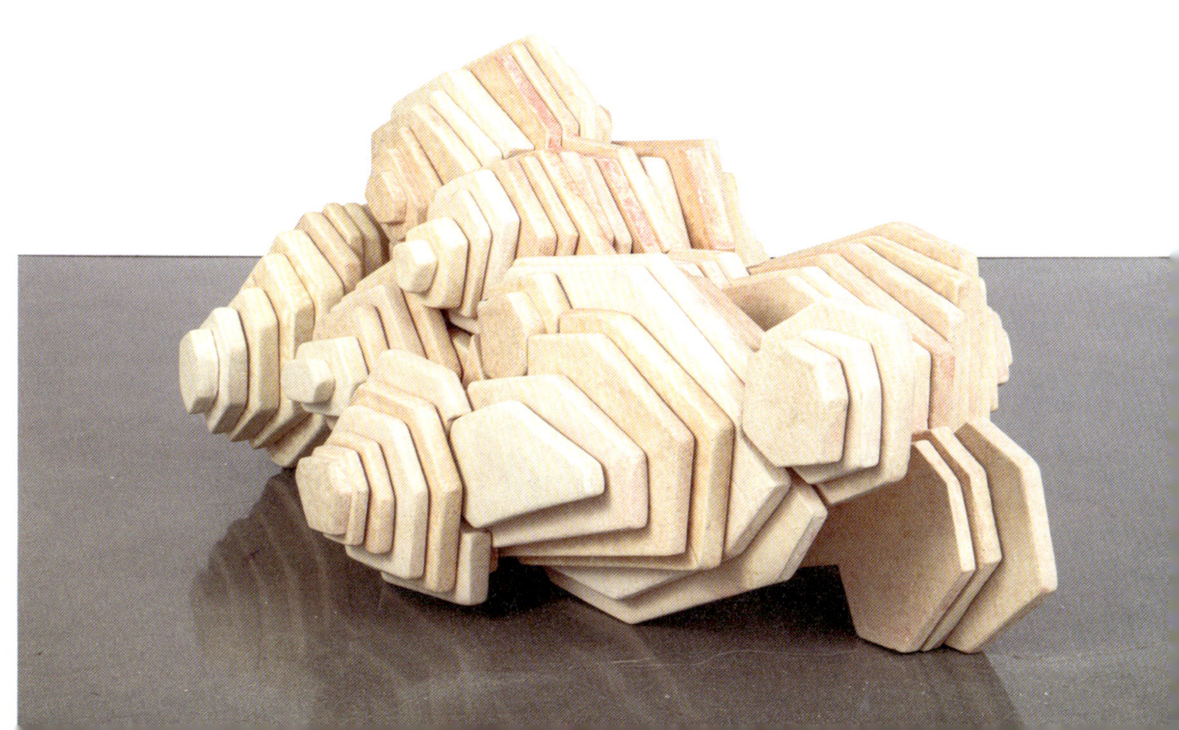

Opposite page *i (calefaction)*, 2014–15 (detail).
Ceramic, glaze, stones, and minerals,
21 × 37 ³/₄ × 8 inches (53.3 × 95.9 × 20.3 cm)

Above *Public Jewel*, 2015 (detail). Stainless
steel, bronze, minerals, 176 × 64 × 71 inches
(447 × 162.6 × 180.3 cm). Byron G. Rogers Federal
Building, Denver

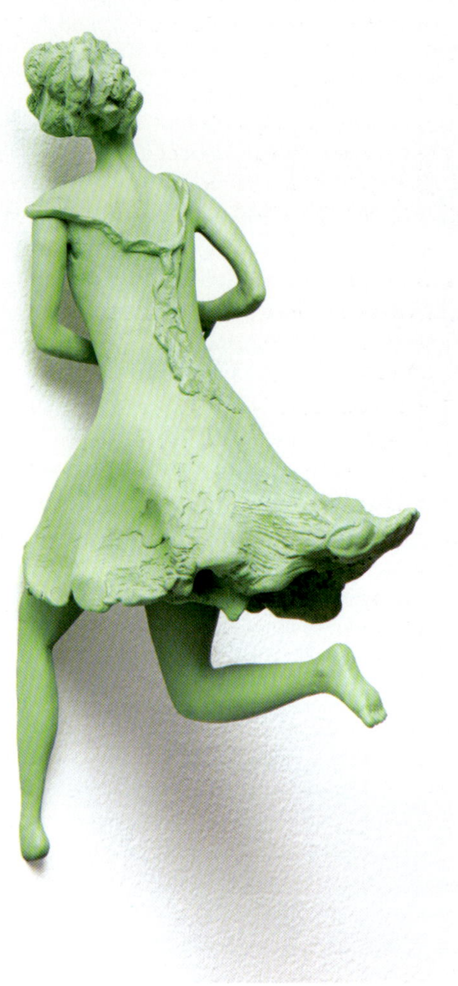

You might have to live like a refugee, 2019

a reclining figure. I researched hematite, which is a brittle form of iron whose crystal system is hexagonal. Since iron is in our blood, I like to think of it as Earth's blood.

I was also thinking about posthuman critical theory and how ecofeminism in the 1970s connected the female with the Earth and about the odalisque and supinity throughout art history. Many of our gestures are not wholly natural but are inflected by gender and by public gaze—what has been represented and is idealized as natural. For *Firestone*, hexagonal ceramic plates puzzle together to evoke a reclining figure.

MC   Art historically, we talk about how certain materials symbolize wealth and power, such as marble or bronze, and we talk about other materials, such as textiles, as being cast as feminine. I'm interested in your choice of bronze for *You might have to live like a refugee* [2019].

LL   I chose bronze for *You might have to live like a refugee*, because it is a figure—a small, articulated, and more classically modeled sculpture of a human being, although I mostly did not use a life model to make it. For many reasons, it was important to use bronze, with its recognizable green patina. I hope that this green calls to mind not only ancient bronze sculptures but also ecofeminism in relation to the current, highly charged moment of immigration around the world. So many people today want or need to move away from their home countries because of climate, economic, governmental, or other oppression. With bronze, the green patina naturally occurs in reaction to the copper in the alloy. I wanted to add some phosphorescence to that material. I wanted this sculpture to correlate to the difficulties so many immigrants and refugees endure and the instability of our social and political structures. *You might have to live like a refugee* is a literal depiction of a woman running through a wall.

MC   I guess that relates to the relationship of the world and the body.

LL   Another way of thinking about the micro and the macro: the individual and everybody.

MC   That makes me think about how *Hands* [1993], which stands out in your work as an unusual representation of the body, calls attention to the ways in which a single hand connects to others. Isolating it actually underscores the ways in which it's attached to other things. The idea of the hand is so tied to individuality—the mark that's made by the hand of the artist and all those things have to do with what makes something unique, original, and specific. But it is only important in its relation to something larger. Can you tell me a little about how you came to make this work?

LL   I was invited to make a work for the international sculpture exhibition Sonsbeek 93 in Arnhem, Netherlands. On a trip there to explore potential sites, I encountered two figurative sculptures across a courtyard from each other outside the Gemeentemuseum, and the hands of each of the figures had broken off. I thought about how hands are fragile and strange, appendages that do so much and express so much. I realized those expressions were no longer part of the sculptures. The missing meaning of those gestures became what those sculptures were about.

I sculpted some hands and cast hands from life and mixed these with commercially produced hands found in novelty and junk stores, creating different scenarios with them in various positions. All were slush-cast in pewter and suspended in relation to one another and in different positions. How do we read bodily gesture, and what is that dependent on? And what does it take to understand a human body in terms of gesture as communication? I didn't end up making this work for Sonsbeek 93, but I did make it for a show at Galerie Jennifer Flay in Paris that same year and showed it again in New York in 1994 under the title *without words*.

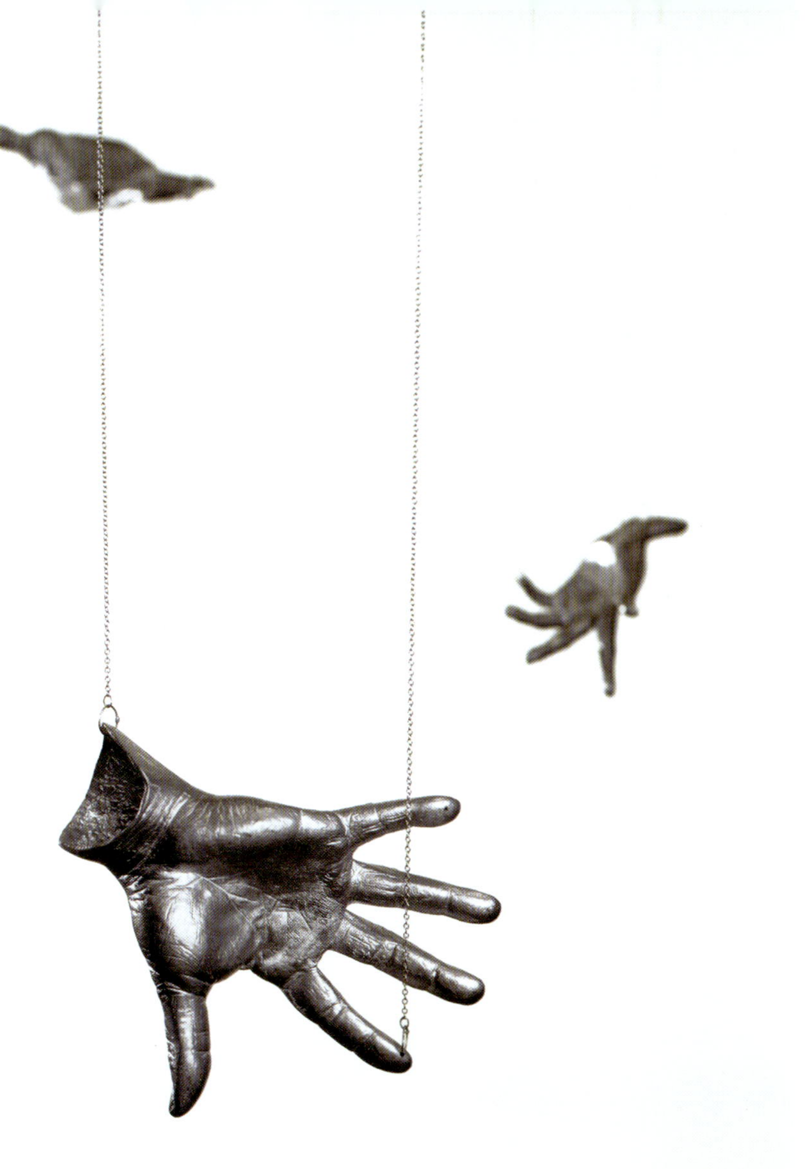

Above *Hands*, 1993 (detail)

Below *Possibilities of the Existence of Meaning Without Words Inside Disorder*, 1993. Installation view, Galerie Jennifer Flay, December 11, 1993–January 22, 1994

MC   I think of the *smile* works [1996–2011] similarly. Connie Butler suggests that they are more anthropomorphic when grouped together than when alone, describing them as images without bodies.

LL   Seeing just one of the *smile* works or a single *Hand* makes it into more of an image. We can think of iconic artworks where smiles and hands are singled out to become the essential aspect of that work—the Mona Lisa or the hand of God in the Sistine Chapel. These are icons, and I was wondering about icons. I wouldn't say that I am deconstructing the body with the *smiles* or *Hands*, even though it could be taken that way; I think of it more as isolating parts—isolating an icon and its locus.

Before I made the *smiles*, I read John Gregory Dunne's novel *The Red White and Blue* and Mark Twain's short story *The Million Pound Bank Note*. In both texts, the authors' use of modifiers before the word *smile*—"perfunctory smile," "victory smile," "one of those large smiles which goes all around over, and has folds in it, wrinkles, and spirals, and looks like the place where you have thrown a brick in a pond"—jumped out at me and gave me the idea to make smile sculptures out of cast porcelain. The heat of the kiln in relation to the material and form acting like a modifier before the word *smile* make each cast form unique.

MC   I feel like these disembodied appendages or expressions sometimes push toward the grotesque.

LL   Yes, something I had to think about in making *Hands* was whether it was going to be grotesque. Is this going to be a horror? I think of Louise Bourgeois, and sometimes that happens in her work. Sometimes it's beautiful, sometimes it's horrible, and sometimes it is both.

MC   For the grotesque to be effective, it must elicit some empathy; we need to be able to connect with it. It can't just be repulsive. Right?

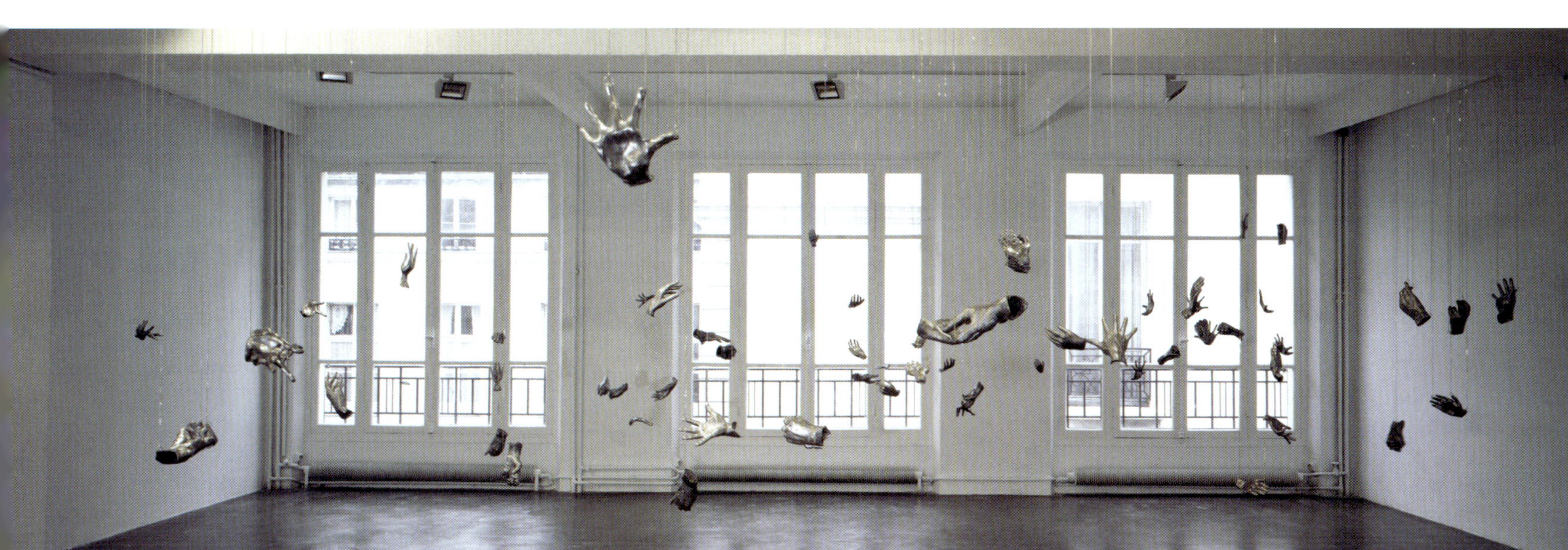

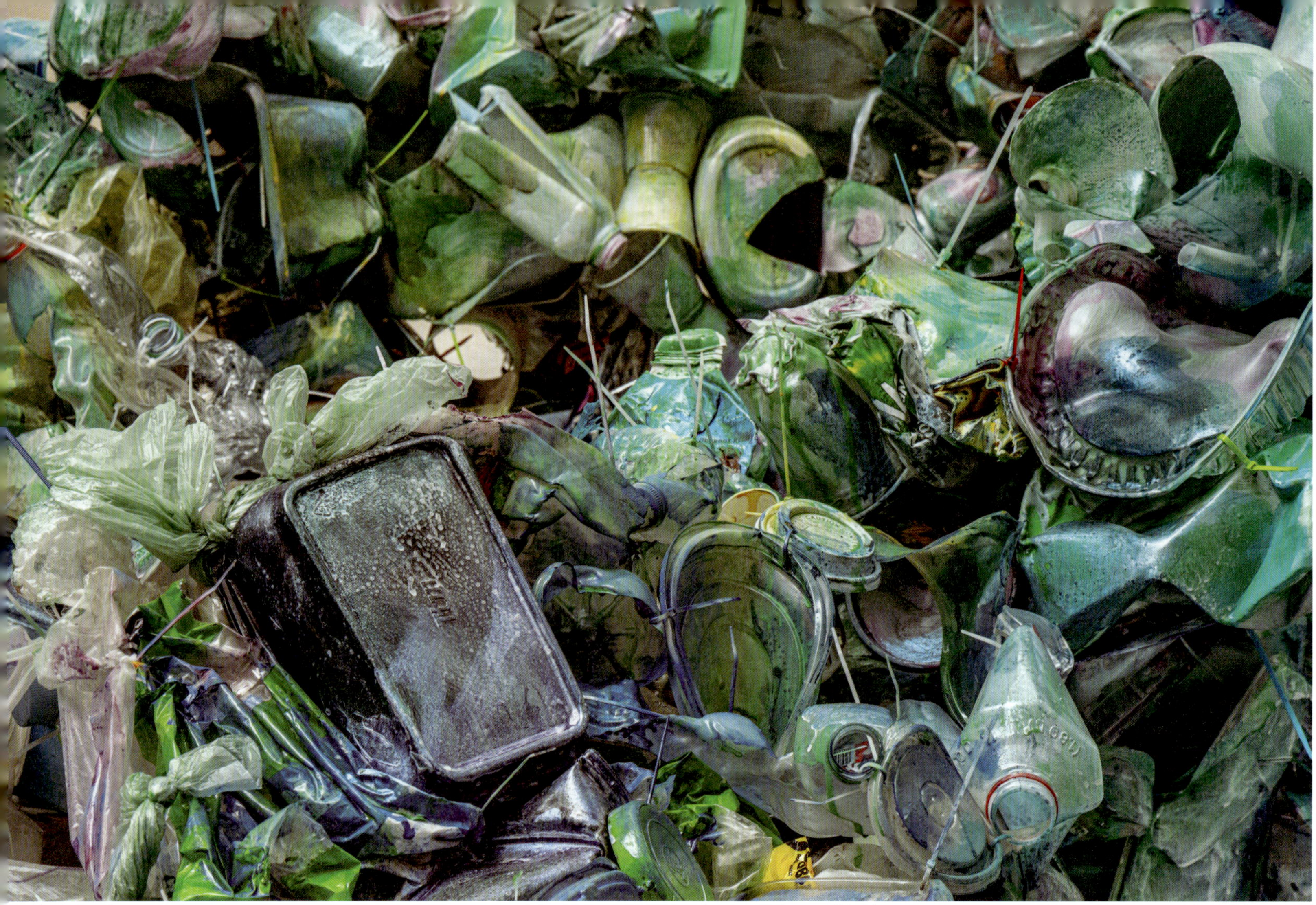

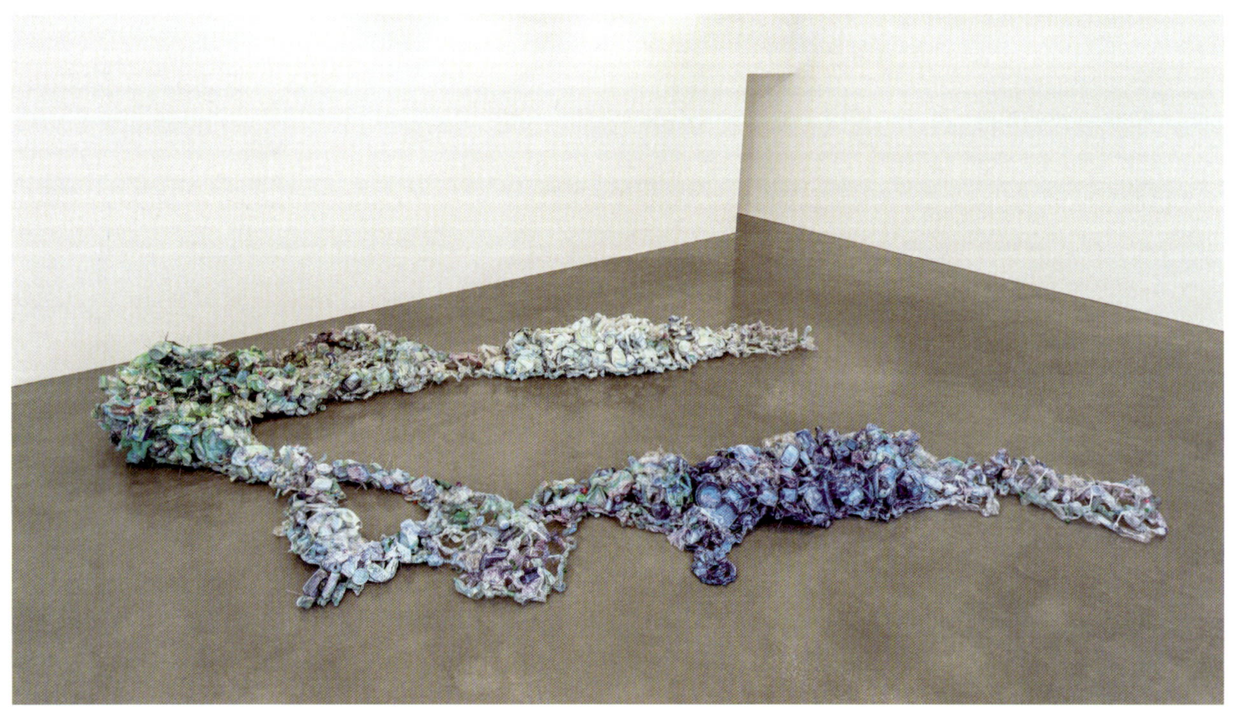

Left and above *Meerschaum Drift (Blue)*, 2020–21. Plastic, 37 × 240 × 346 ³⁄₄ inches (94 × 609.6 × 880.7 cm)

Opposite *2001*, 2001. Fiberglass, stainless steel and automotive paint, 144 × 144 × 144 inches (365.8 × 365.8 × 365.8 cm). Doris C. Freedman Plaza, Central Park, New York, November 29, 2006— January 5, 2007

LL I guess there is some horror that can induce empathy or pathos. I'm trying to evoke both in a material, formal, and fictional way. The real and the unreal can show each other off to great effect. In animation, they call that effect the uncanny valley. Sometimes a resemblance that is too close to the real is uncanny and becomes terrifying or repulsive. I'm exploring that line with the *smile* works and, especially, *Hands*. The hands that I sculpted were at a smaller scale than the life-cast hands. I am interested in science fiction and fantasy, too.

    The show I'm making for the Kunsthalle Zurich in June 2022 will conjure an impossible, fictional place where outer space and our oceans come together. The *asteroids* and *meerschaum drifts* in the installation will unmistakably hold the sense of the material they are made of—respectively, ceramic and a new material I am working with, refuse plastic. The petroleum used to produce plastics contributes to global warming, but our inability to contend with our use of plastics is out of control and its own crisis. There are two to five different plastics in a typical container, and only one of them is marked, usually. And nobody has the time to take every item that they use, break it down, and put it in the right place for recycling. It can't be dealt with on an individual or micro scale. In the capitalist world, all the responsibility will be on the consumer until this huge amount of trash can be turned into commodity. Some say that only 9 percent of all plastic ever used has been recycled, but I've read that the number may be closer to just 2 percent. The only way we're going to get to reuse systems, to vegetable plastics that are truly biodegradable, or to recycling that actually works is to focus on the whole cycle and the consequences of making objects with such materials. This can only happen at the macro level of governments and international agreements. There is some movement on holding producers to account through a governmental-policy approach to treating and disposing of postconsumer products known as Extended Producer Responsibility (EPR).

MC Right. The cycle needs to start with production and the source of materials.

LL Most artists don't want their work to disappear, to biodegrade. But I think this is something that artists, like everyone else, will have to start dealing with: the time scale of objects— their artworks. The question is: what material can I use that is biodegradable, that is not toxic, and that can be brought back into the system without a toxic effect on microscopic life, fish, plants, and animals?

MC We think of the organic and the inorganic as completely separate things, but you overlay them in a way that destabilizes both. It changes our understanding of both.

LL Yes, a lot of different works, including *2 as 3 and Some, Too, Public Jewel, 2001* [2001], and the *smiles* combine inorganic and organic forms, too. I think this is evident throughout. It's also in the *Cultures* [1987–], in a way.

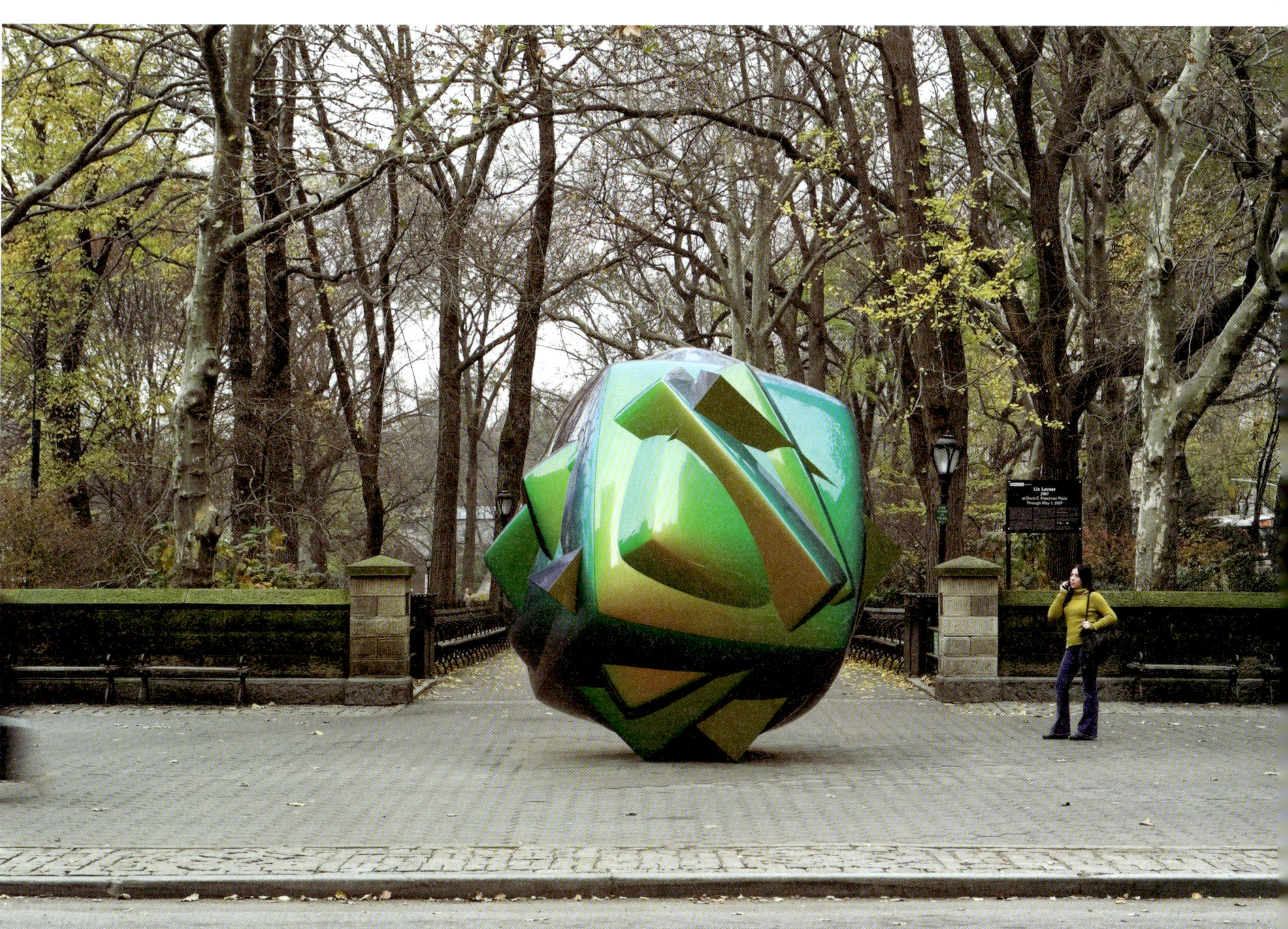

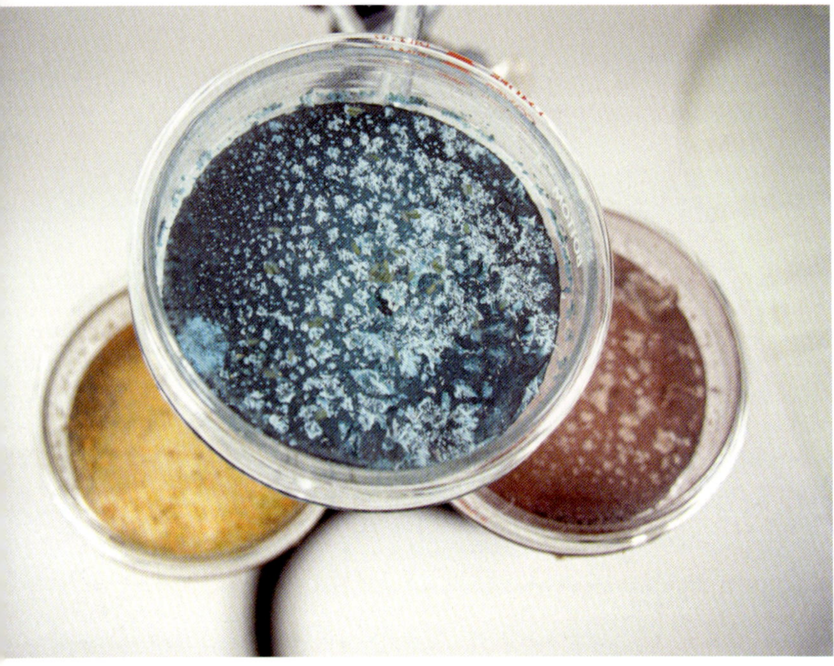

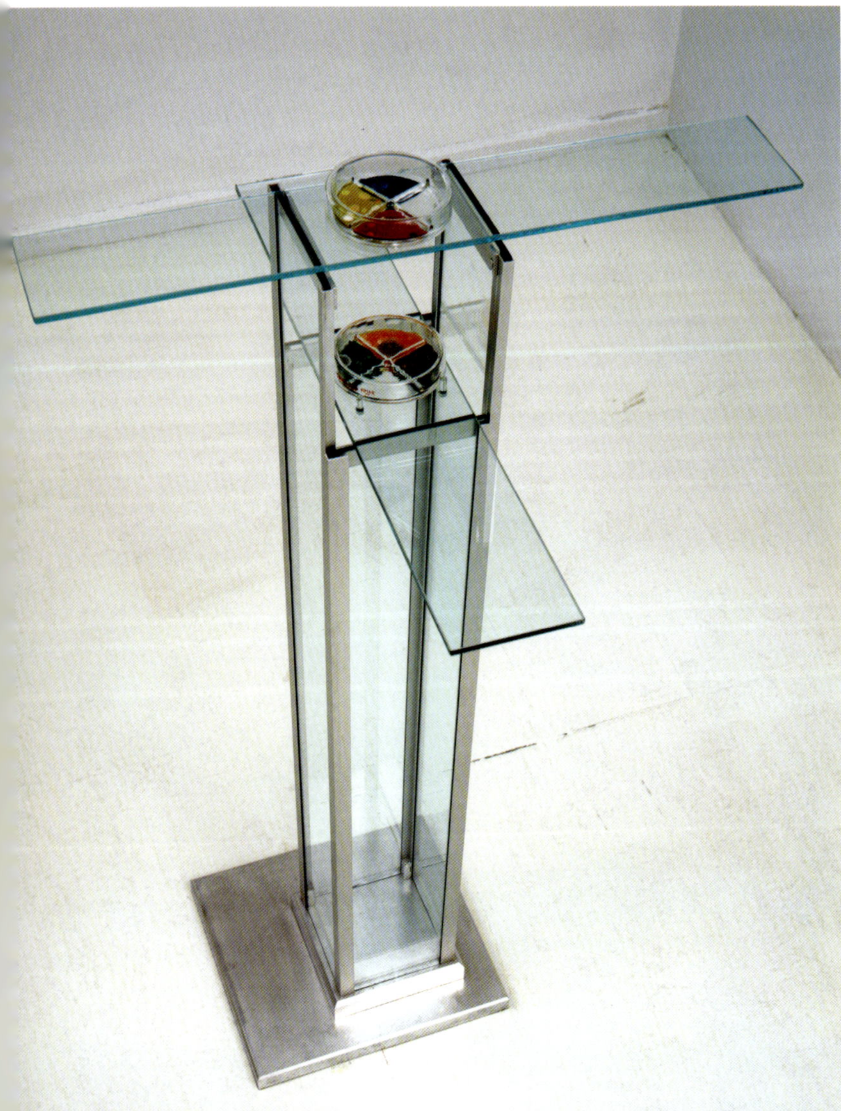

MC When I saw the *Culture* pieces for the first time, which was after I'd already seen your work in various contexts for ten years or so, something clicked for me. Ideas and approaches were seeded in those works. They are controlled regenerative processes that incorporate real organic decay, but you call them *Cultures*. Even with the science-lab connotation, it's a natural, inevitable process. What does that mean about nature and culture, or nature and art?

LL The *Cultures* are assembled with several substances and forms that all contribute to the understanding of the object as a work of art. *Orchid, Buttermilk, Penny* [1987] was originally composed from those materials placed over a thin media of nutrient agar in a large glass petri dish. I took photos of it poolside at the Tropicana Motel the morning after a one-night exhibition called *Room 9* [1987] in one of the motel rooms. I took another photo of it three months later in my studio. That was when I had to come to terms with the death of that culture. It seems myopic not to have anticipated the evanescent aspect of the material, but when I opened the box and saw it, I was shocked.

Eventually, I introduced materials like food coloring or microorganisms with an inoculation wand. In this way, I could "culture" anything, and the combinations would grow and "bloom" by digesting the colored nutrient agar. As the nutrient was exhausted, they would slowly decay. Waferlike colored discs would be left in the petri dishes—they will eventually turn to colored dust, though this hasn't really happened yet. The titles of these works are taken from the names of the materials, places, objects, or subjects where the microorganisms that I used to inoculate the colored agar in the petri dishes were located. The poetics of the titles combine with the pathos of the short-lived, energetic, resplendent world in the petri dish, as well as its afterlife as an art object.

MC The *Cultures* go back to the idea that, as individuals, we can't control everything about how we live in culture and in nature.

LL What you say about culture and nature brings to mind a talk I listened to the other day given by the farmer-gardener Harald Hoven, who has been working with plants for sixty years. He talked about how much that we depend on to keep us alive are things that we don't have control over. He was talking about all that a gardener doesn't have much to do with—the life in the soil, what's in the water and air, the climate, the seeds. Hoven suggested that we can admire these things beyond our control and how we're taking more than we're giving. That is an aspect of the human condition we don't admit to often. You and I have talked before about the extractive aspect of mining and how much we take from the planet to survive and live as we are accustomed to and aspire to. This is where we find ourselves in the Anthropocene.

Top to bottom
Culture of Marvin Heiferman, 1988.
Glass, nutrient agar, food coloring,
cast iron, steel, height: 48 inches (121.9 cm)
*Primary, Secondary: Culture of Empire
State Building and Twin Towers*, 1988

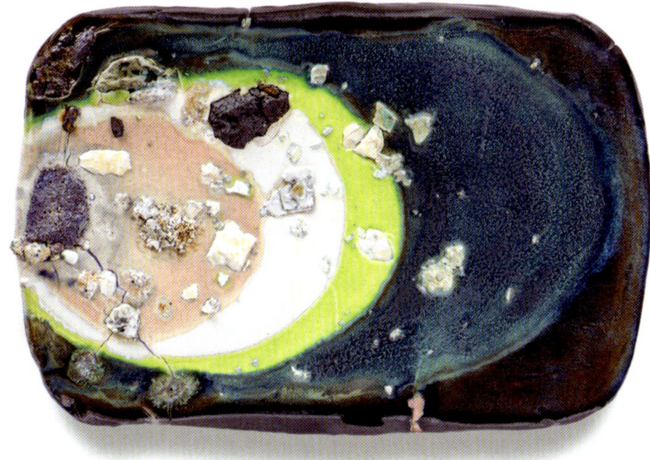

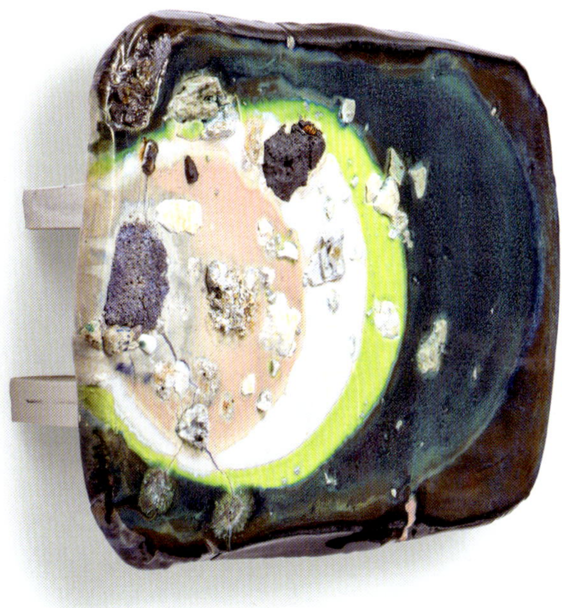

x (calefaction), 2016 (front and three-quarter view)

MC   In looking at your work over time, I'm drawn to how you posit agency, both from the perspective of your intent as an artist and how much you are willing to turn over to the visitor. In a work like *Corner Basher*, the visitor can control the piece. By turning over the operation of the work, you're calling attention to where we, as individuals, may or may not have agency. This relates to how you talk about mastery relative to a material or technique. I'm thinking about ceramics, of course, and the *Culture* pieces, which are a form of process art: you set something in motion, and then the piece makes itself.

LL   Yes, in some ways that I cannot control. There are parameters, though.

MC   Right, you establish parameters, and then it's a somewhat controlled process that you let take its own path. When you're glazing ceramics, you can learn a lot about how a glaze will react, but some unpredictable things are going to happen.

LL   Yes. When I started making the ceramic wall pieces, I didn't use glaze; I used pigmented epoxy. I could work with that process but not really control it. It took seven hours for the epoxy to cure, as it slowly flowed over and through the topography of the ceramic forms. I'd come back in the morning and take it from there. Ceramics is its own world. It is a deep technique—so deep, nobody could try everything that has already been mastered. You need to find your way inside all that technique. I can do all the planning I want, but there's something that happens in the making that can never really be anticipated, which honestly is just the way it is with making art and a big part of its pleasure and surprise. One decision leads to the next thing. For me, it is just the way I move forward. I suppose this also has something to do with what people take from it—and I don't want to control what people take from it.

Cornering
the Setup

CATHERINE LIU

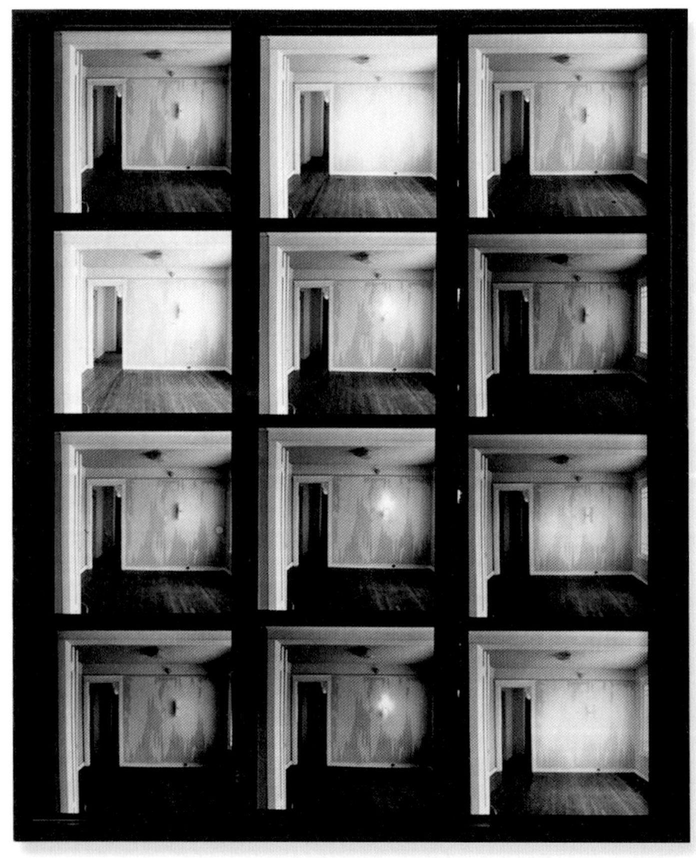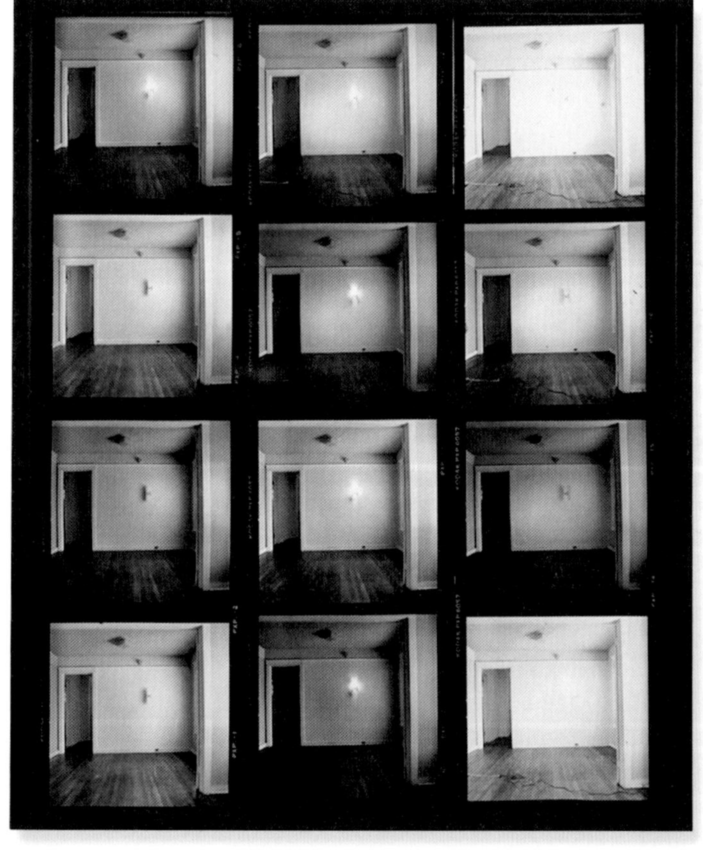

Untitled, 1985. Black-and-white photographs; three
parts, 24 $\frac{1}{4}$ × 20 $\frac{1}{4}$ inches (61.6 × 51.4 cm) each

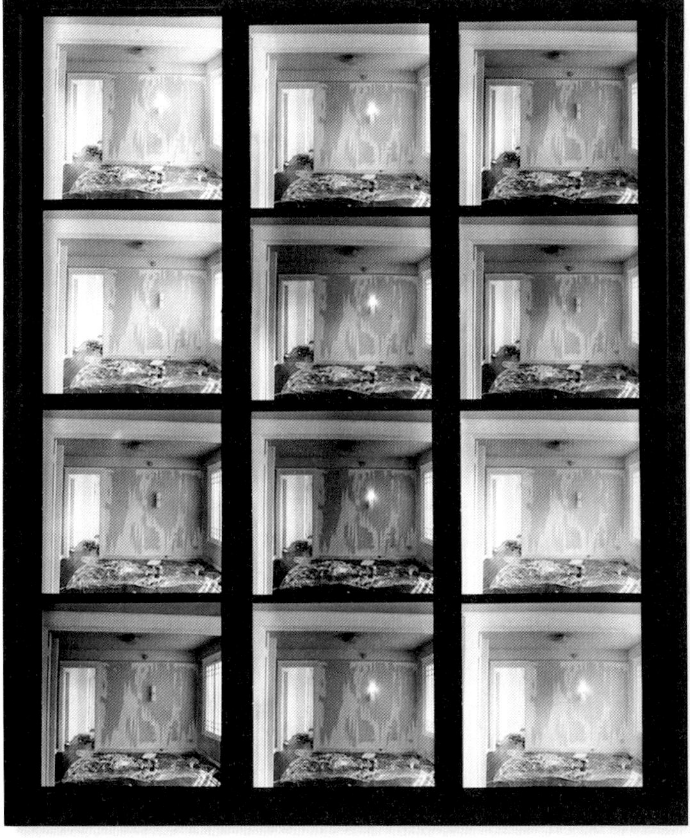

There is a level of sculptural abstraction that is produced by an artist's intervention—an intervention that disrupts the very space of viewership itself. A sculptor once said that good sculpture should deny photography: that is, it should be unphotographable, because it defies stasis and eludes capture, because its very presence in the space of representation makes the seizing of such space impossible for any technique of camera obscura. Liz Larner's work engages in a project of disrupting the construction of the space of the artwork and, in the process, challenges the viewer to enter the space of the exhibition in a different manner.

Larner has used the strategies of installation to create powerful allegories of the way in which the experience of visual representation is constructed. The questions that her work raises are directly related to the way in which the gaze is detachable from the body. In *Chain Perspective: Reversed, Reflected, Extended* (1992), she uses chains to "draw" the lines of sight in classical perspective that create an illusion of depth in two-dimensional media.[1] By playing with such techniques of classical representation, she, in her own words, "gives another perspective on perspective." The properties of the material with which she works are also always highly charged and polyvalent. Chains call to mind a myriad of associations around servitude, restraint, and constraint; laying down the law; and drawing limits and lines of exclusion. Larner's work has always alluded to and used force and tension in ways that invite philosophical reflection. If her work resists and seduces the viewer at the same time, it is because it uses the force of resistance inherent in the materials themselves to evoke their aesthetic and theoretical potential. Larner's installations often work with the mutual resistance that objects exert upon the space and that space exerts upon objects. A mutual incomprehension and a reciprocal indifference are overcome through the creation of productive tensions—tensions that are produced by pliable materials drawn taut, and tensions that can produce almost invisible reactions over time. These tensions and resistances can be interpreted in the context of Sigmund Freud's take on ambivalence and Friedrich Nietzsche's take on force and resentment, but we cannot do any more in here than allude to them as some of the difficult and intellectually exciting associations that Larner's work calls up. Larner's work is close to theory and to philosophy, but it keeps its distance regarding an explicit engagement with discourse.[2] An excess of proximity often generates a force field that keeps at bay that which is closest.

1 This piece was part of *Helter Skelter: LA Art in the 1990s,* a show at the Museum of Contemporary Art, Los Angeles, January 26, 1992–April 26, 1992. An early version of the work, *Chain Perspective Reflected,* was shown at 303 Gallery, New York, in 1990.
2 See Jacques Derrida, *The Post Card: From Socrates to Freud and Beyond,* trans. Alan Bass (Chicago: University of Chicago Press, 1987), 263.

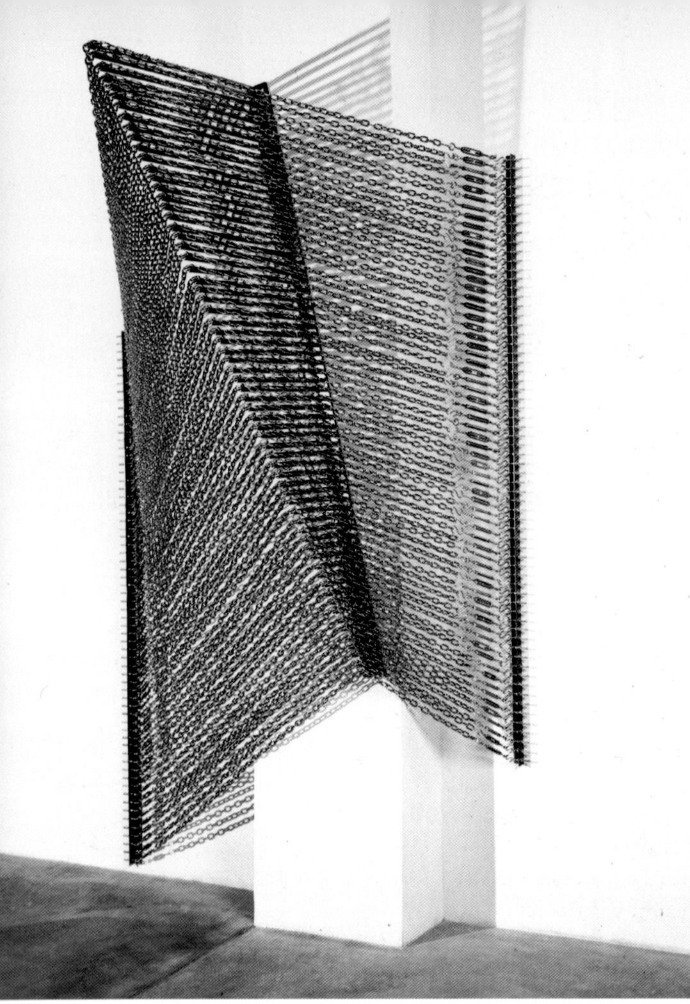

Chained Form on the Diagonal Interrupted by Humans, 1990. Chain, steel, hardware, 84 × 66 × 42 inches (213.4 × 167.6 × 106.7 cm)

The notion of "place" in the work of Larner is explored in a rigorous and inevitably theoretical manner through techniques of installation. Installation is a setup that disturbs all notions of setting up. In his essay "Upsetting the Setup: Remarks on Heidegger's Questing after Technics," Samuel Weber suggests that we understand the Heideggerian use of *Gestell* in terms of "emplacement" by working through a certain notion of "installation."[3] Technology for Weber is about the frame, about the situation of a horizon and the setting of place; the notion of emplacement, then, collects and assembles the various ways in which everything, human beings included, is "cornered" (*gestellt*) and set in place. But since the places thus set up are the result of emplacement, they can never simply be taken for granted. Places must be continually established, orders continually placed. As emplacements, the goings-on of modern technics thus display a markedly ambivalent character: they arrest, bring to a halt, by setting in place, but this placement itself gives way to other settings, to the incessant replacing of orders through which new places are set up and upset.[4]

The question of the corner is interesting here because Larner has consistently been working through the notion of how to cut a corner in a room—in the exhibition space of what has been idealized as the white cube. She often installs her work in corners, framing these spaces with chains, machines, a game of mirrors, and even words painted on both walls and floors. The corner acts as both support and obstacle; she makes us acutely aware of their sharpness, of their marginality to the room and their structural relationship to all notions and aesthetics of centeredness. For Weber, the setup that needs to be questioned is one that has been evoked by what he translates as the Heideggerian notion of technics. Technics install the human being on a horizon: this "installation" allows for the human being to have a certain coherent relationship with nature, available to him or her either as a resource to be exploited or a ruin to be mourned.

Larner's installation plays with the notion of an idealized, static space of representation by evoking the effects and marks of time. Time begins to play an important factor when force is exerted on the very supports of the white cube itself: in the case of *Wall Scratcher* (1988) and *Chain between Wall* (1990), a projected destruction of the infrastructure of the exhibition space is contained in the sculptures themselves. Attention is called to the very conditions of installation: an art object is supported literally

3 Samuel Weber, "Upsetting the Setup: Remarks on Heidegger's Questing after Technics," in *Mass Mediauras: Form, Technics, Media* (Stanford, CA: Stanford University Press, 1996), 55–75.
4 Ibid., 72.

5 *Corner Basher* is operated by an ON-OFF switch and a speed control dial on a control box mounted on the wall about twenty feet away from the machine of the work. The destruction of the architecture is always variable and depends on the material of the walls, the amount of time the machine is in operation, and the rate at which it runs.

and metaphorically by a complex of infrastructural institutions. The marking of time within the art object takes place in the tension of projected, inevitable destruction. The chain installations can pull down the corners of the white cube, given enough time; the *Corner Basher* (1988) can work on its dogged little path of destruction, and if given enough time, it too will destroy the support of the space of representation.[5] The machine marks the intervention of time upon space. This points to the way in which supports, both figurative and metaphorical, are supposed to be effaced, made invisible even, by traditional techniques of art installation.

In the age of corporate sponsorship, a certain amount of institutional prudishness has been shed when museums must use corporate logos in their advertisements for a show, but the normal sequence of affairs still demands that a certain kind of "support" be as unobtrusive as possible in the display of art objects. There are artists who take on these paradoxes directly in a mode of critique; these strategies are ideological, and Larner's are allegorical. In ideological critique, the framing of visual representation is almost never questioned—this is why activism in the art world almost always functions in modalities of inclusion and identification, whereas allegorical critique questions the very conditions of representation itself. Viewership and "communication" of a political message are predicated upon the transparent space in which the art object has been placed, and transparency is precisely what Larner asks us to question.

In Larner's project *Machine* (1998–2001), the use of the latest automobile motion-sensor technology allows her to continue to work through questions of presence, topographies that shape representation and principles of destruction. This machine/installation, still as yet in blueprint form, is one of the strongest interventions in the field of the inevitable encounter between technology and Freud's "Beyond the Pleasure Principle." Contemporary artists and contemporary theorists can be too close for comfort, in ways that are not immediately recognizable. This kind of uncanny intimacy, however, can take the form of mutual resistances that make for the most productive of tensions. Art must always in some sense resist theory, and theory art.

Larner is an artist who has never stopped reflecting on the place, the frame, the emplacement of the art object, and the methods, techniques, and supports for its display. It is impossible, therefore, when writing on her work, to avoid the question of what it means to write "on" an artist's work in general. What kind of surface offers itself up and to what kind of inscription? Larner's work challenges the writer to think of these issues because she is always working on the status of the art object in relation to its structural and infrastructural support system. We say without thinking that someone has "written" on Larner, but what does such a thing mean? If writing "on" art is not to be merely a prosthetic practice, it has to take on the challenge offered by Larner's work to think through the forms and constraints that shape and support writing itself.

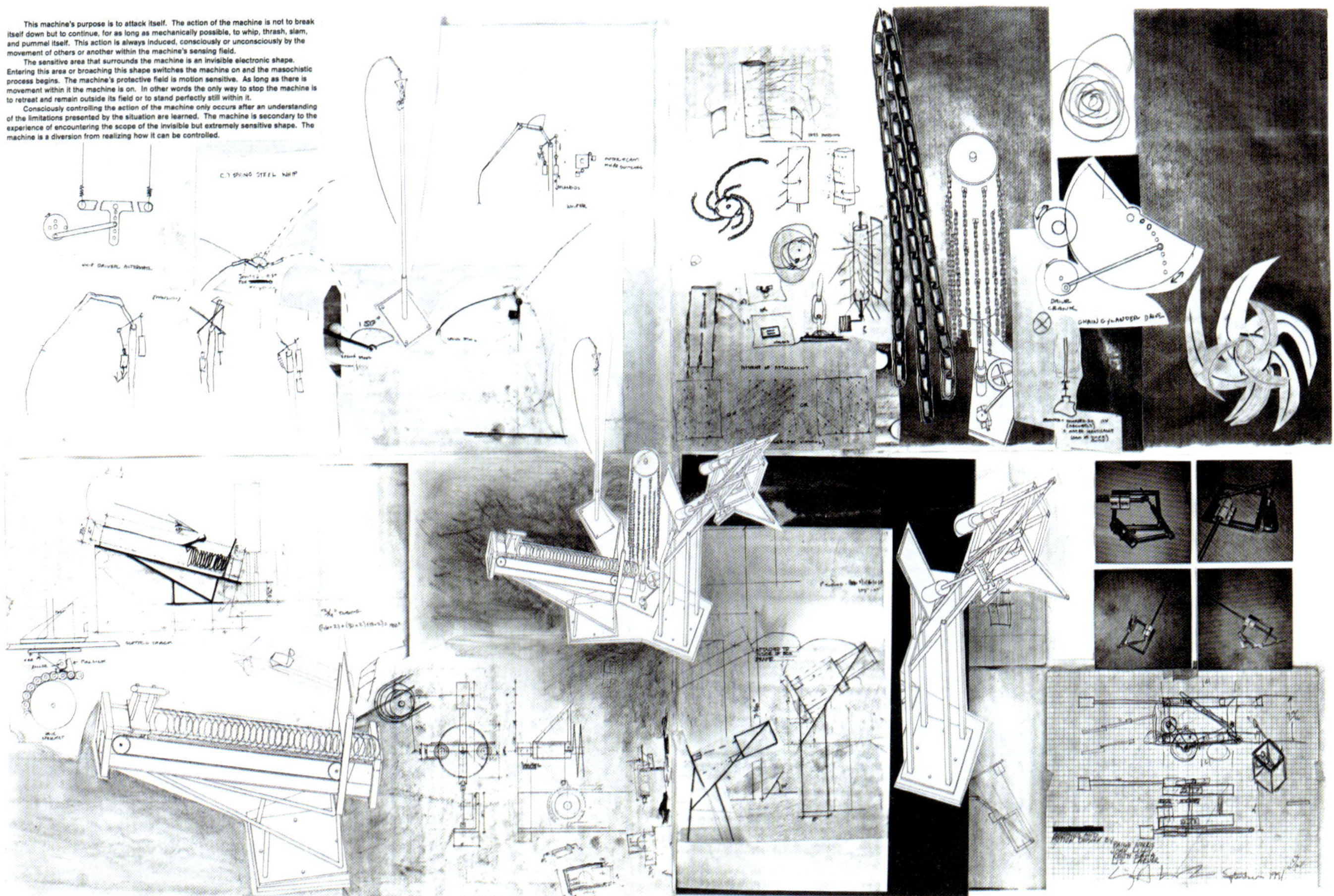

Collage for Machine, 1991. Photocopy, graphite, collage on paper, 22 × 33 7/8 inches (55.9 × 86 cm)

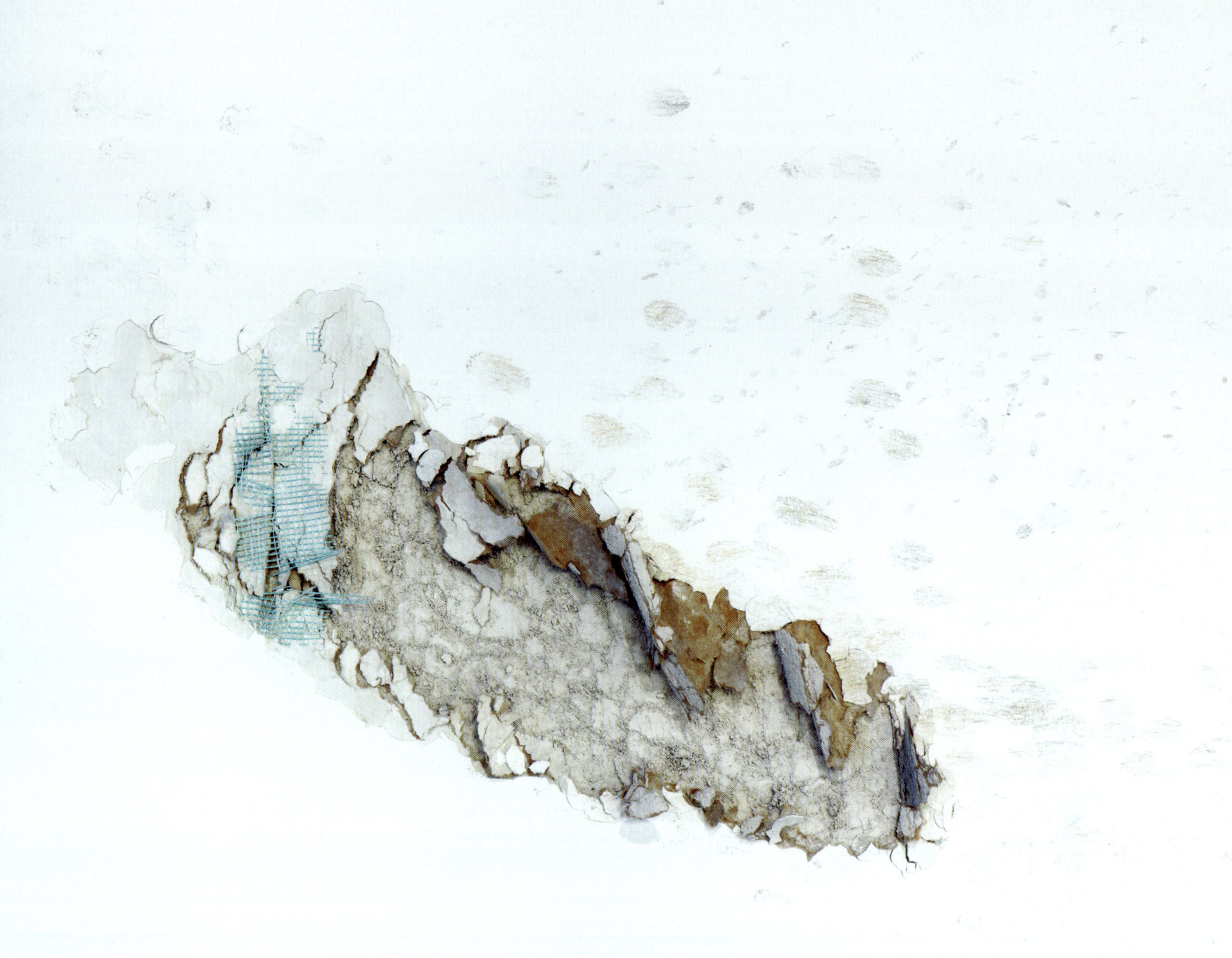

Liz Larner: Don't put it back like it was
SculptureCenter   January 20–March 28, 2022
Photographs by Cathy Carver

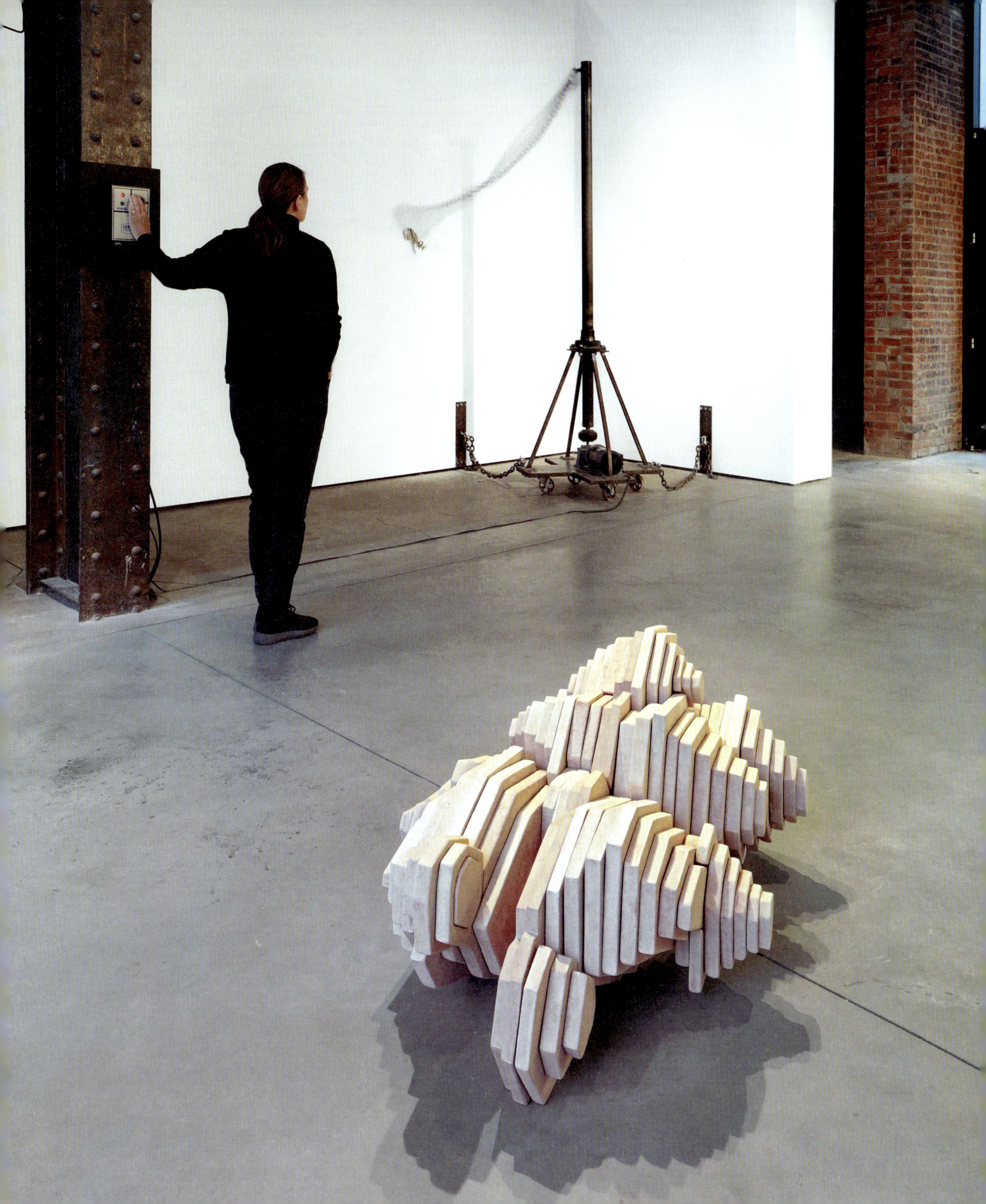

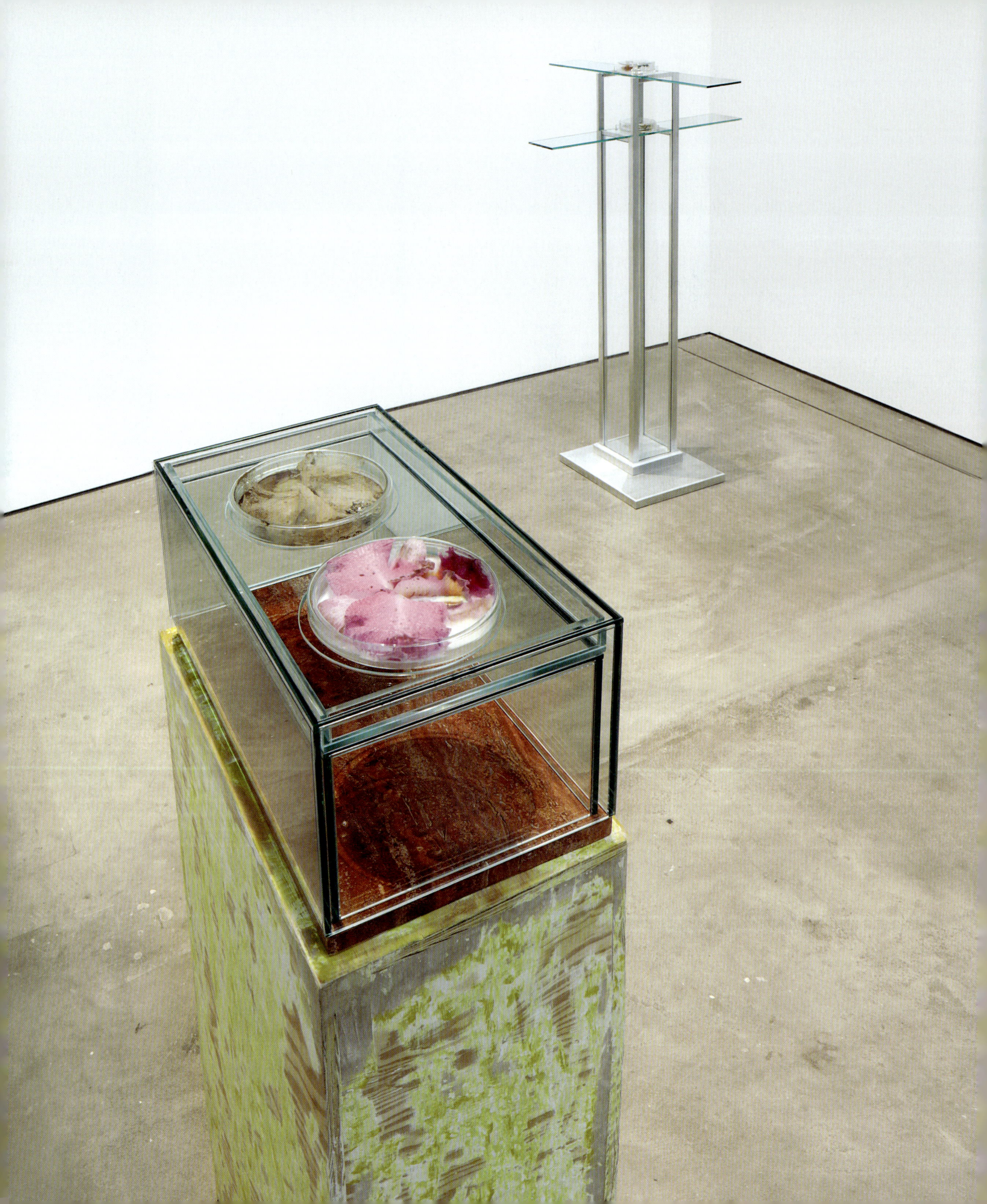

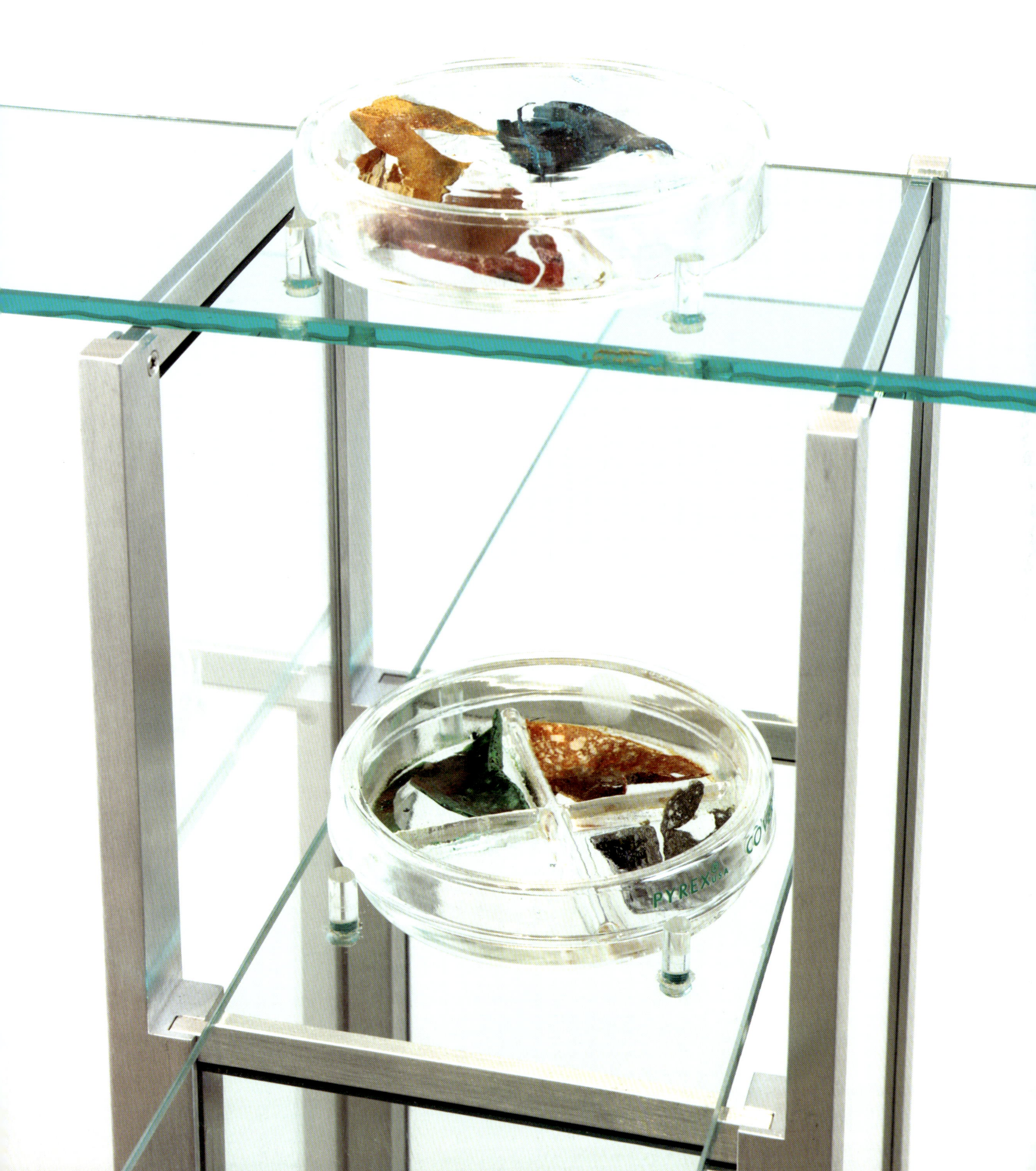

PYREX USA
COV

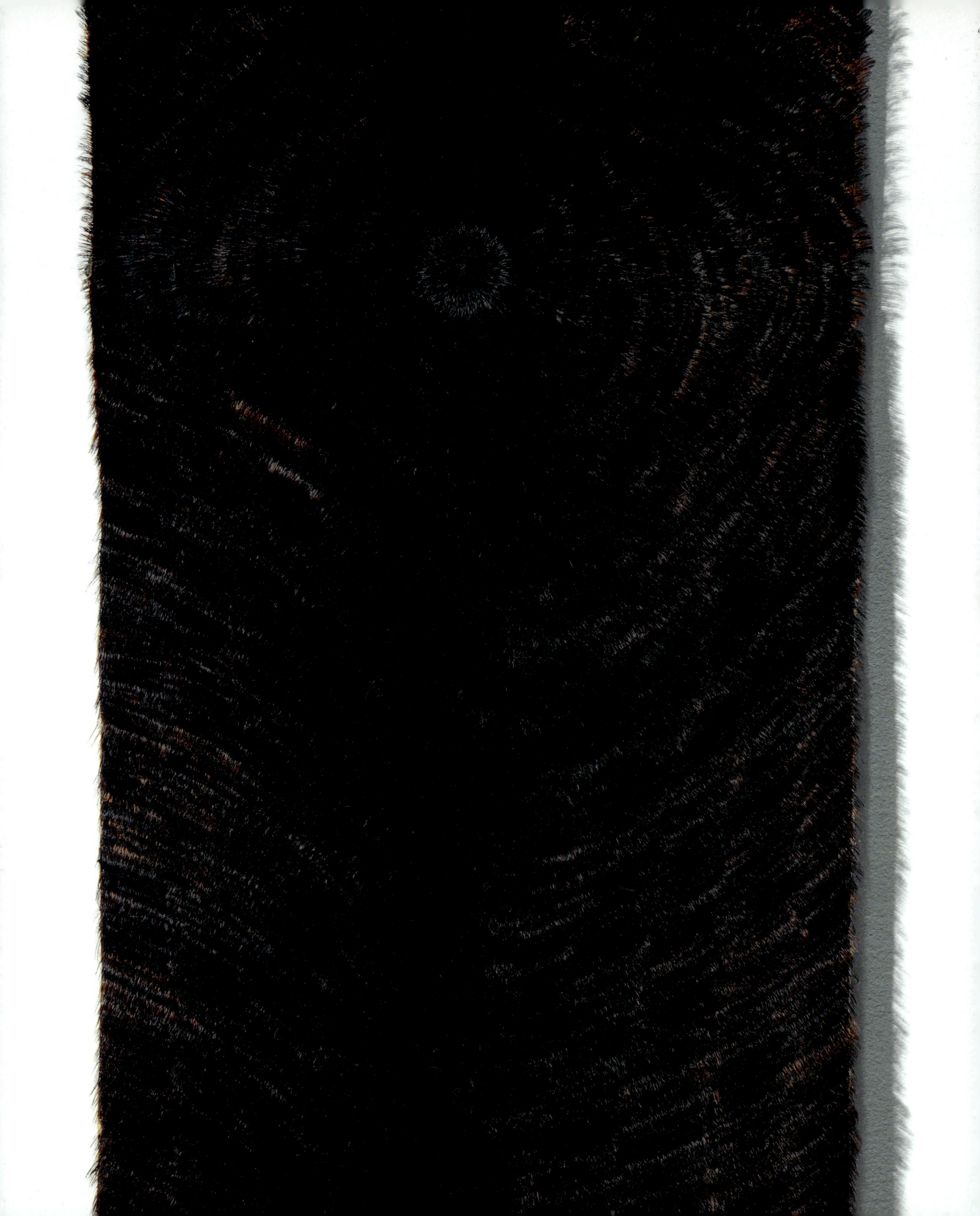

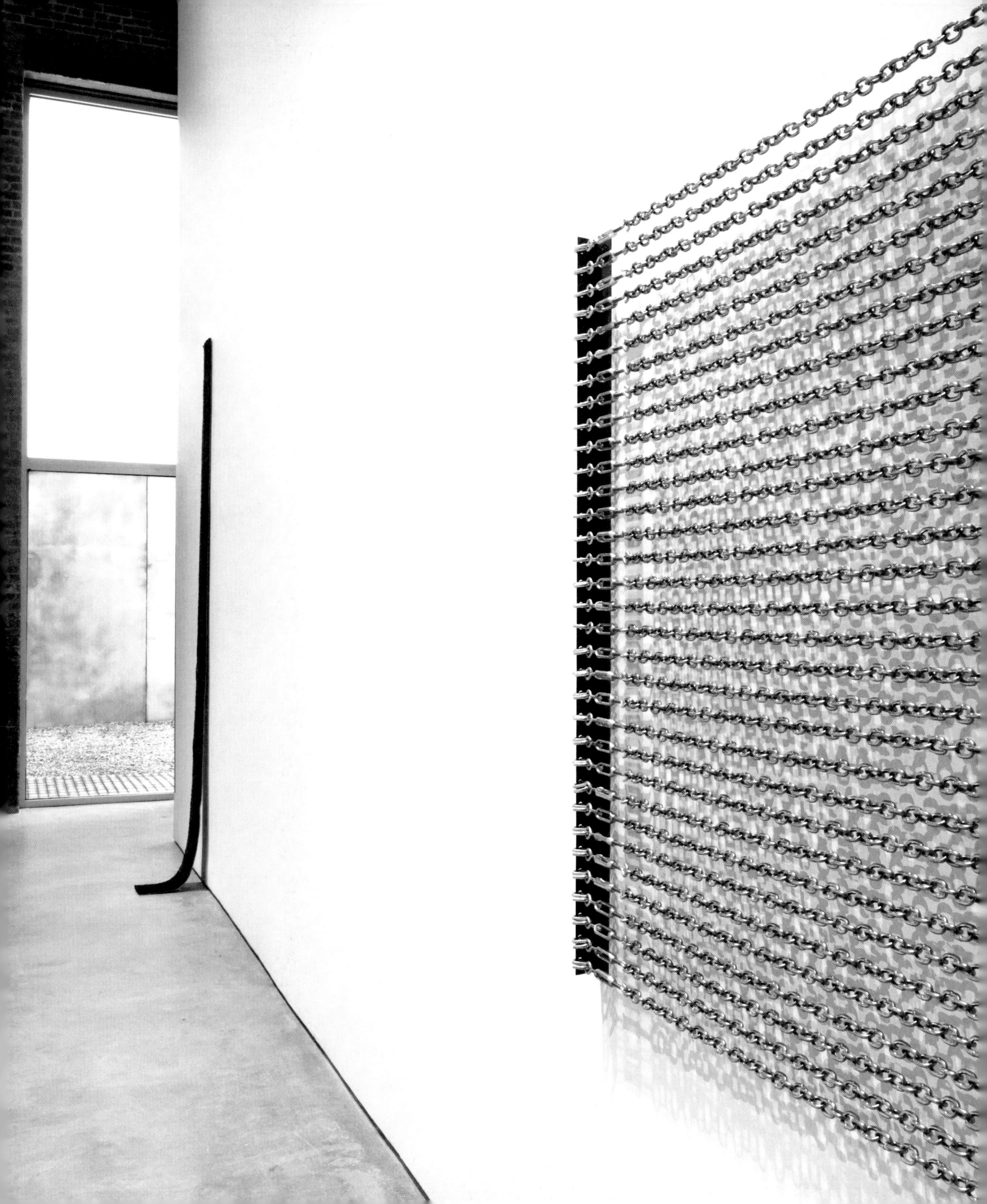

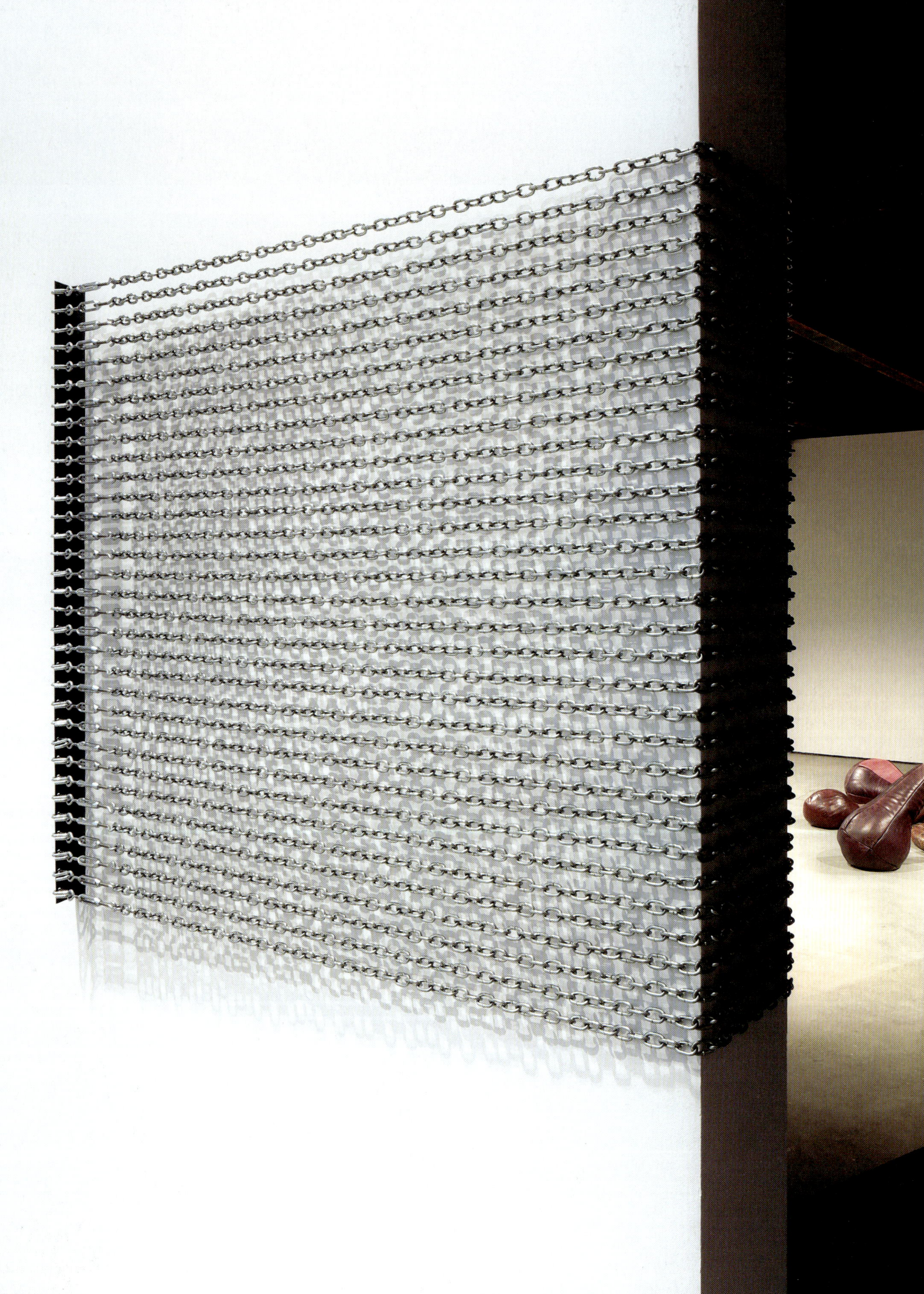

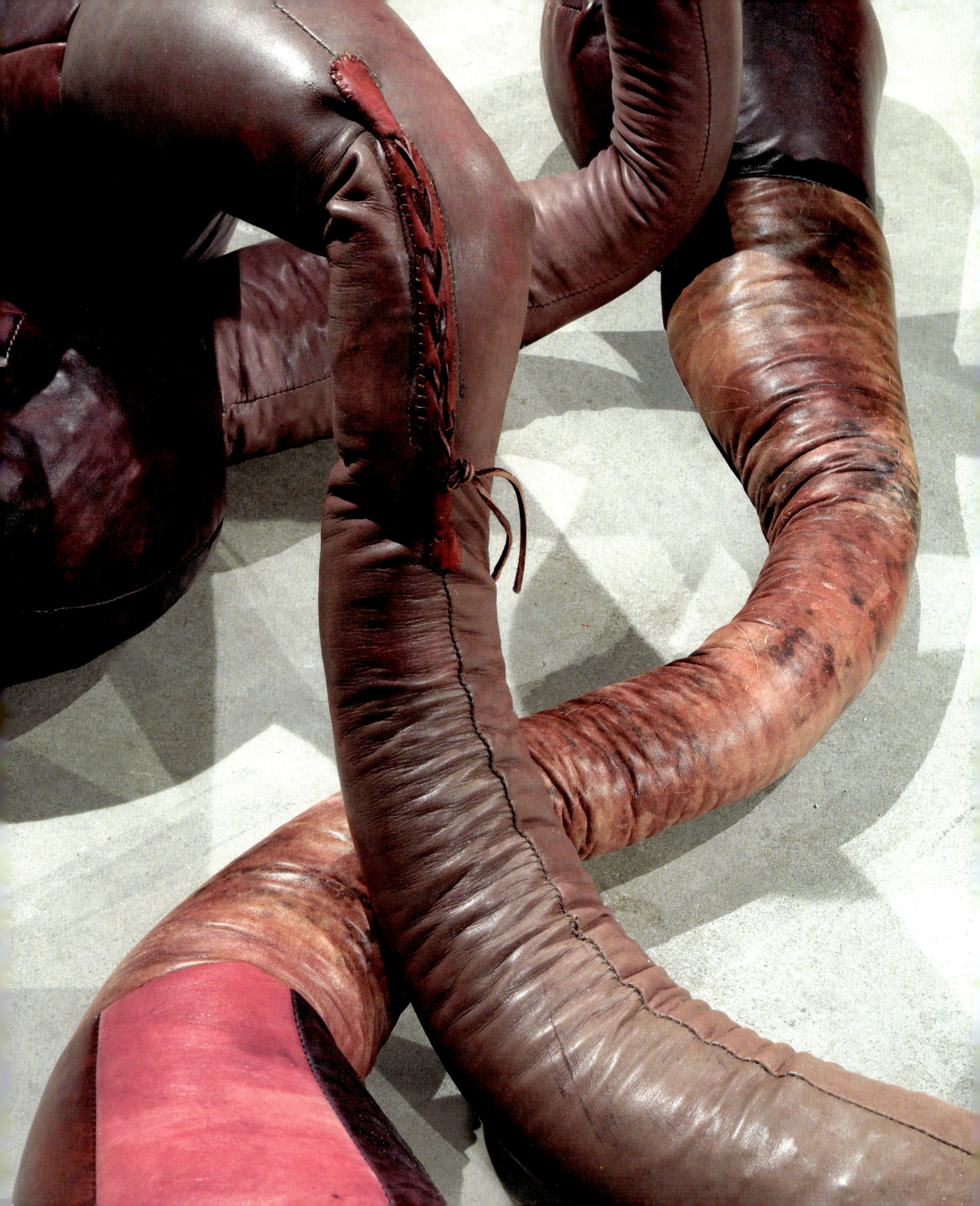

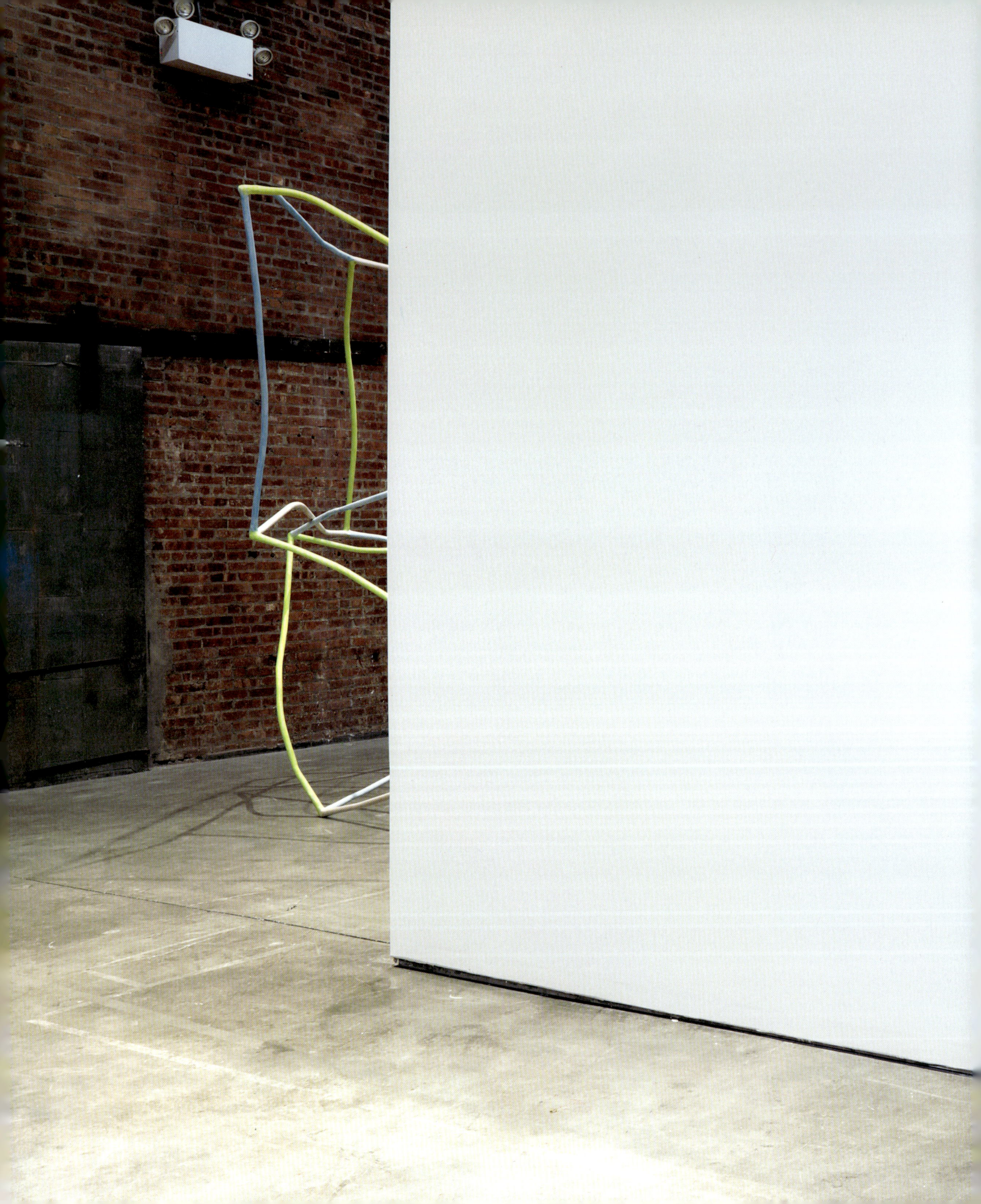

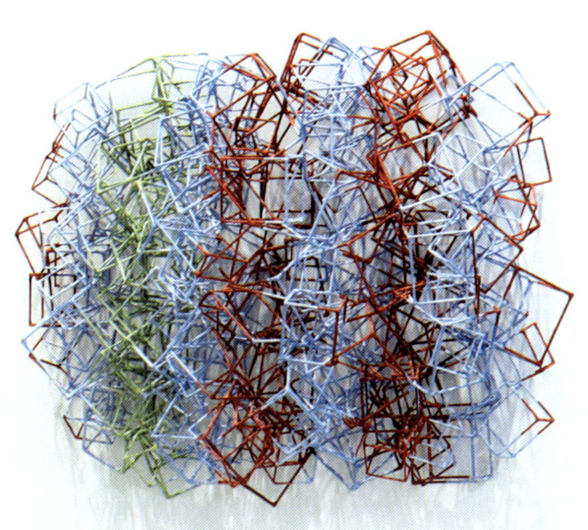

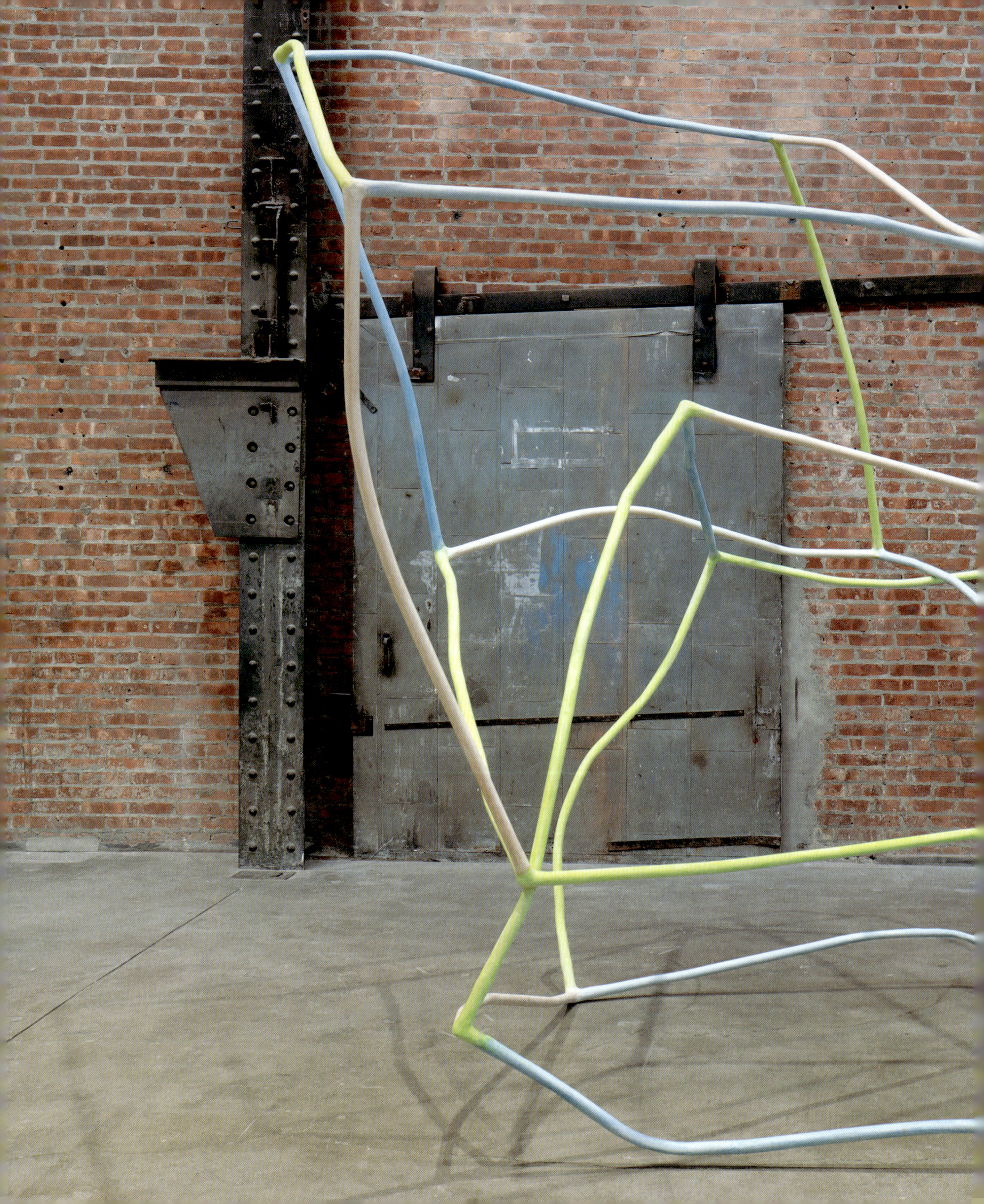

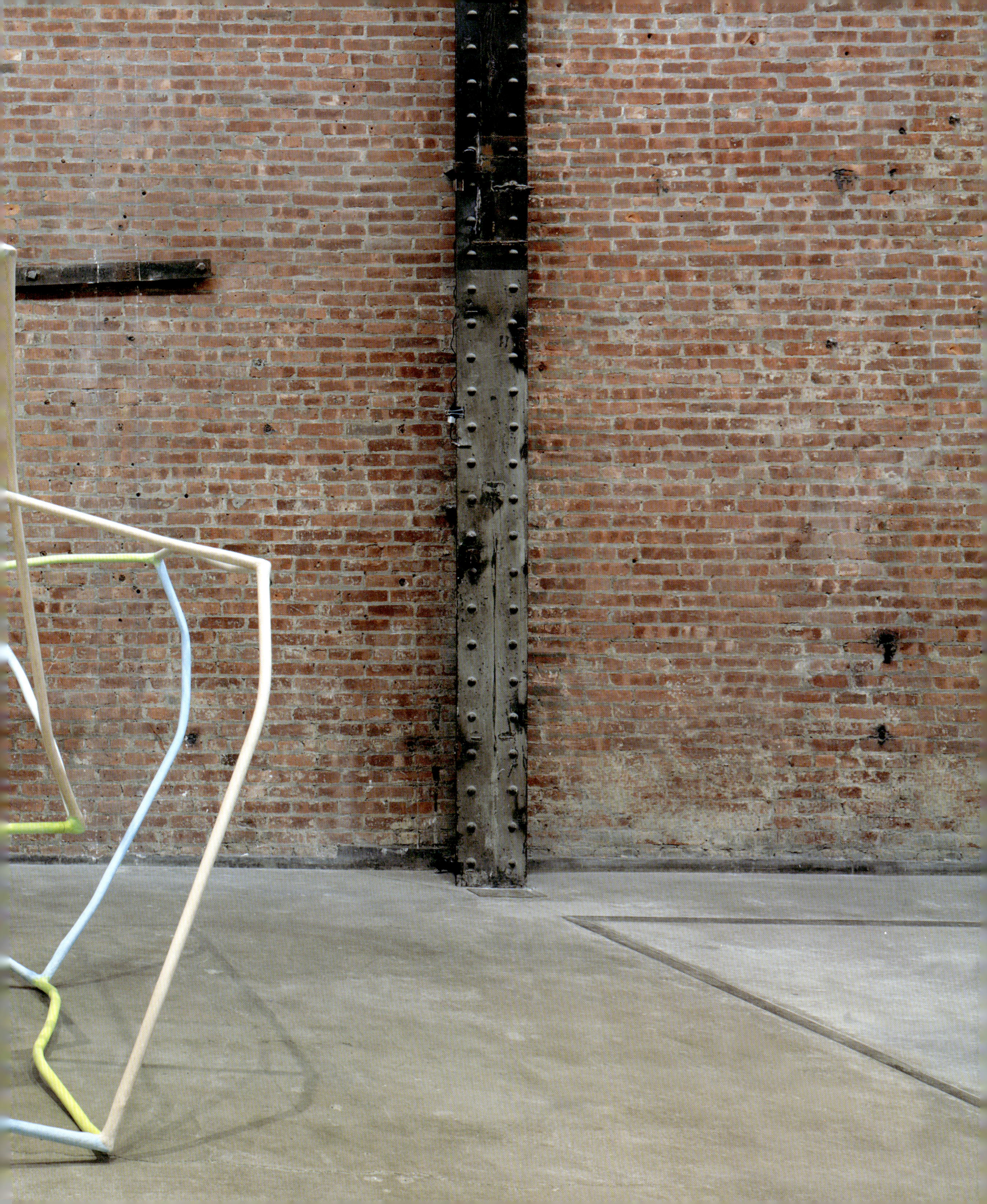

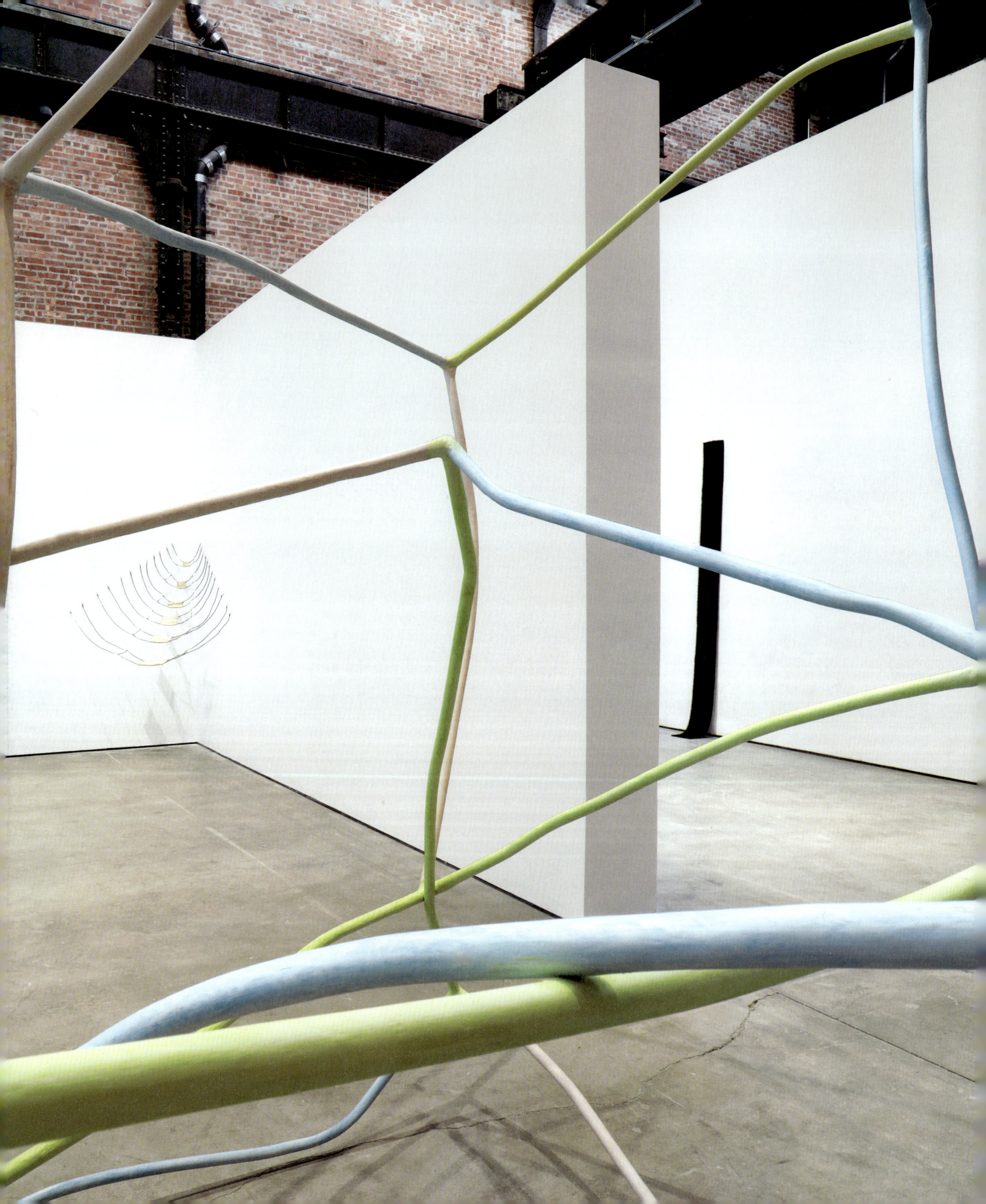

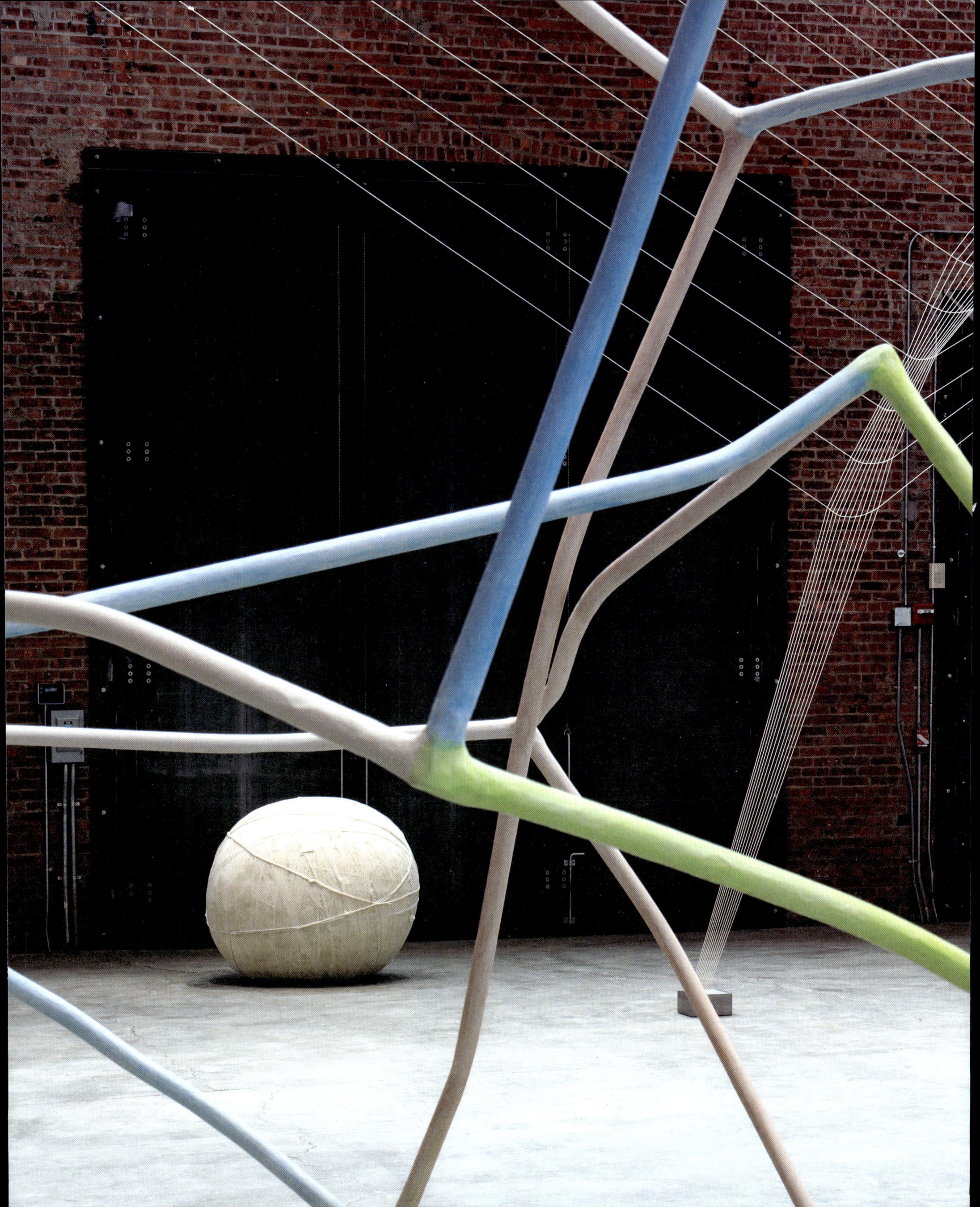

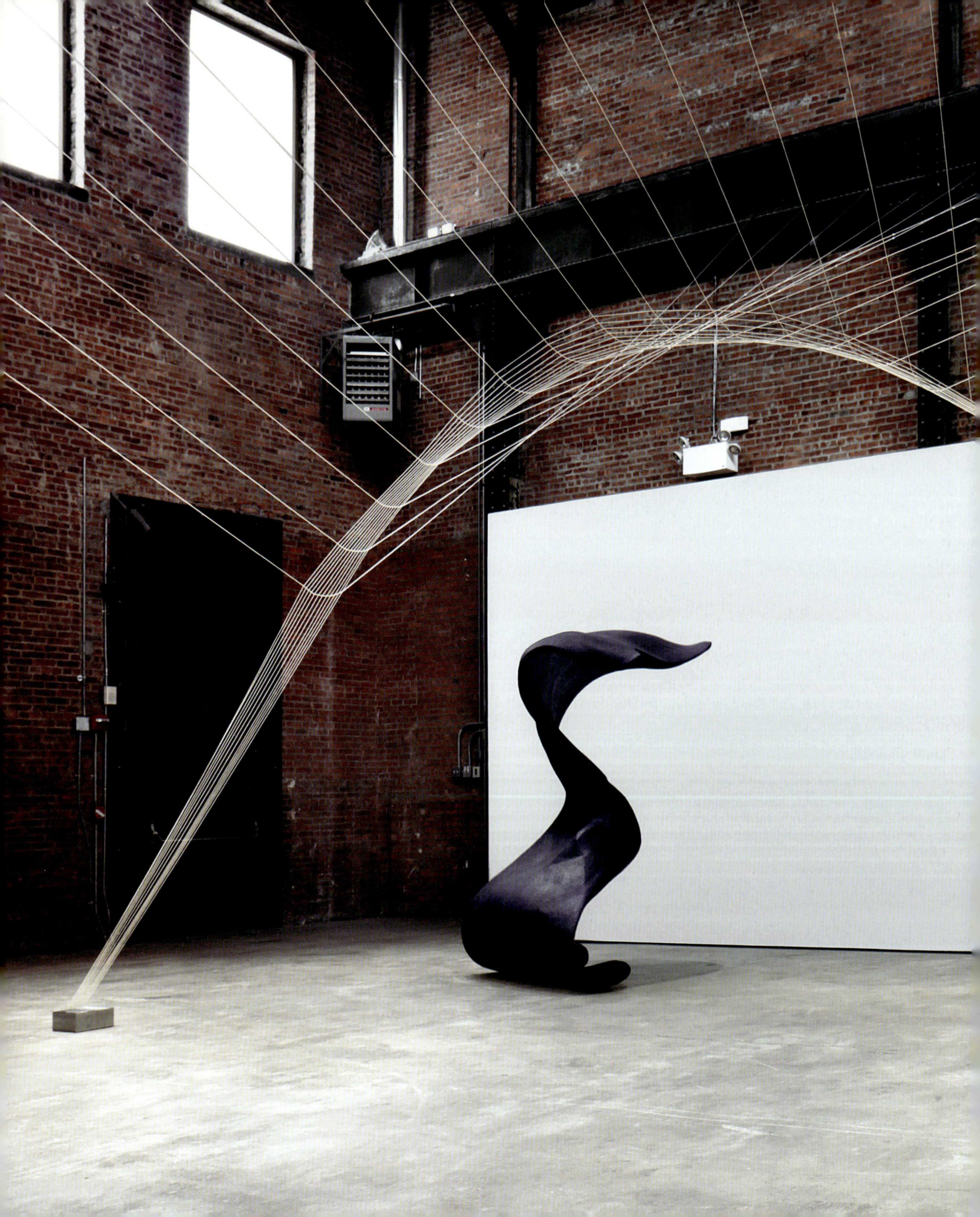

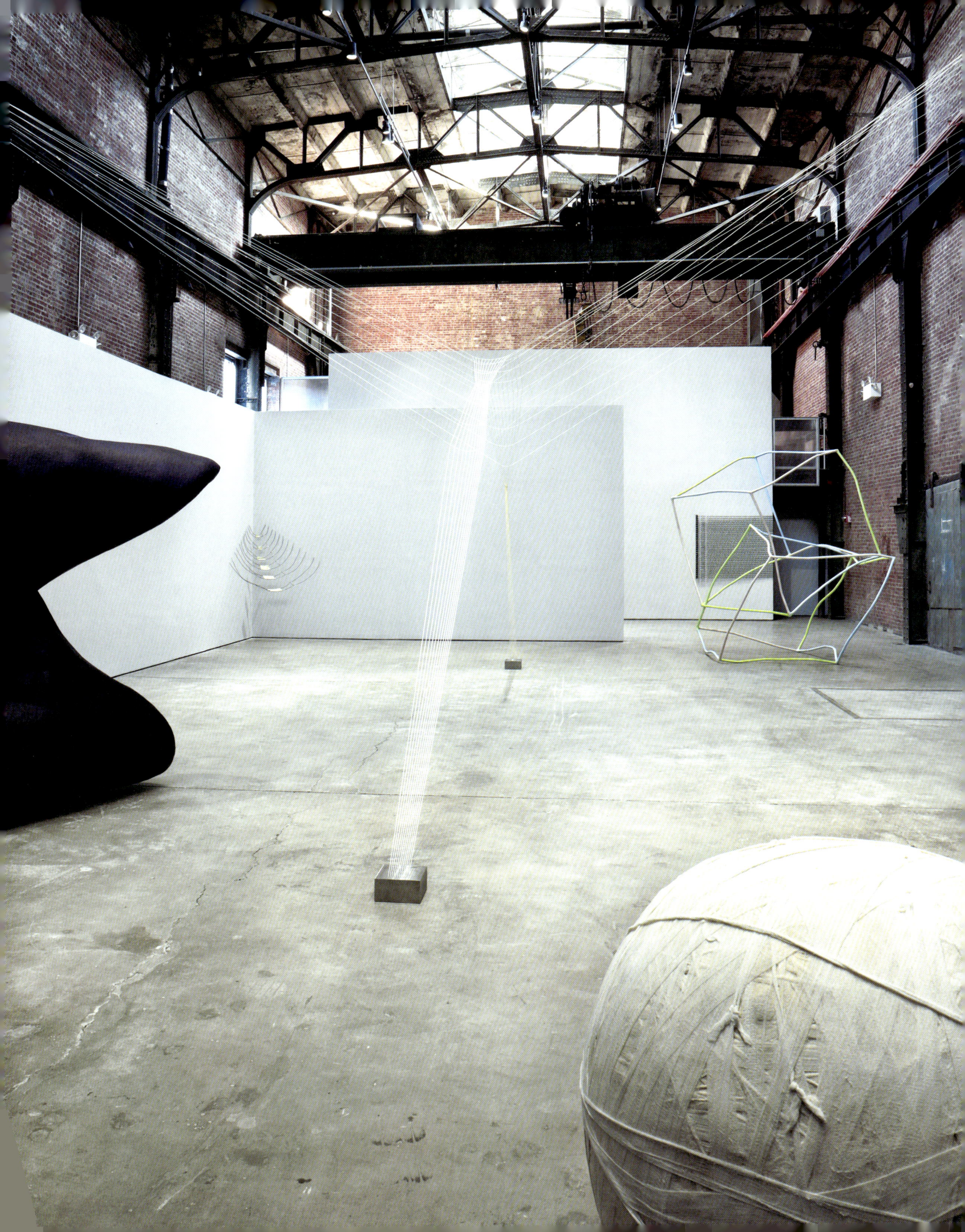

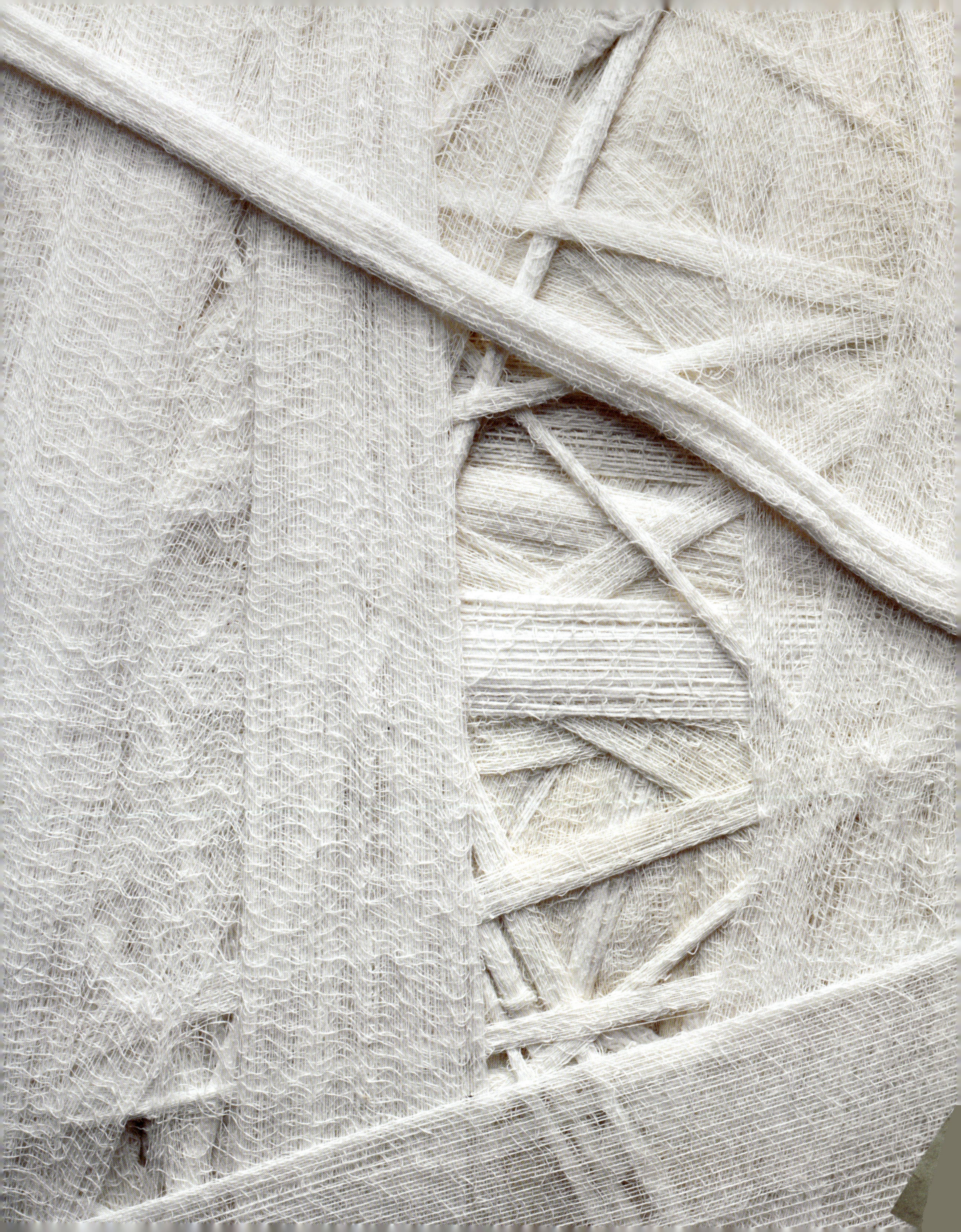

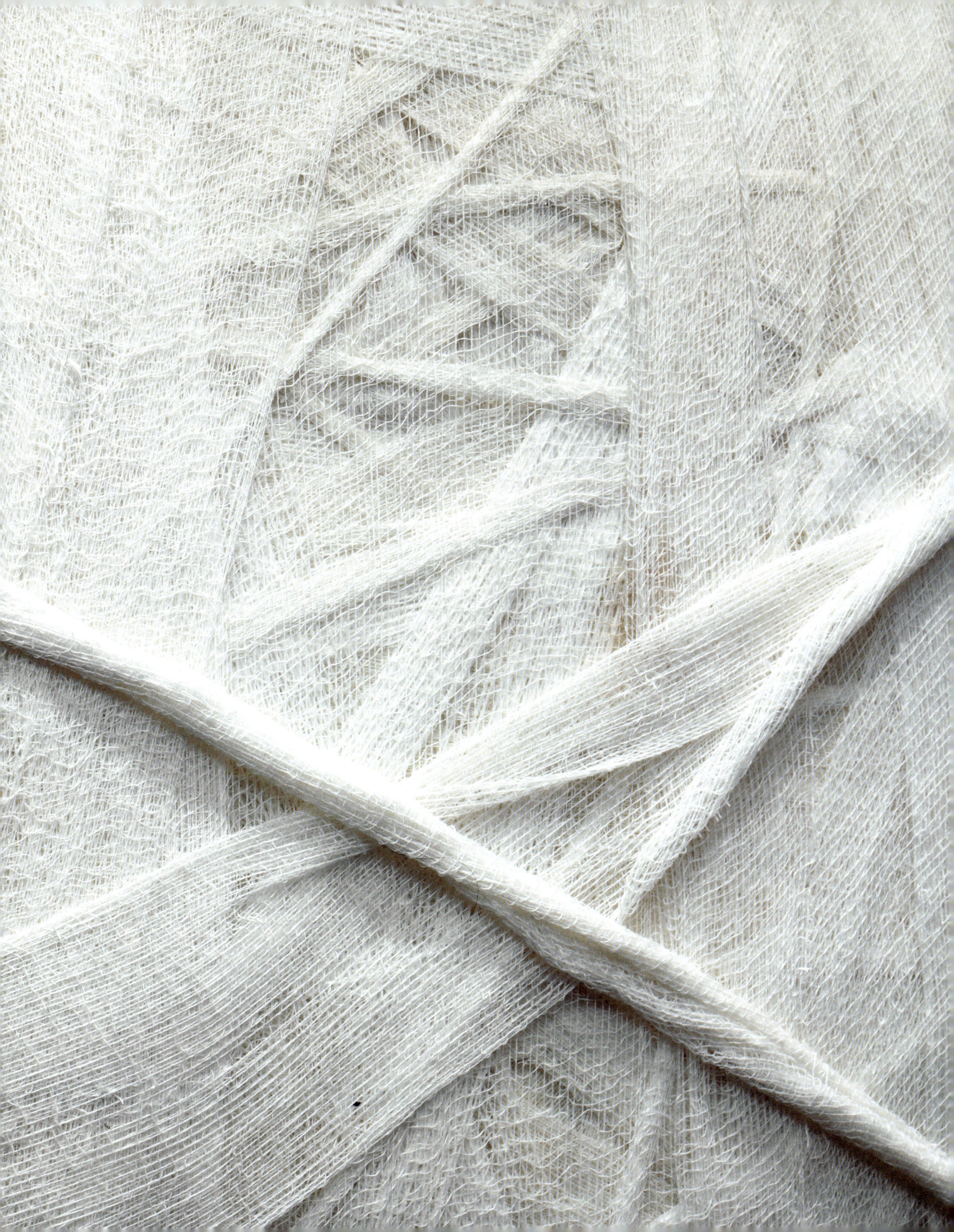

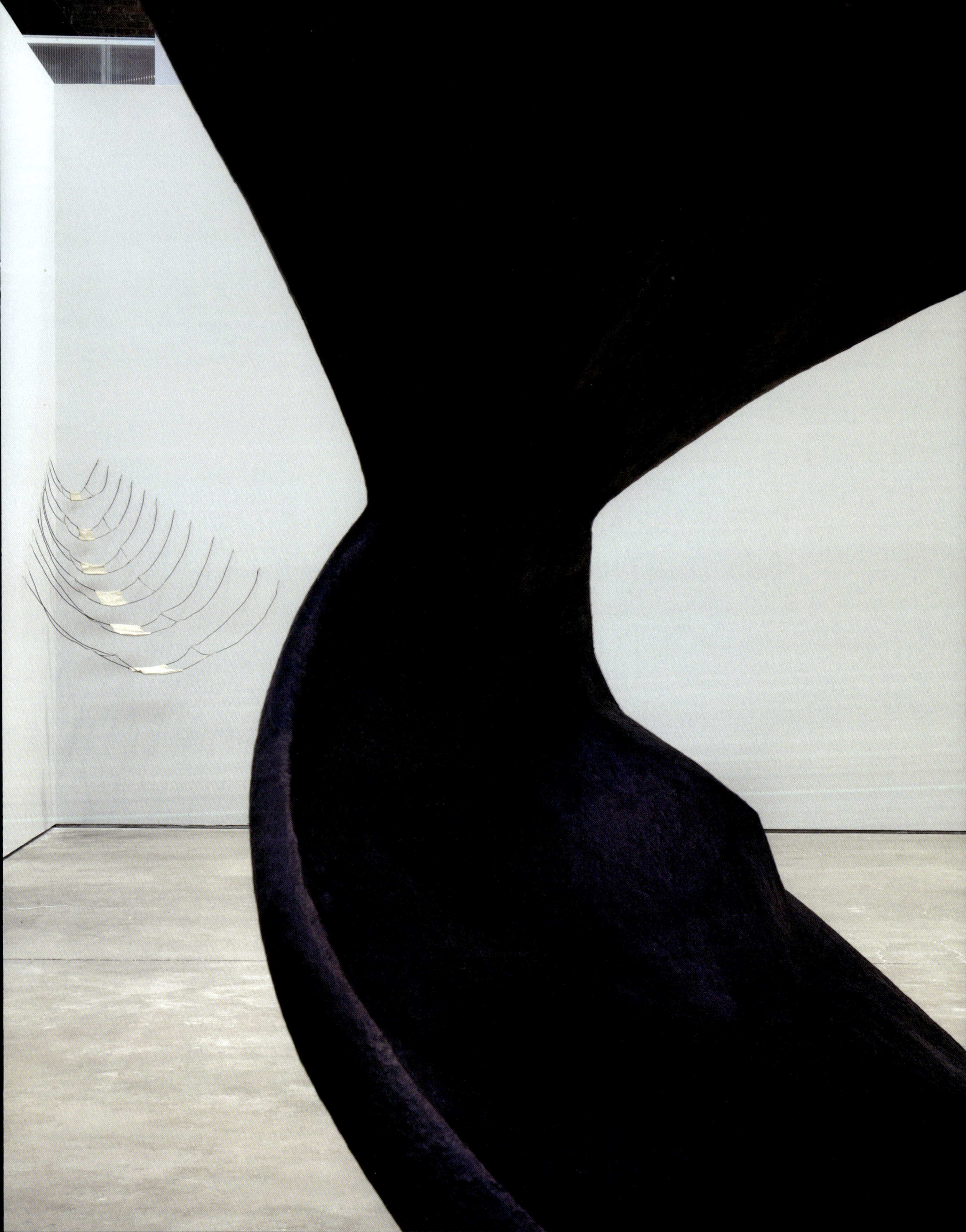

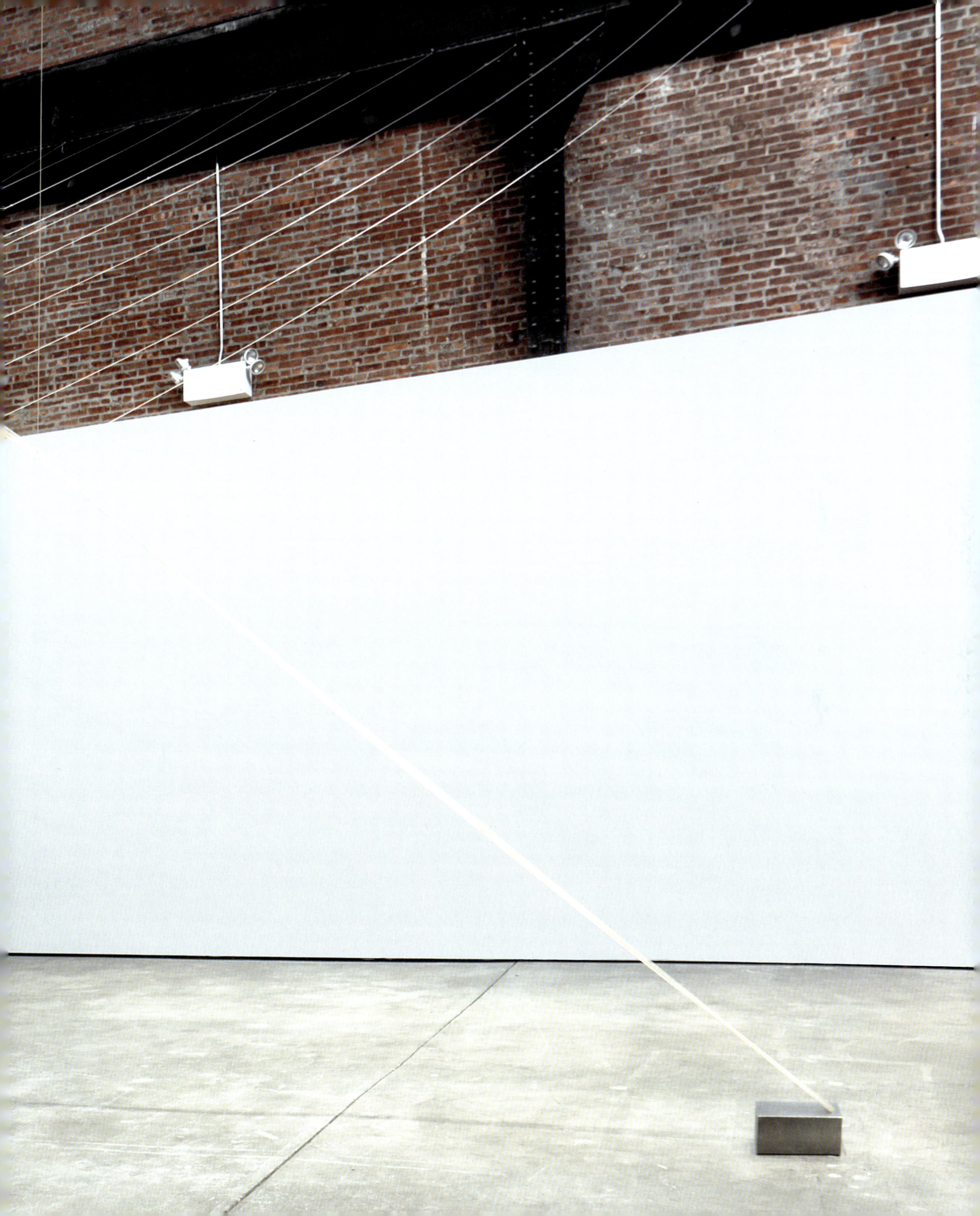

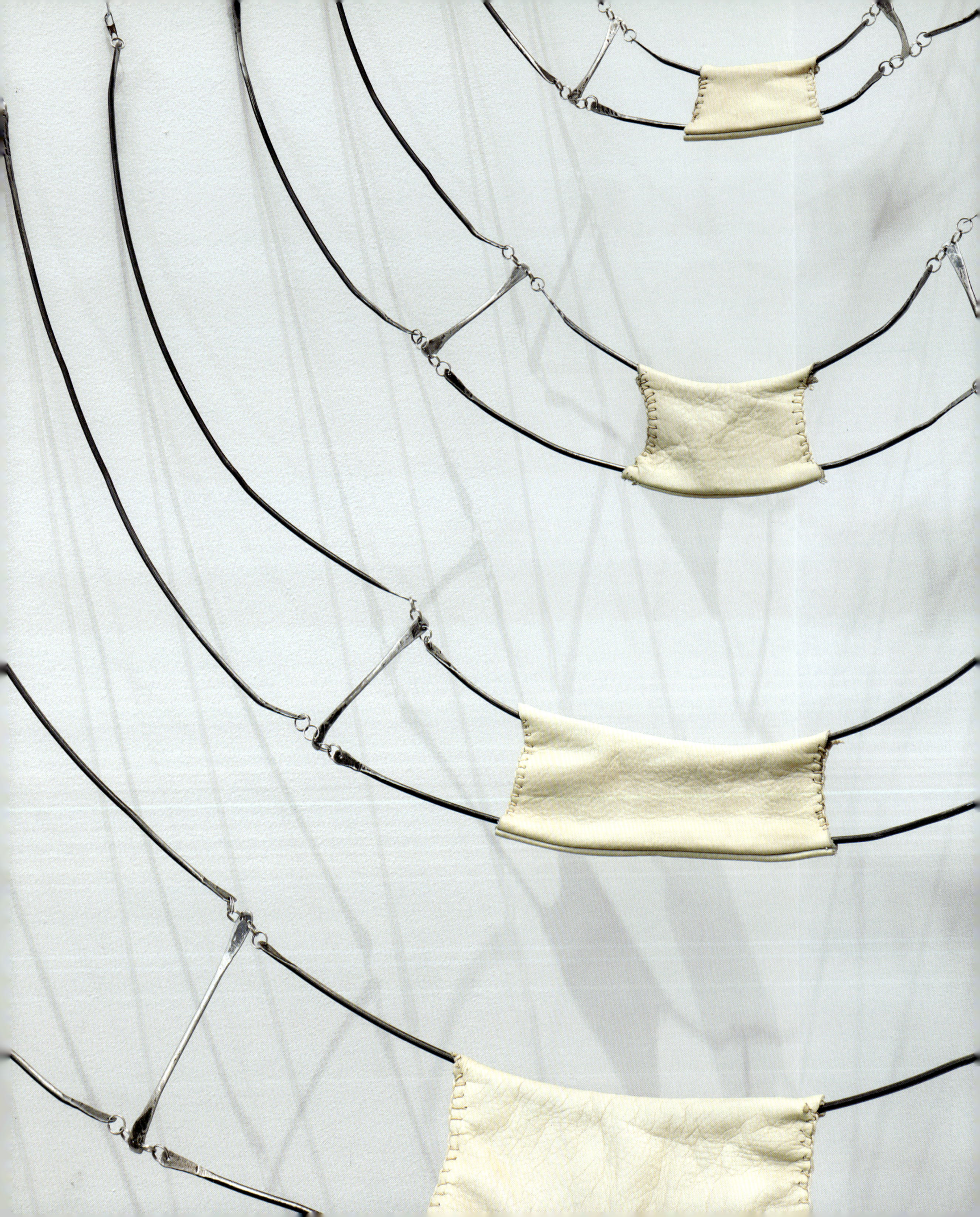

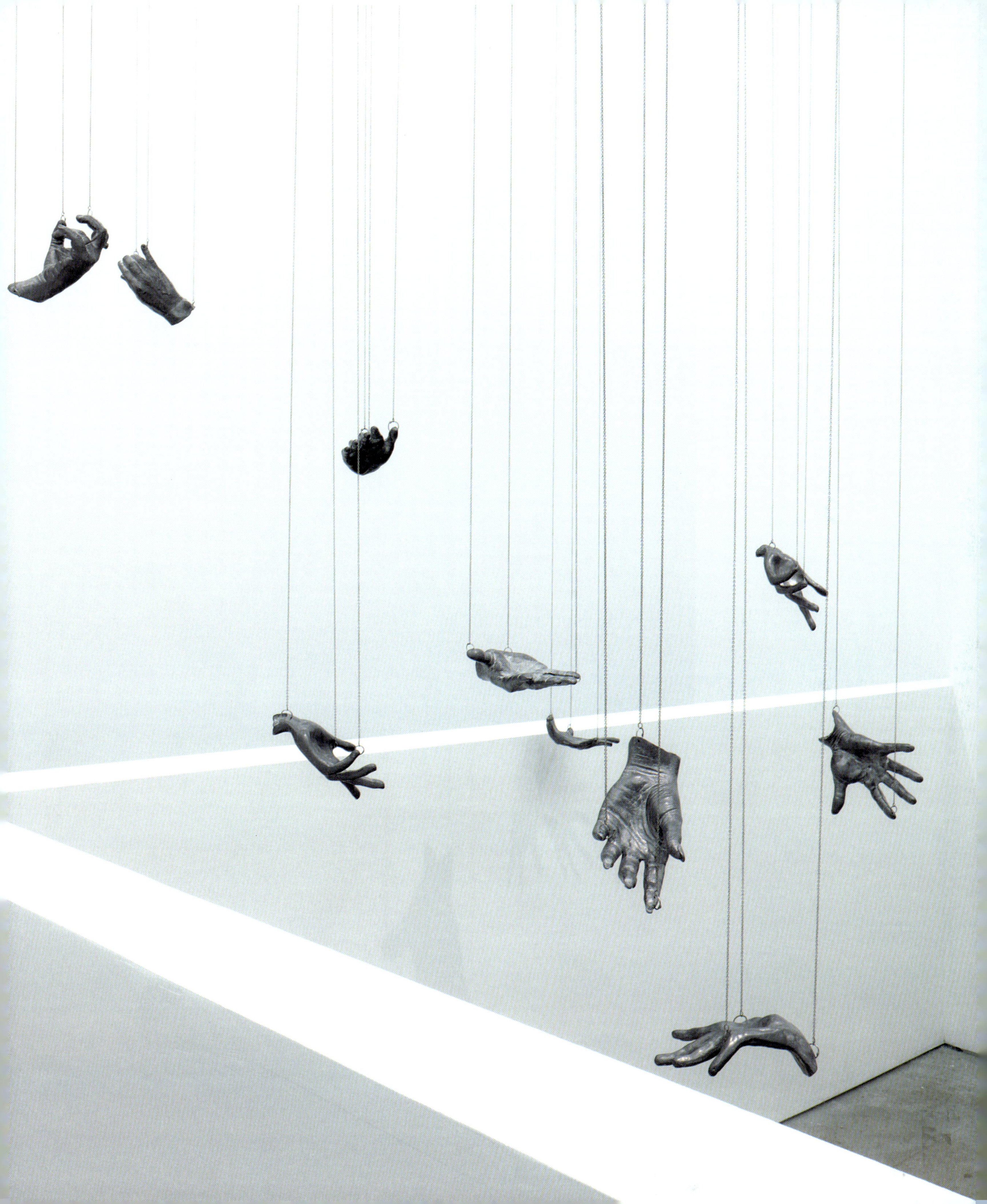

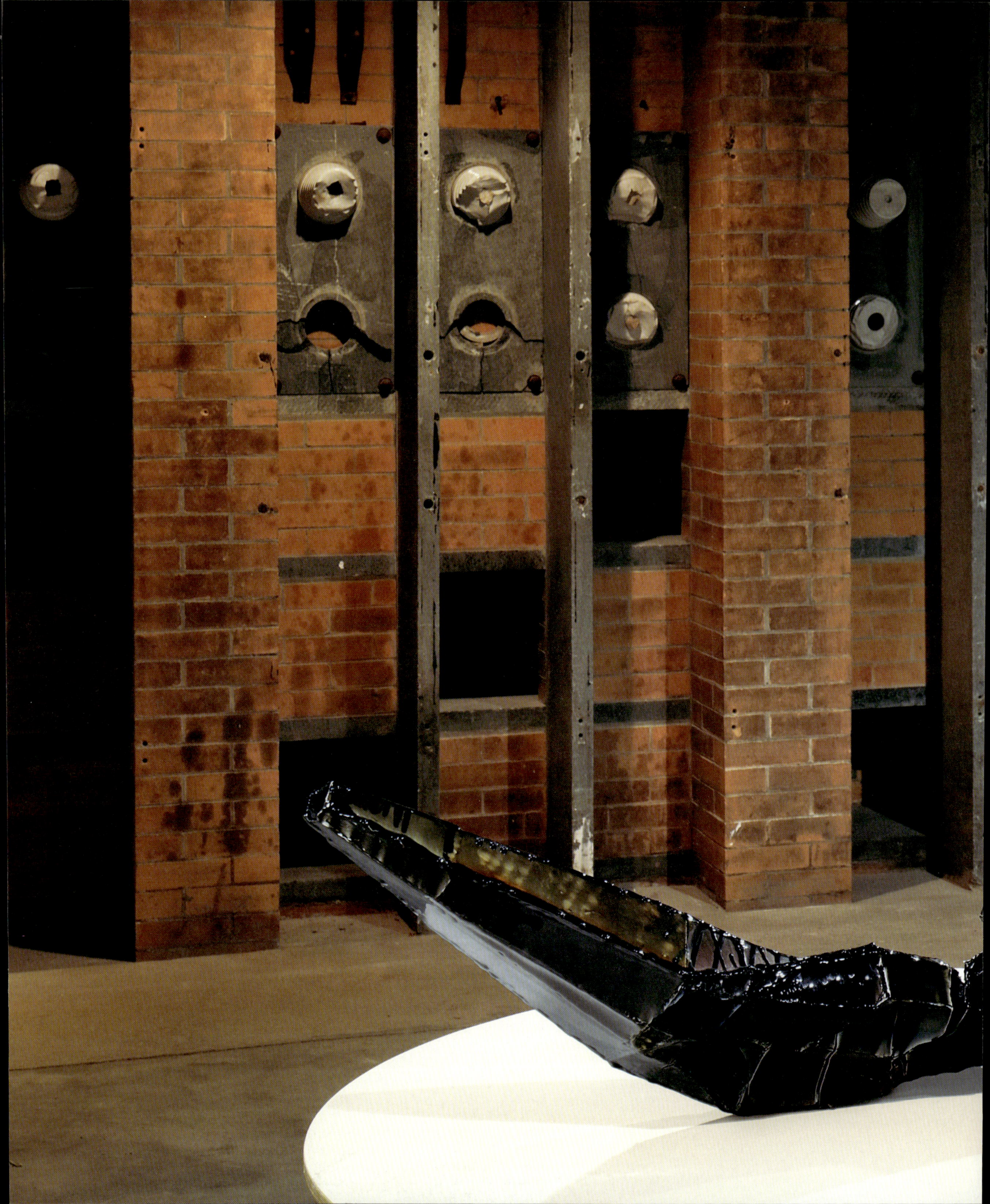

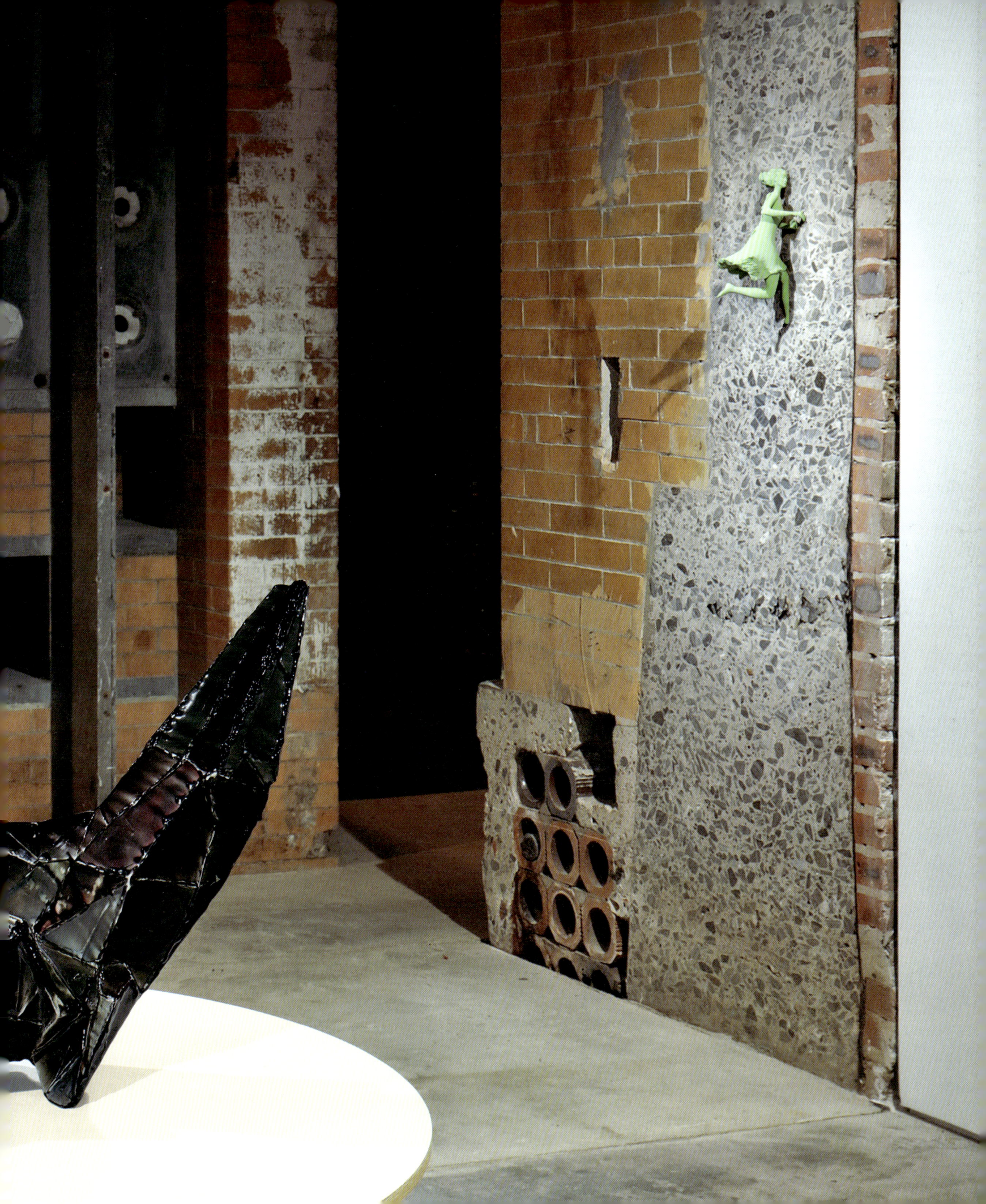

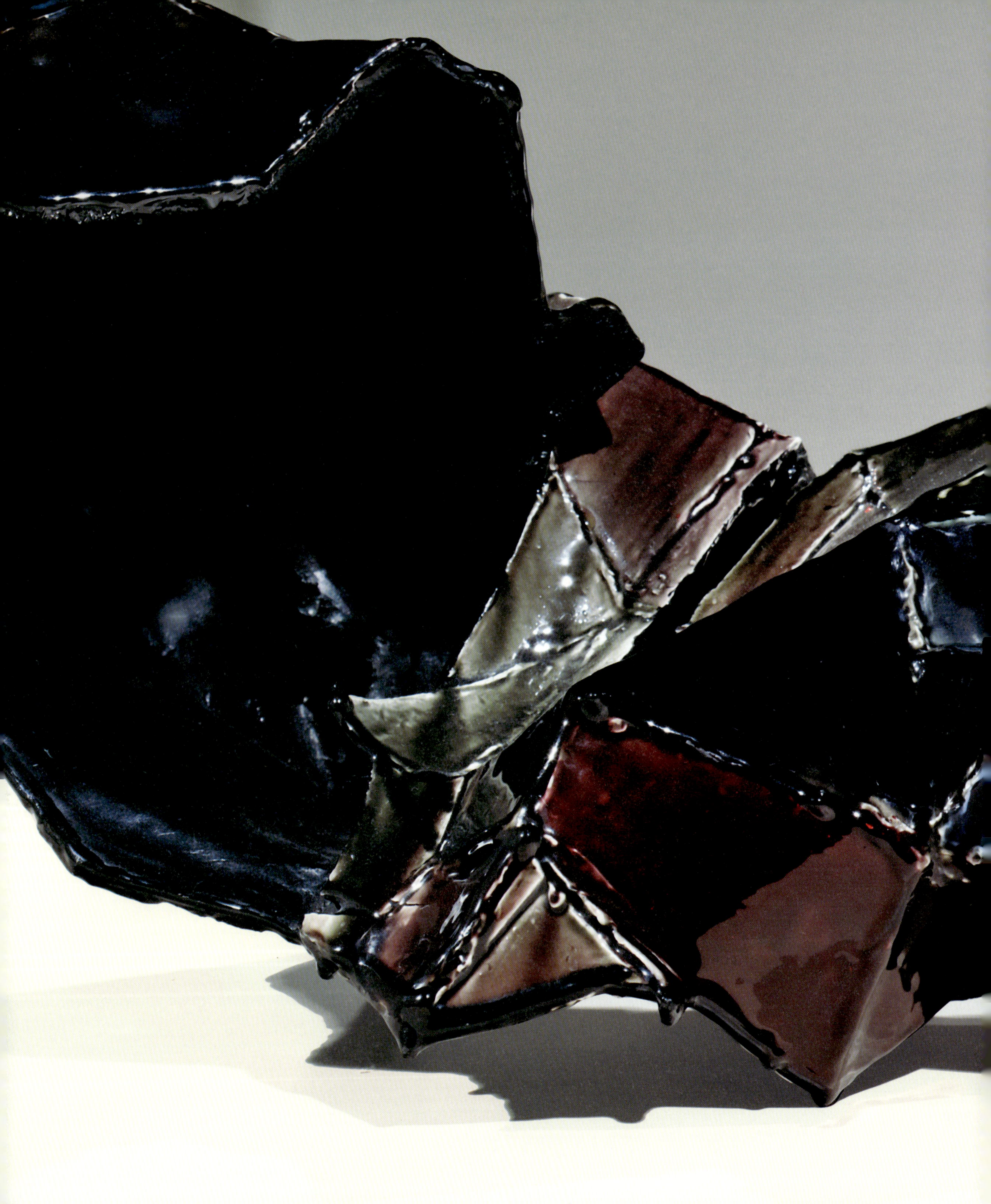

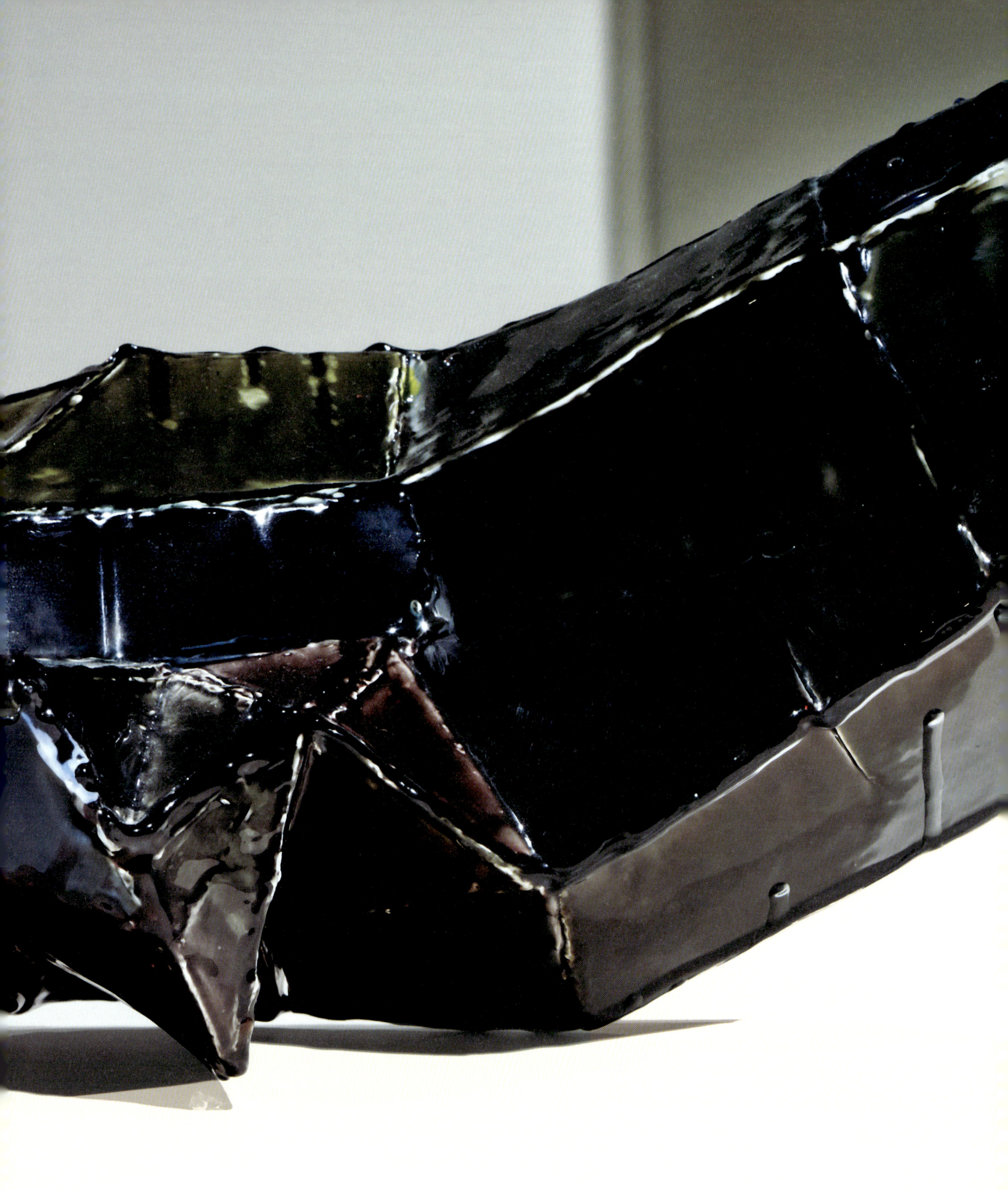

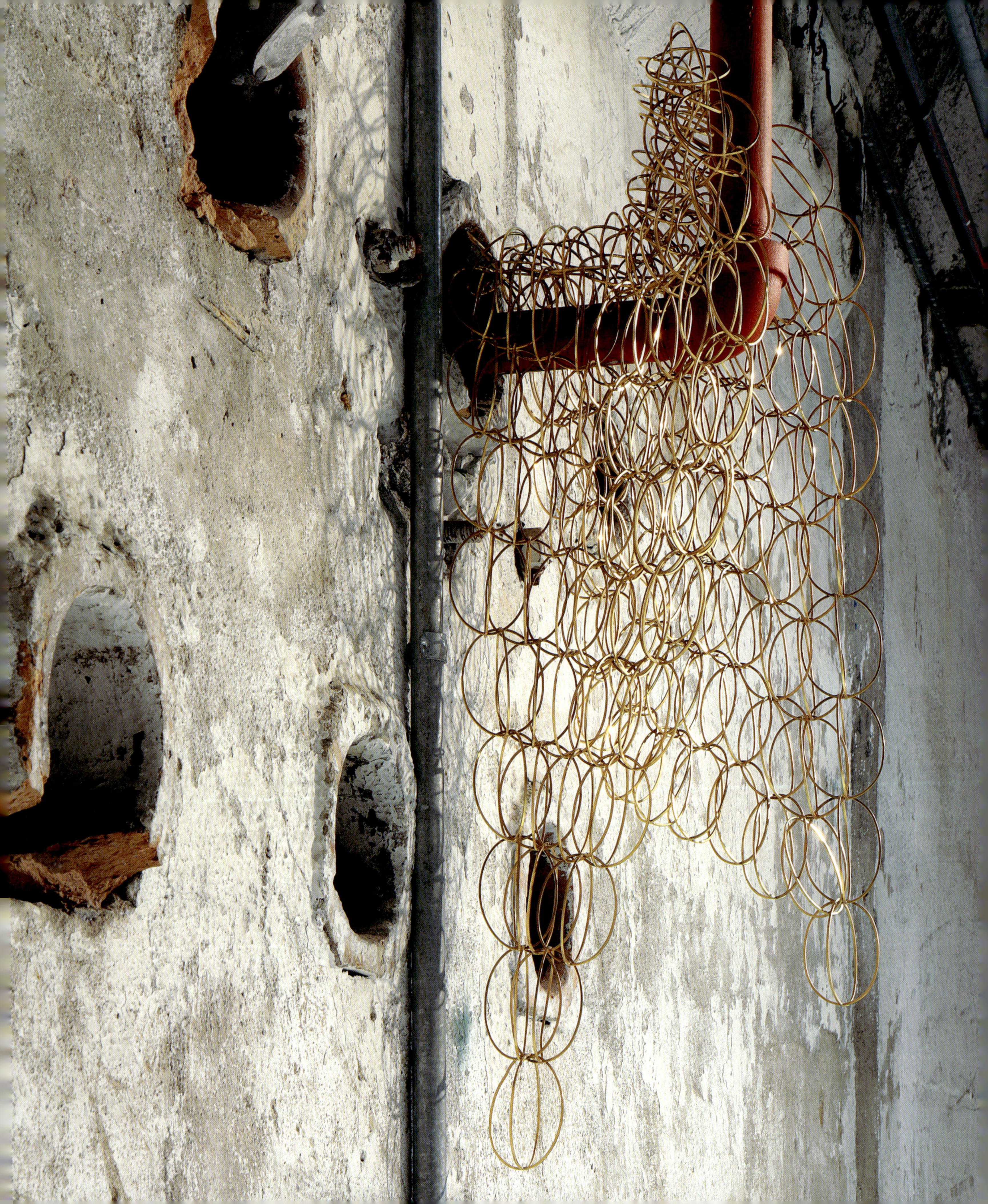

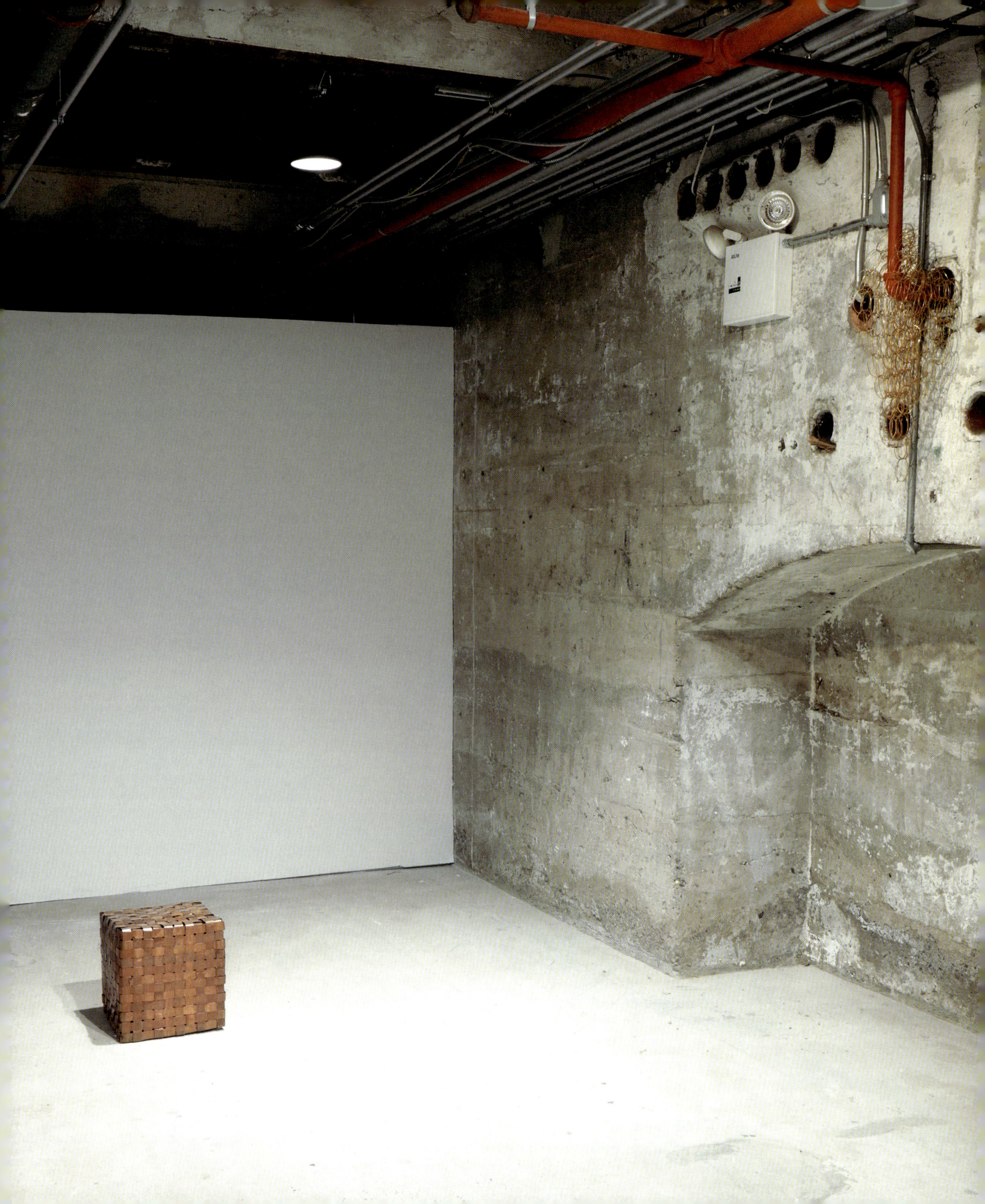

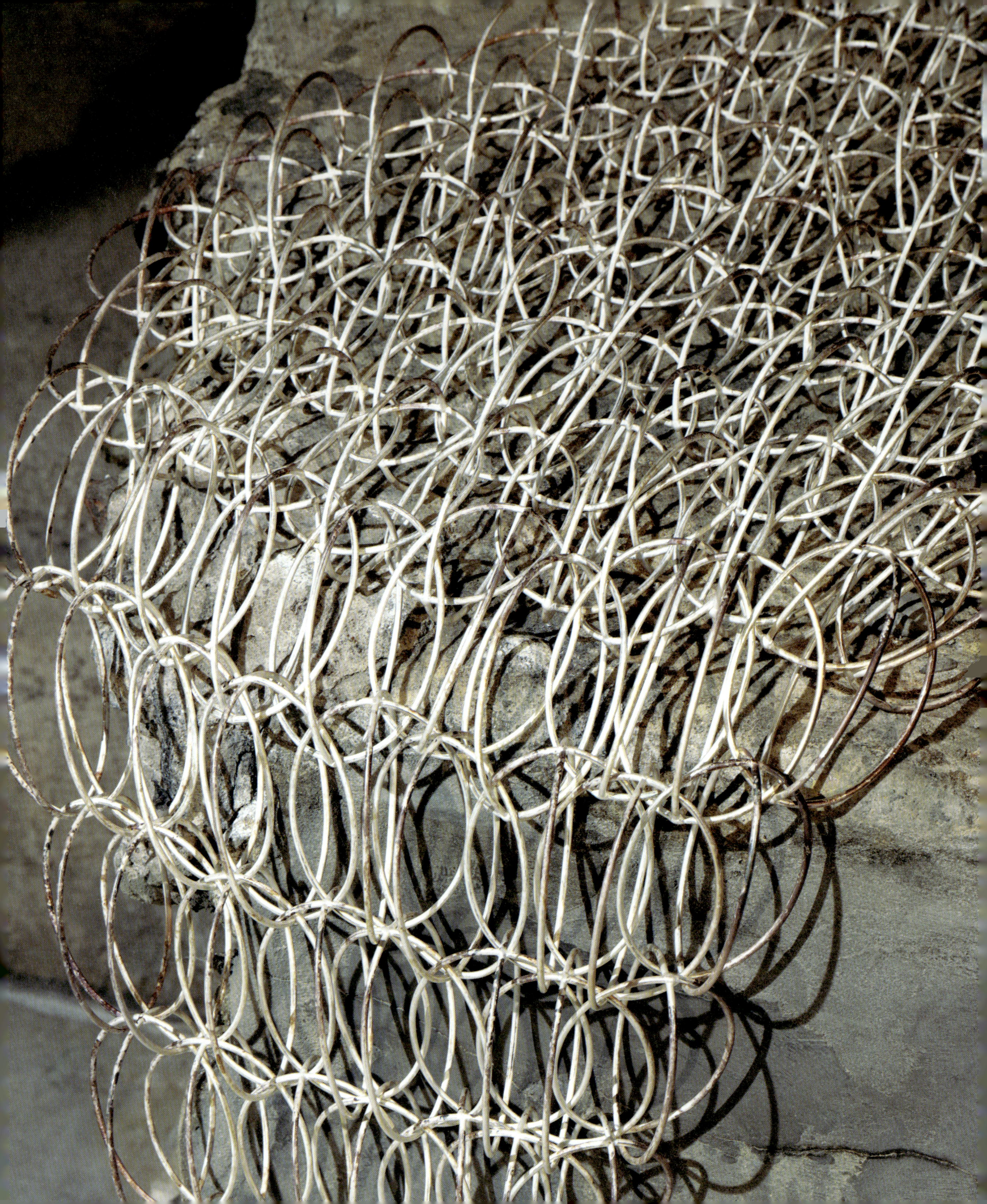

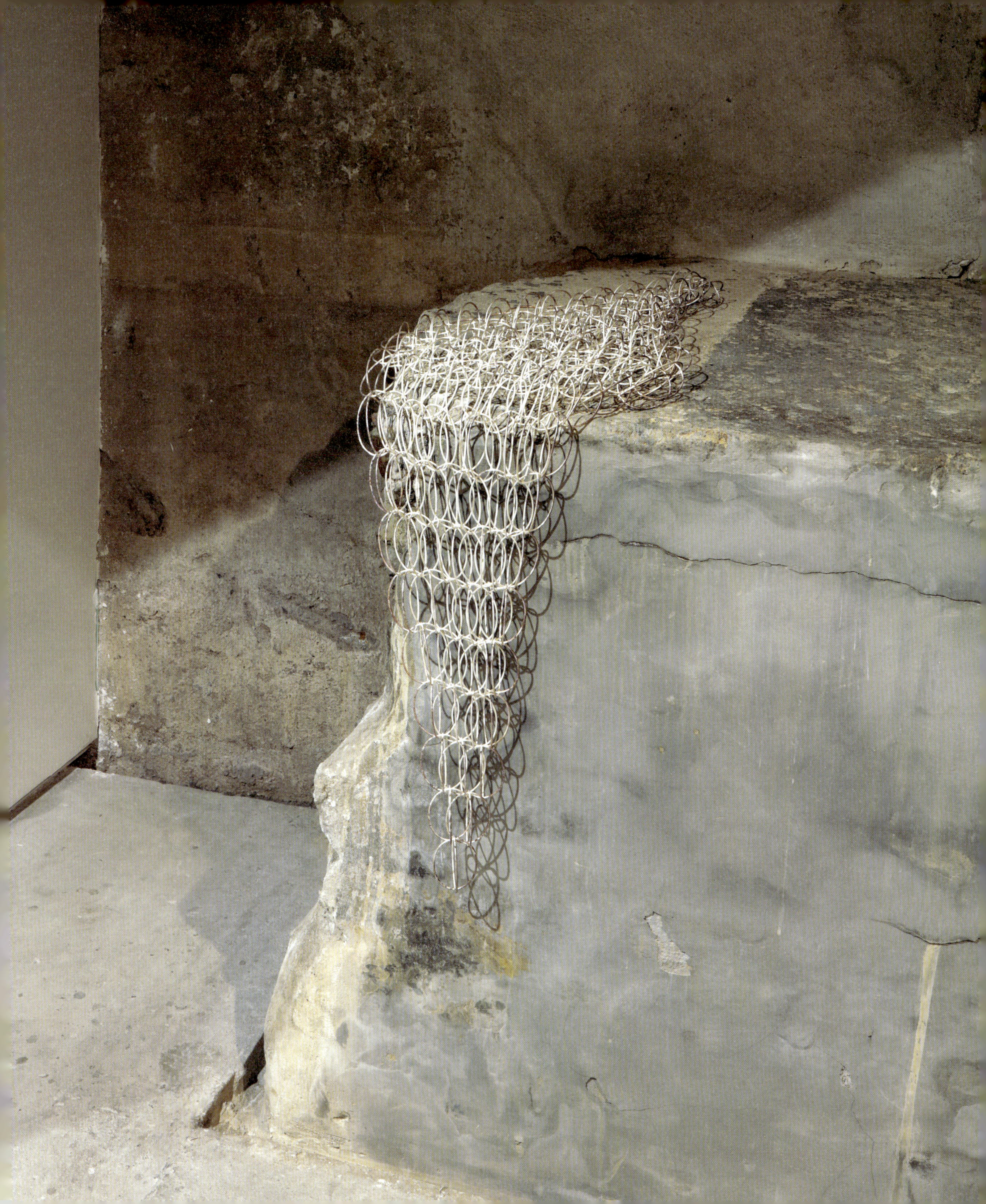

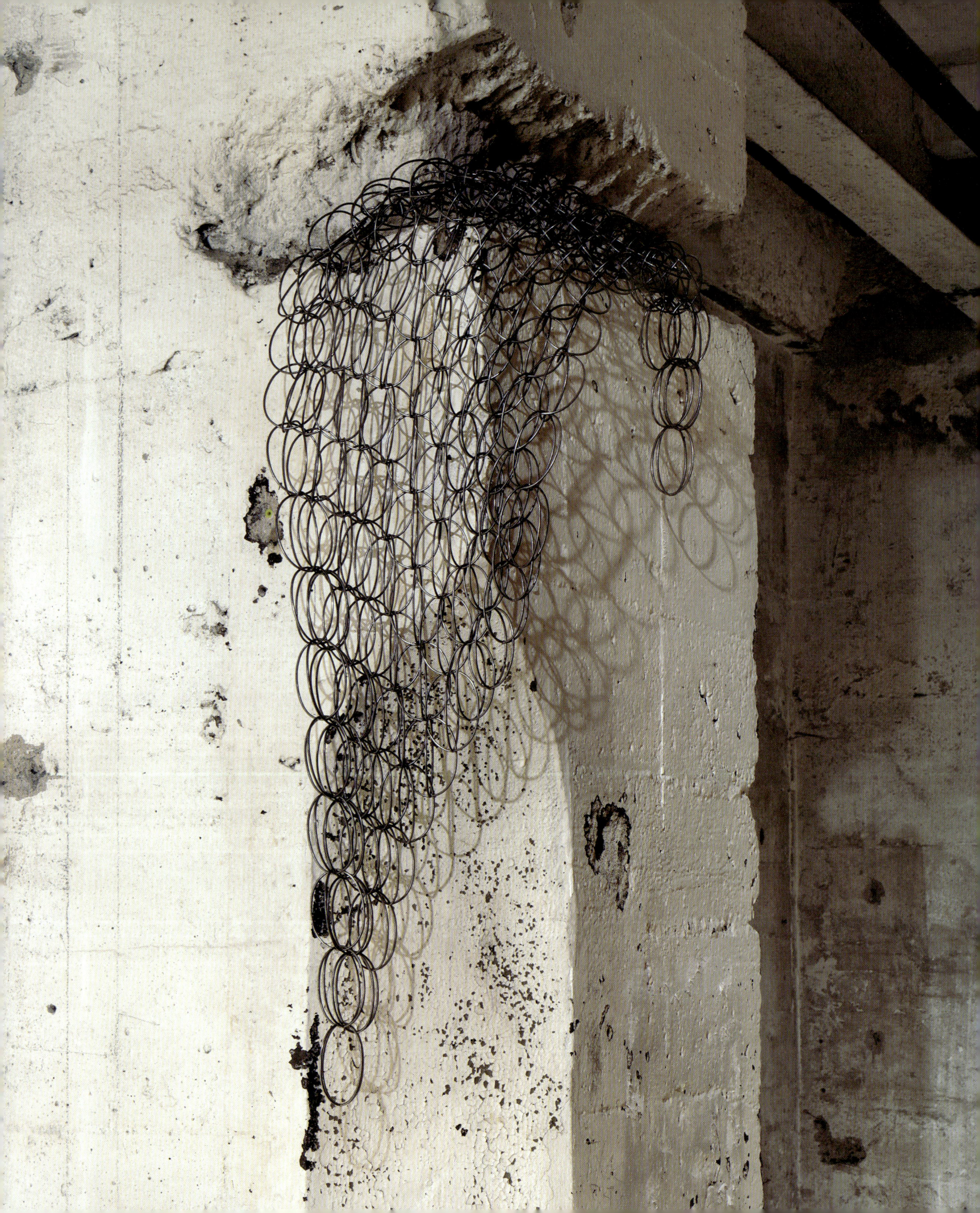

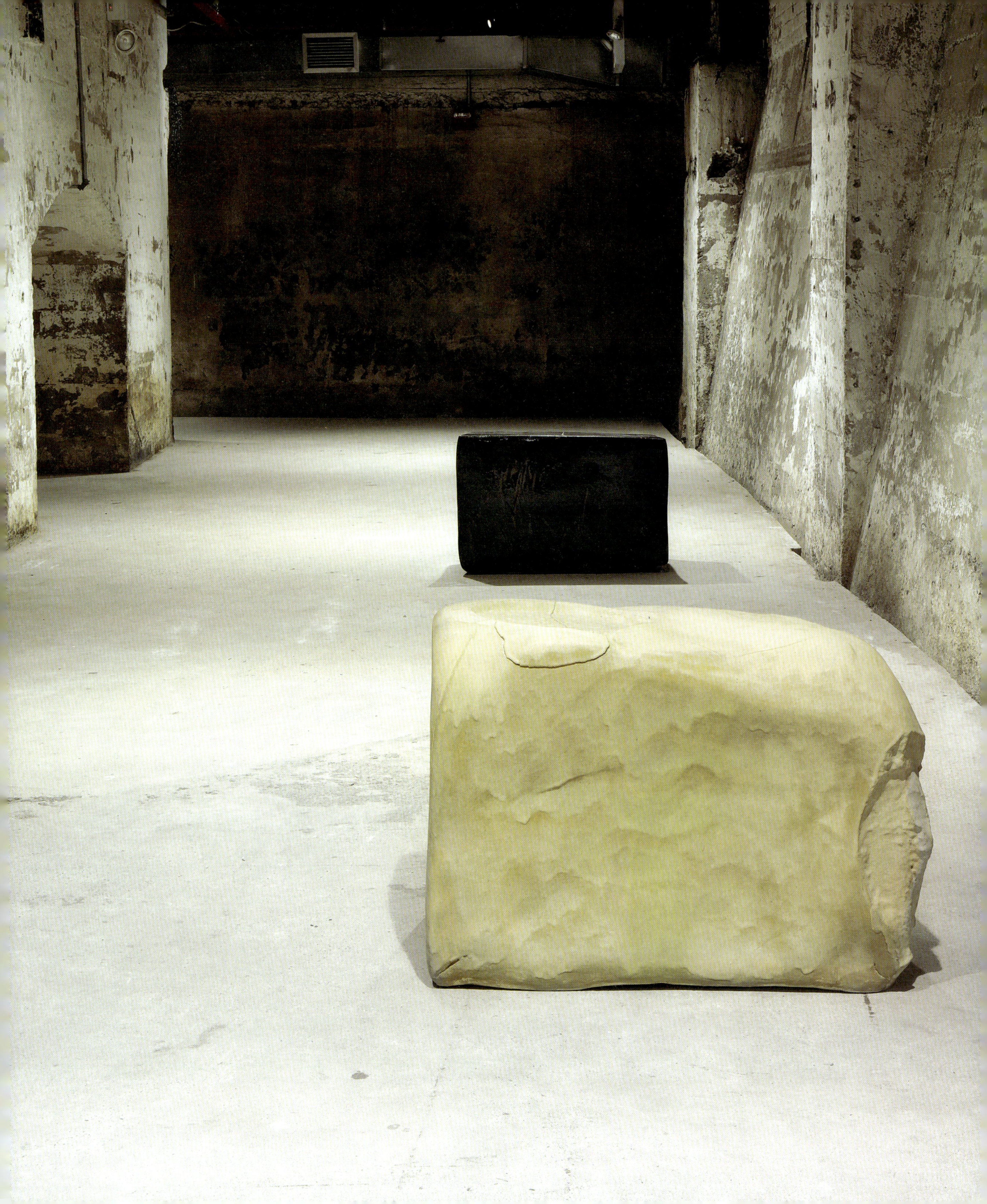

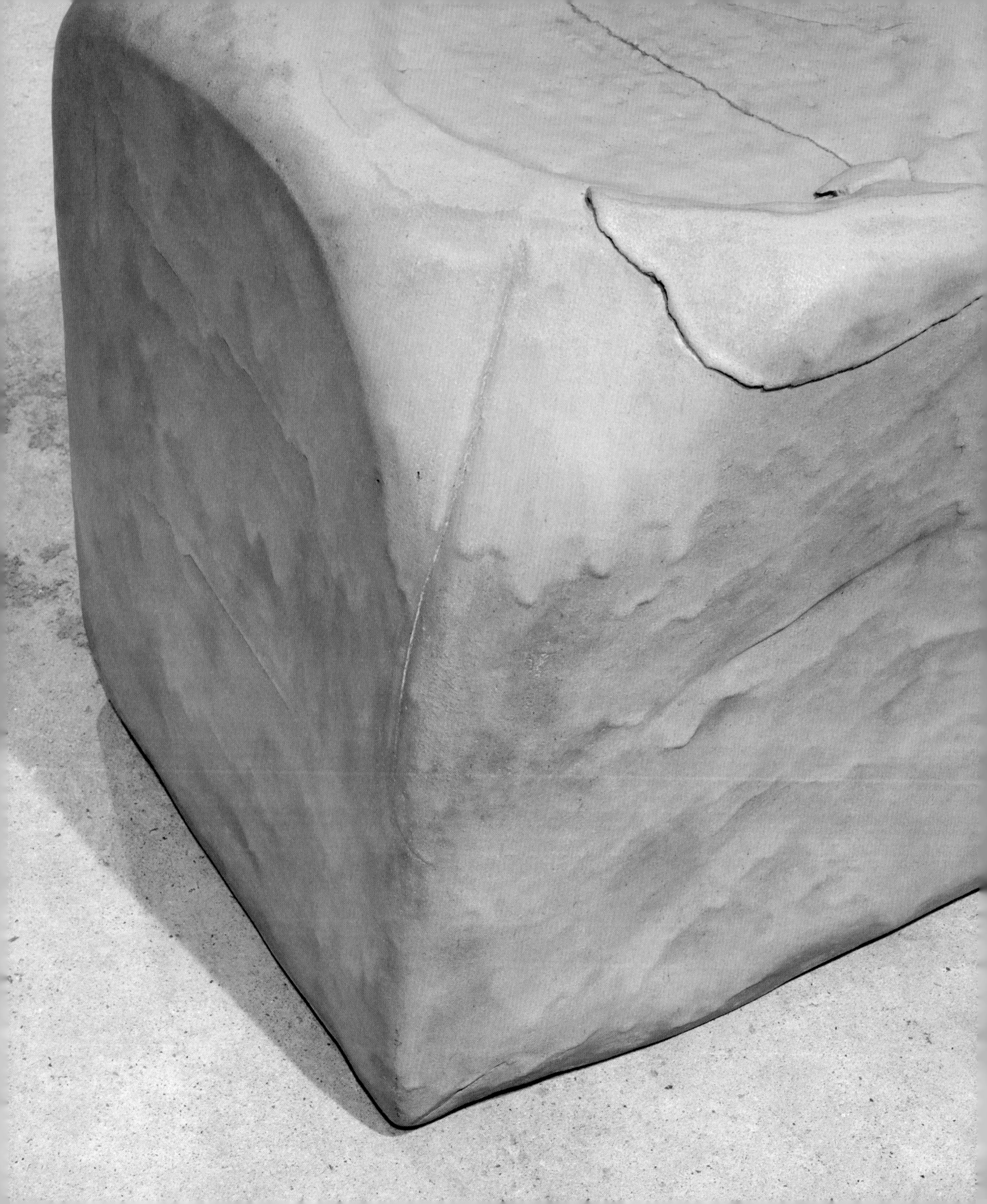

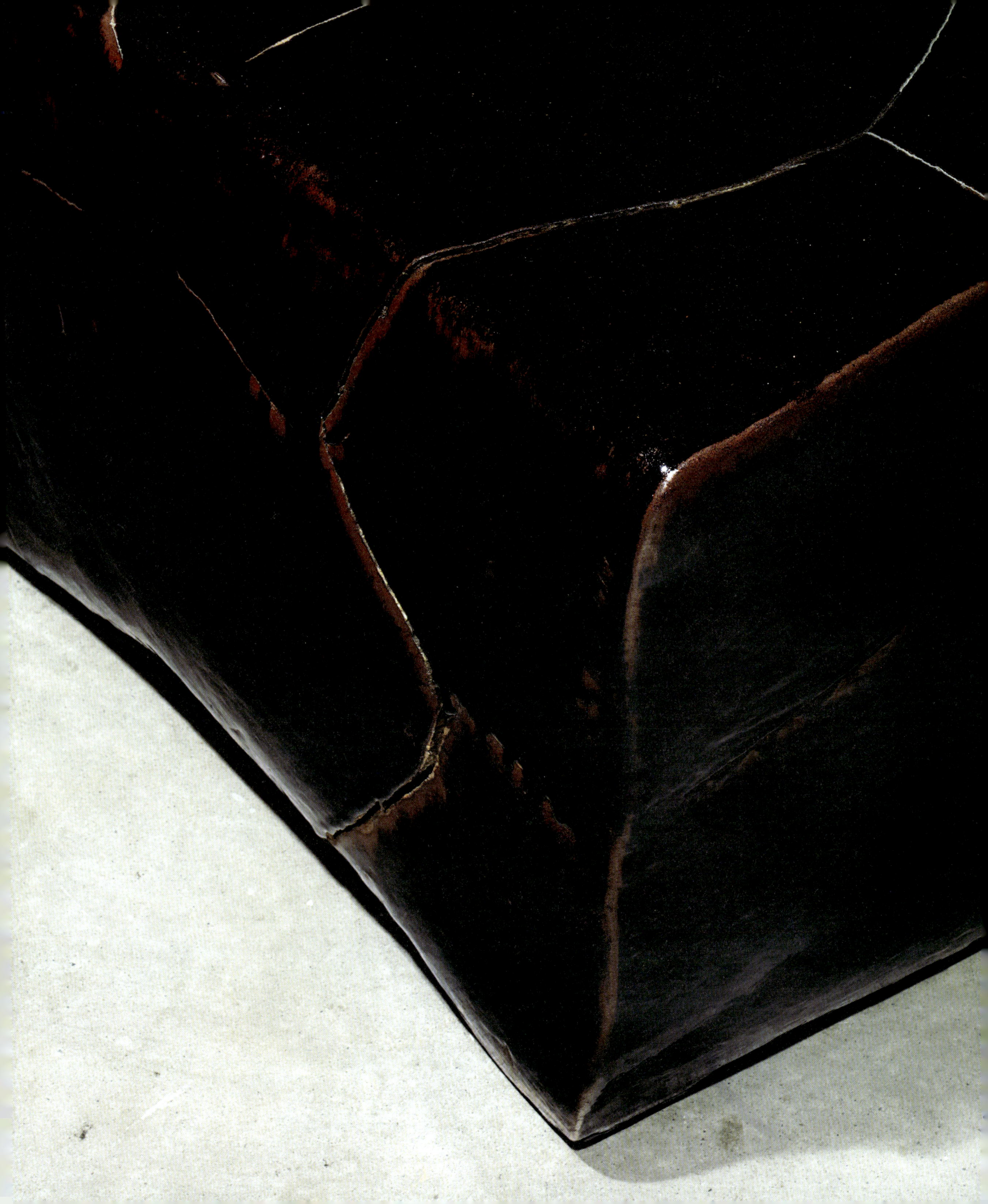

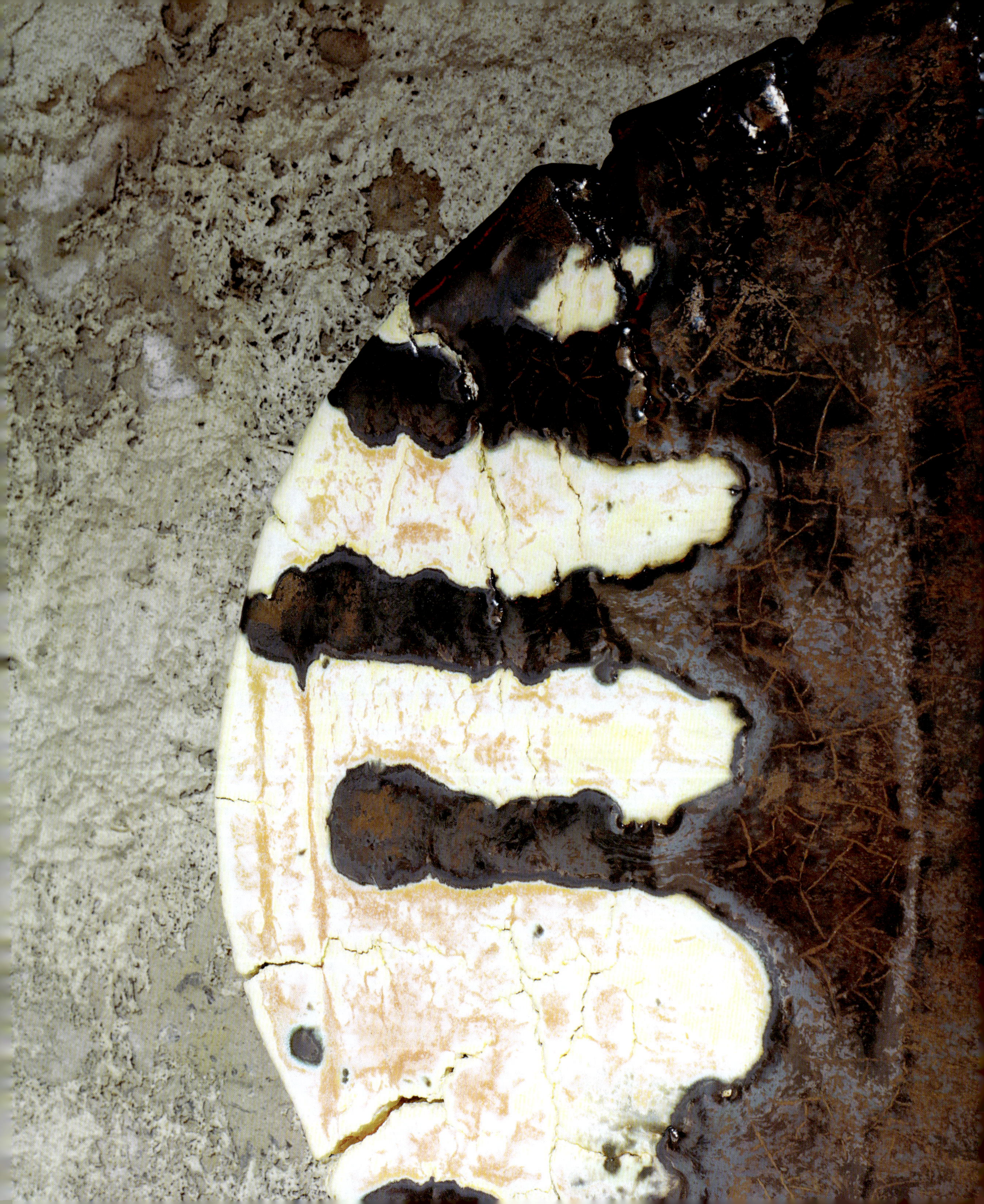

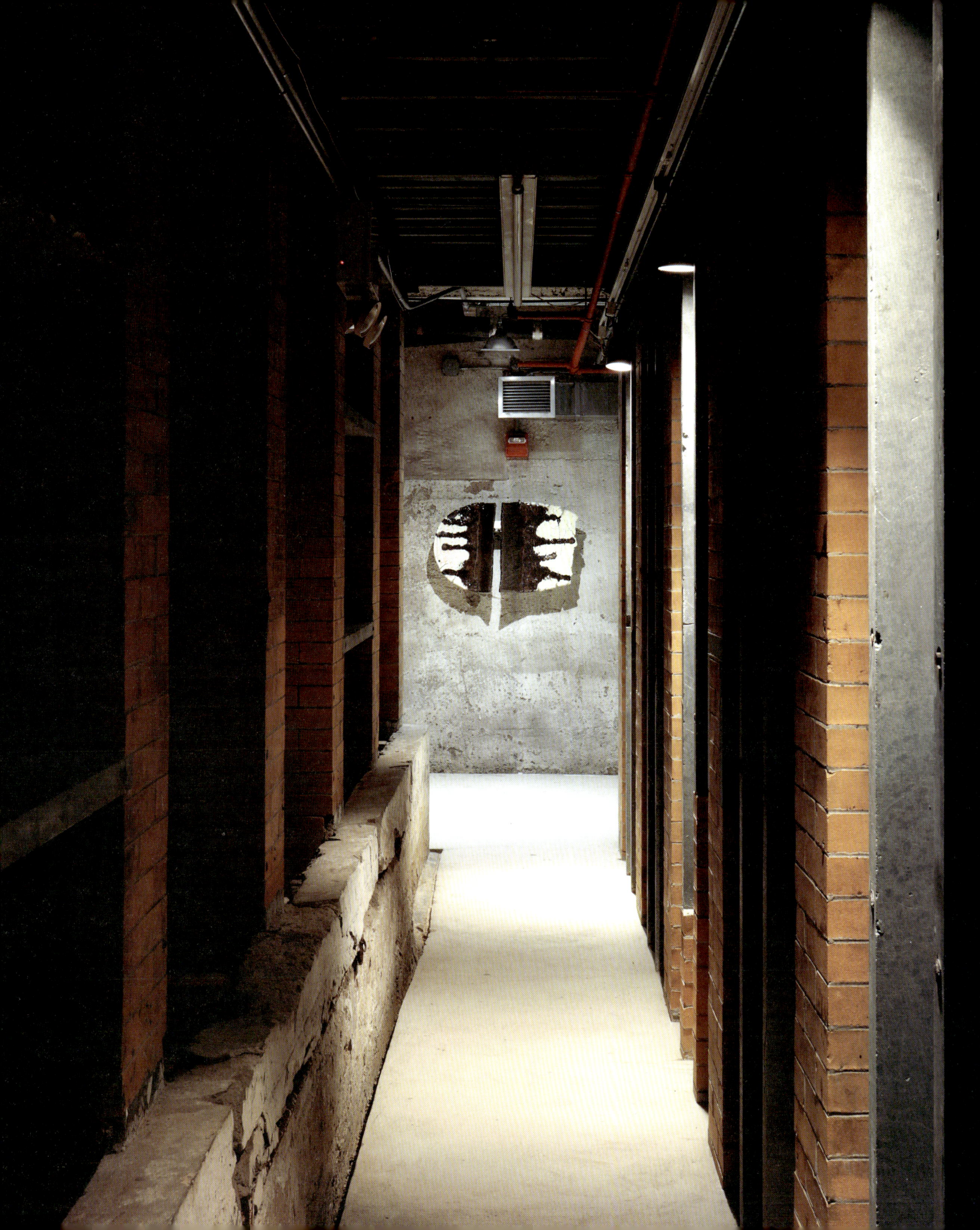

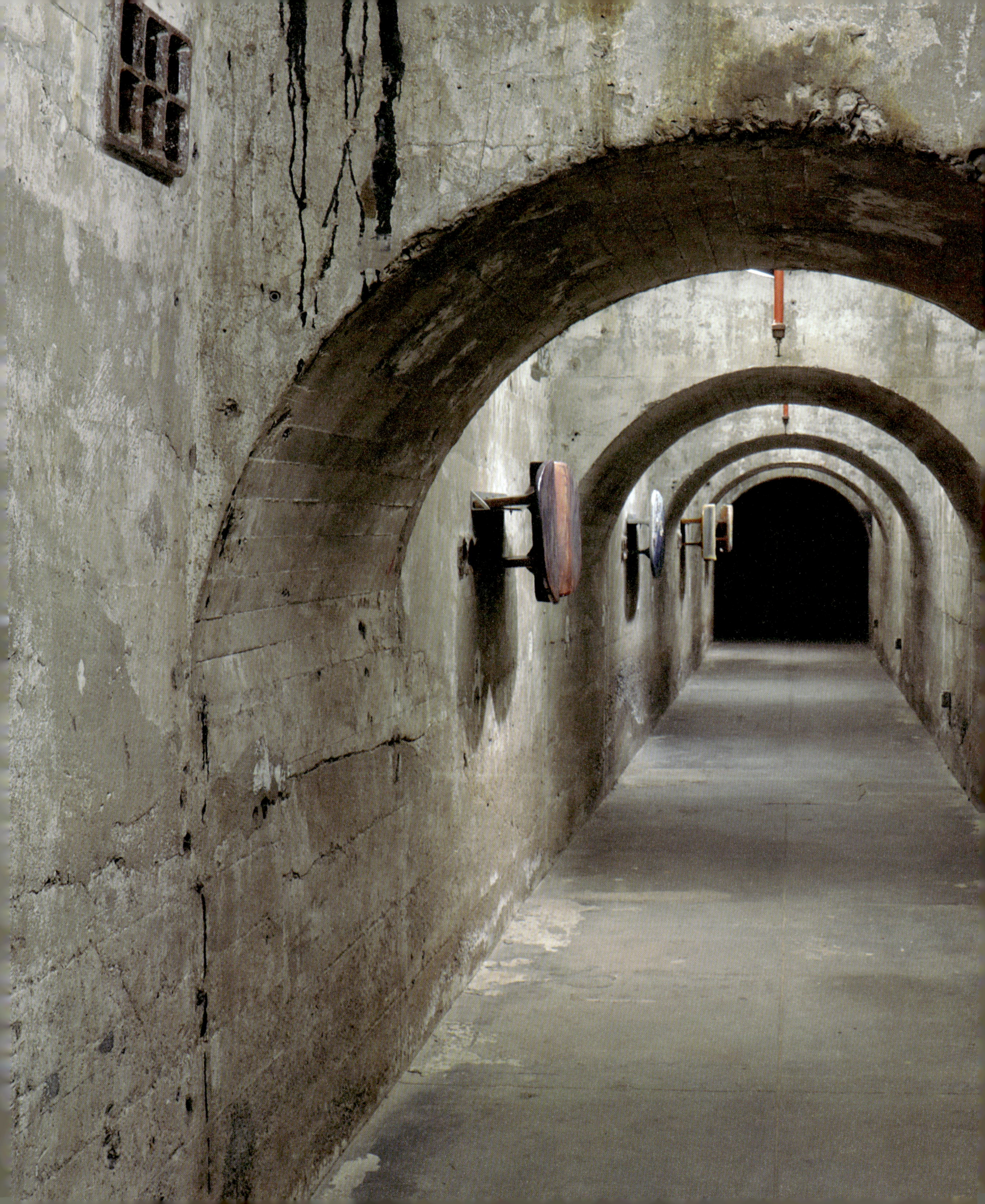

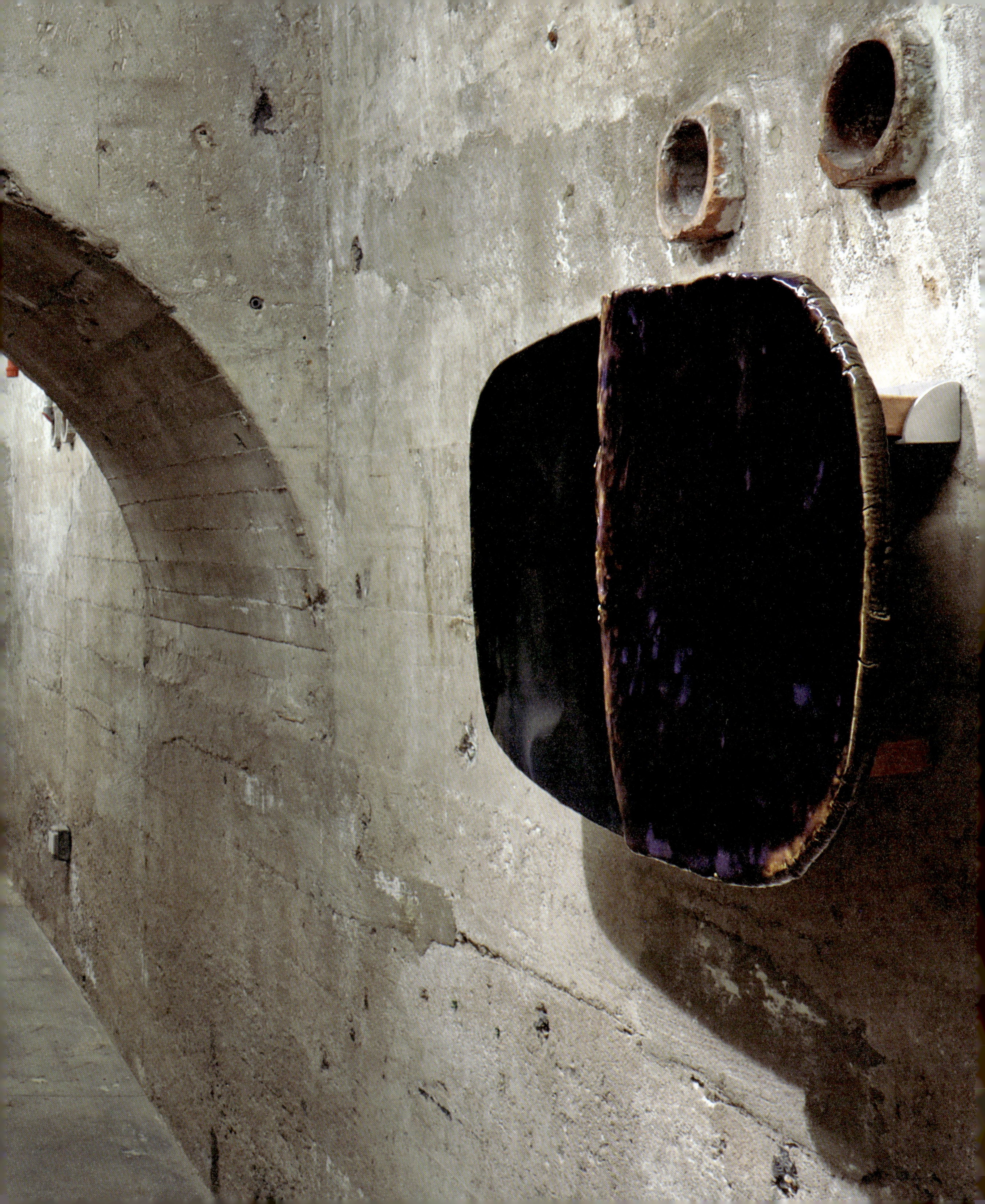

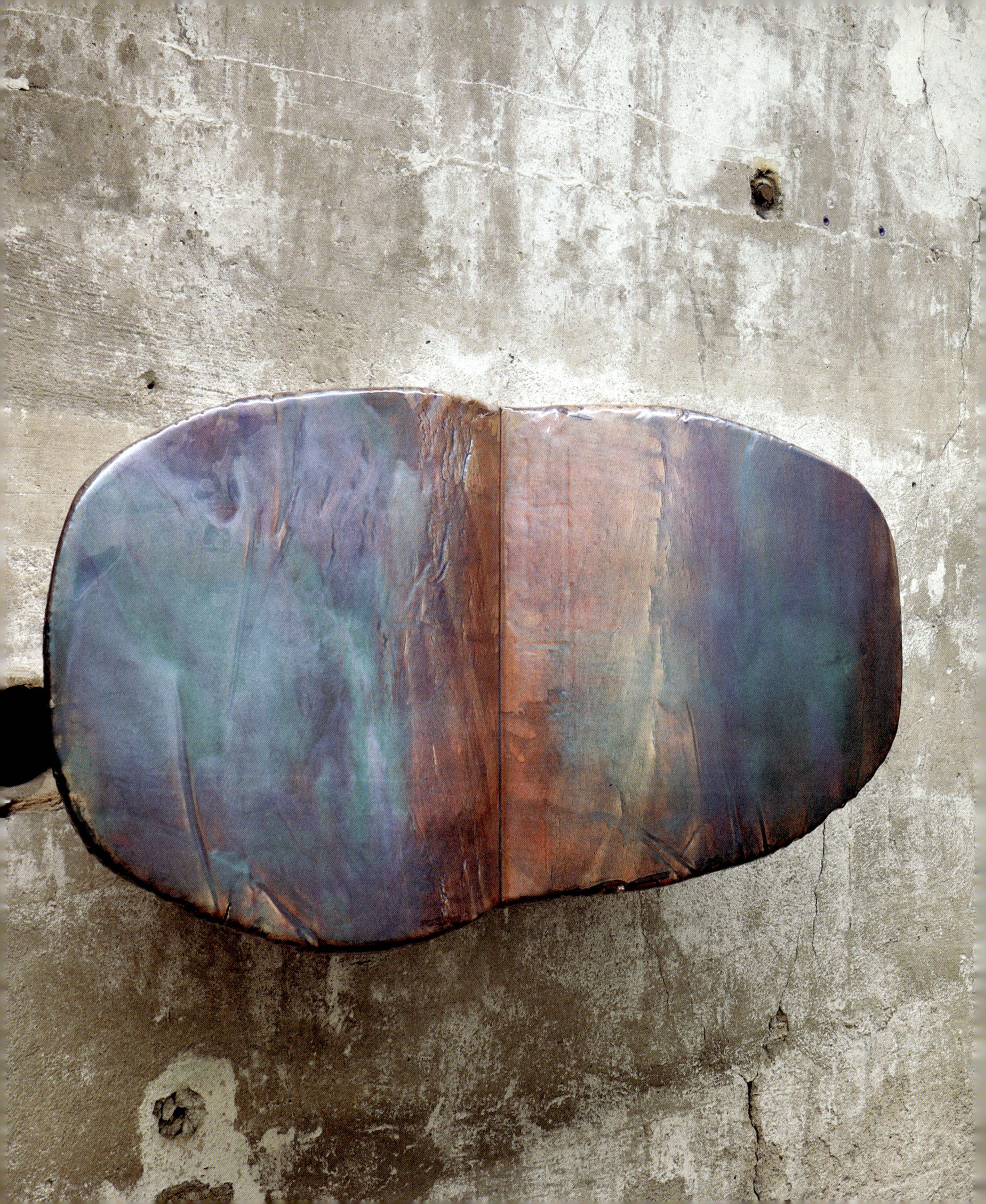

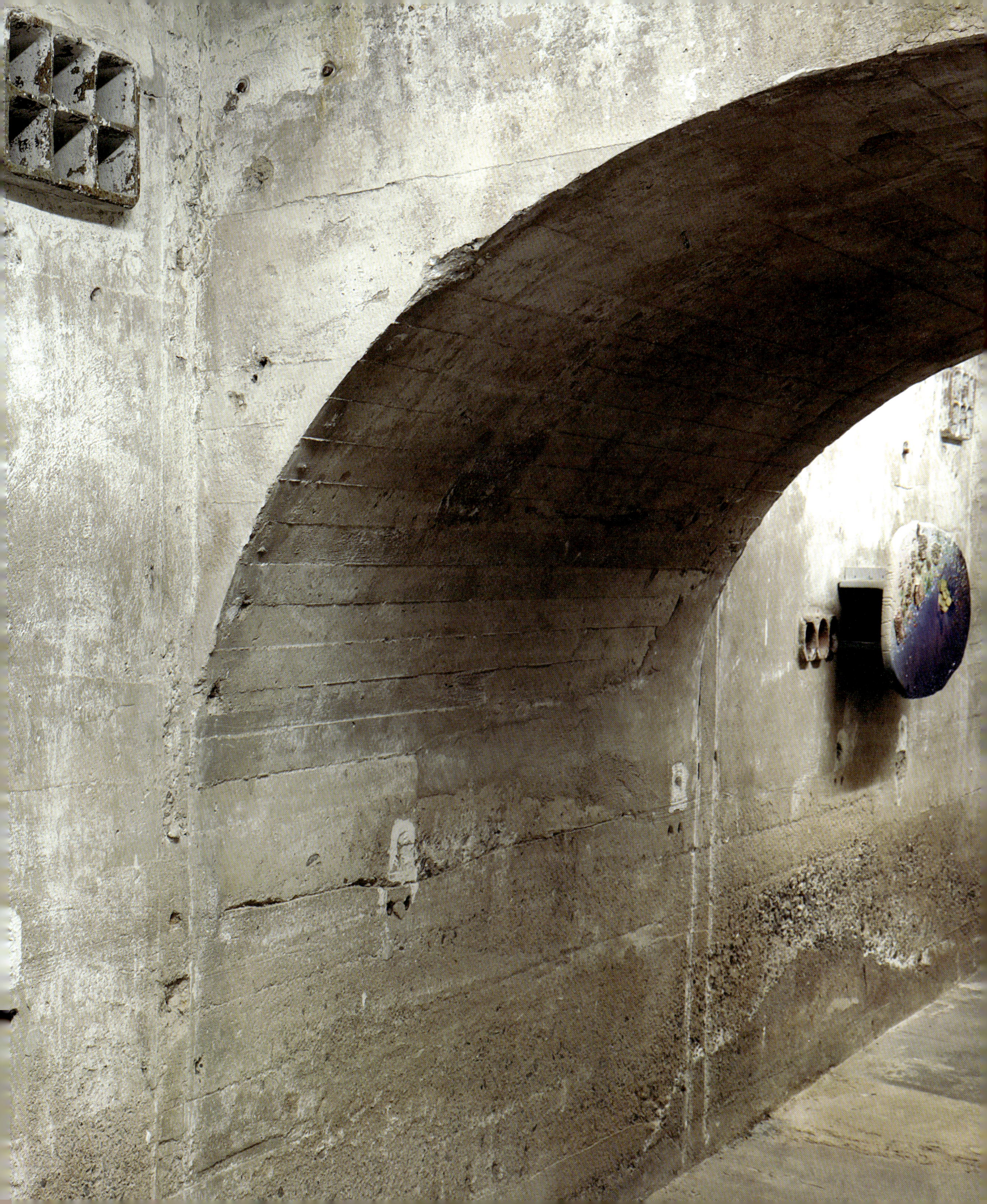

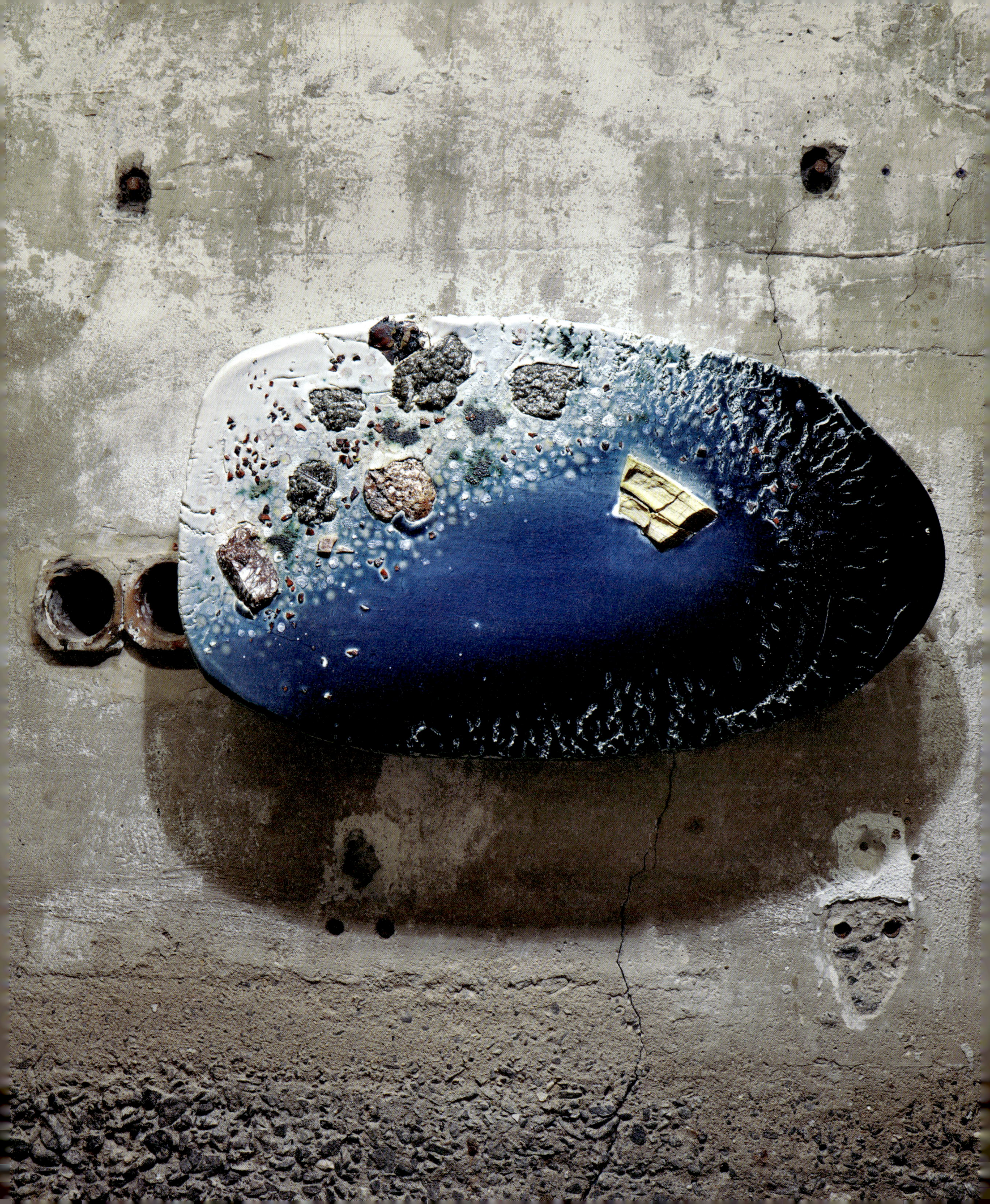

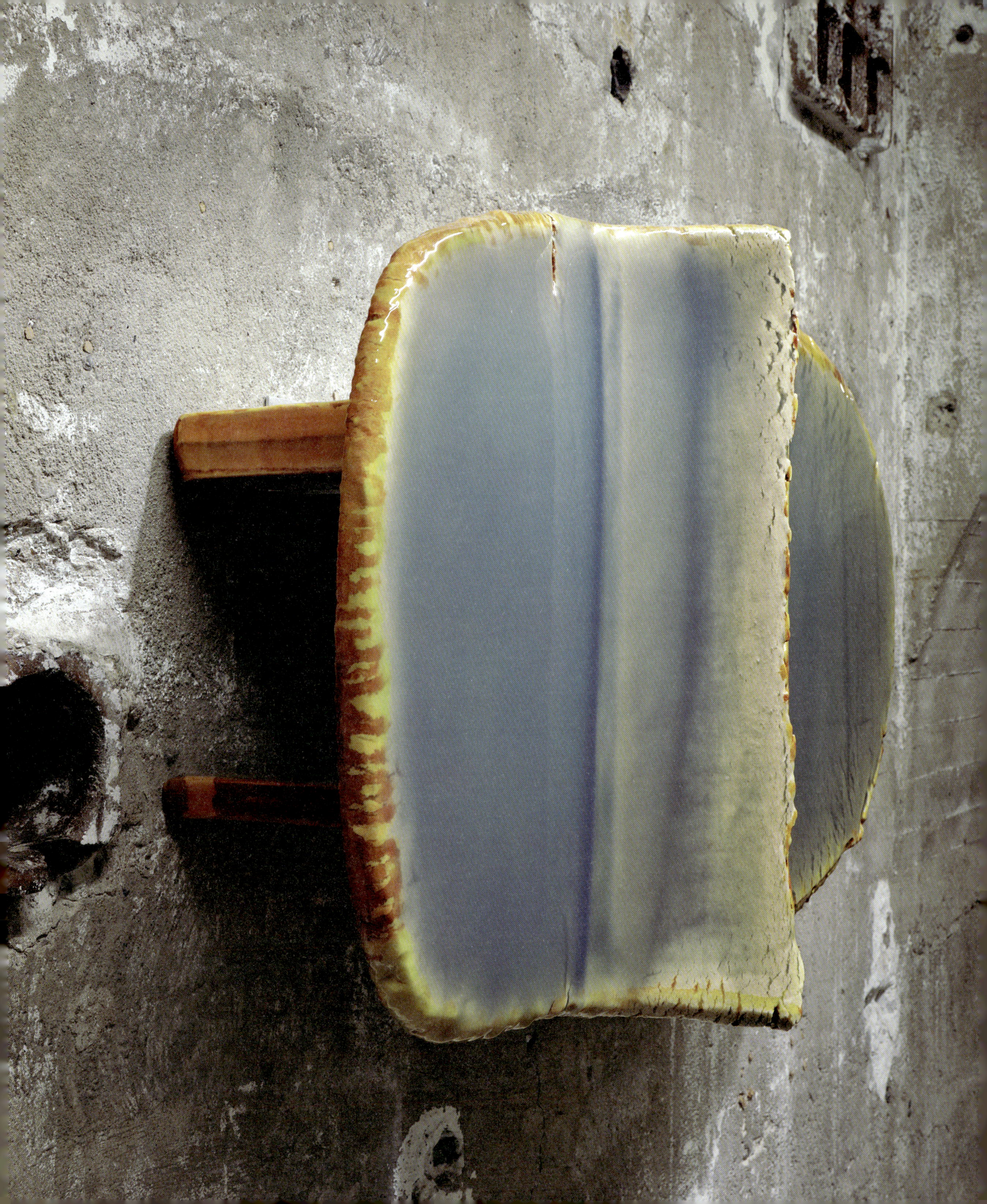

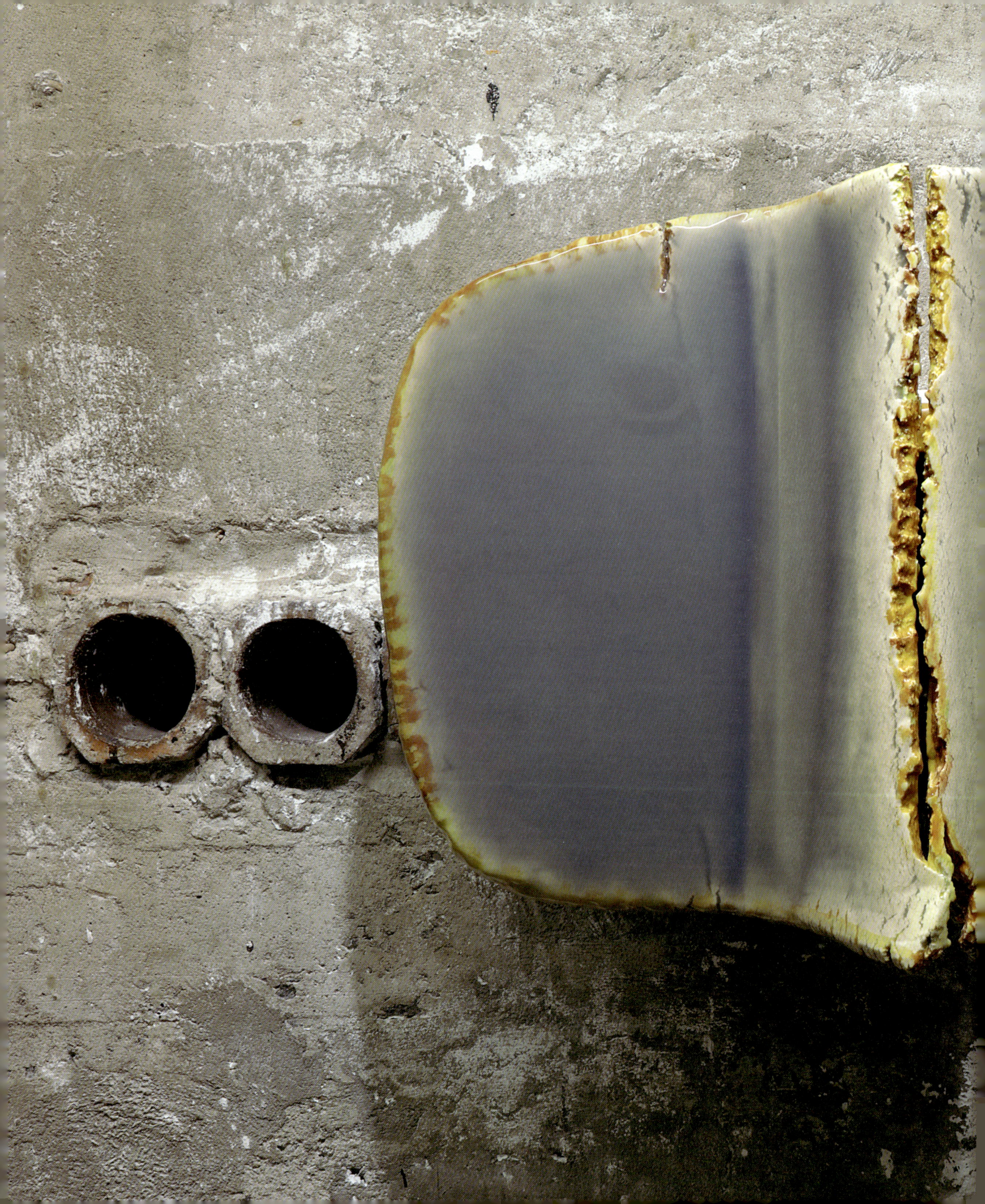

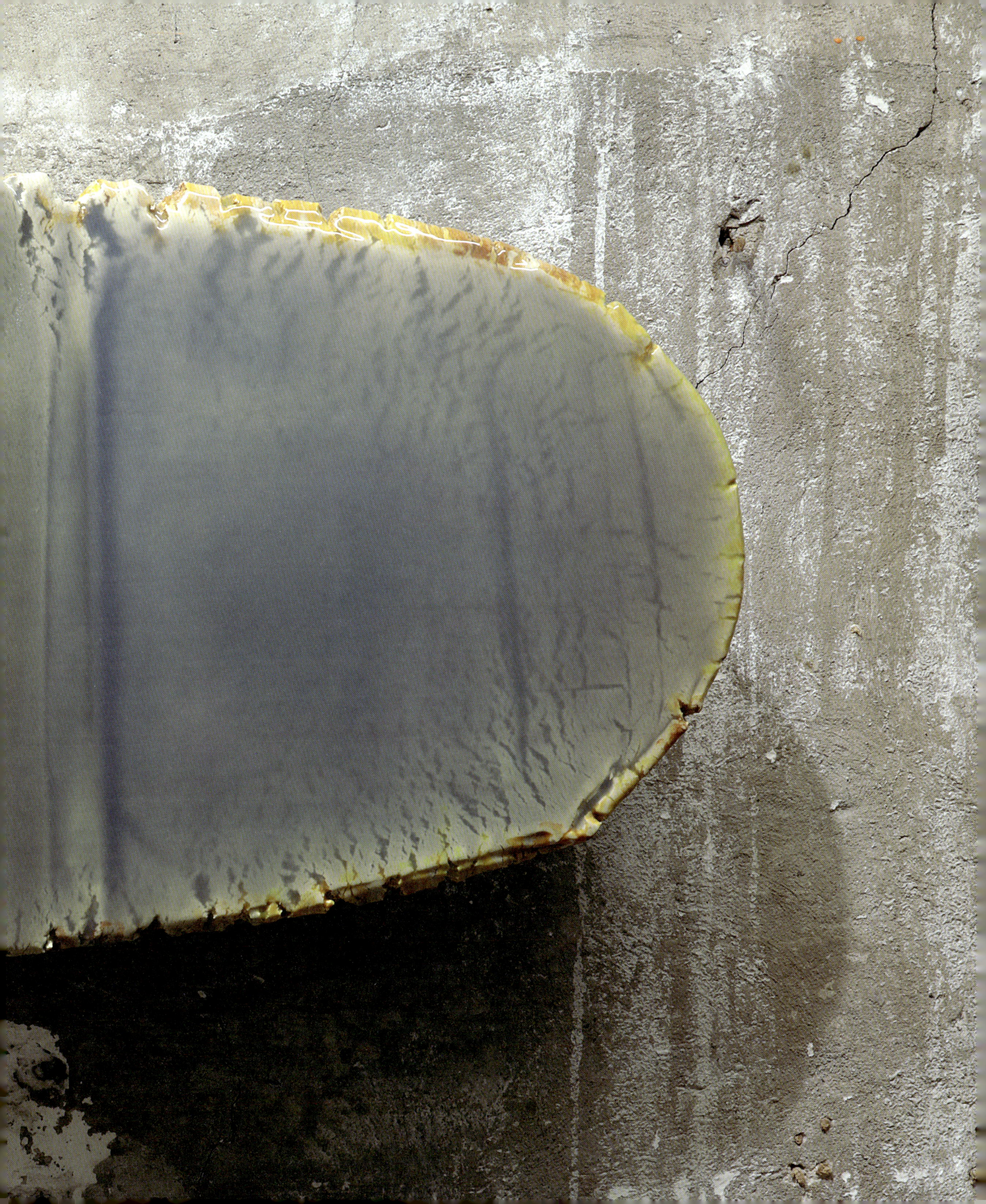

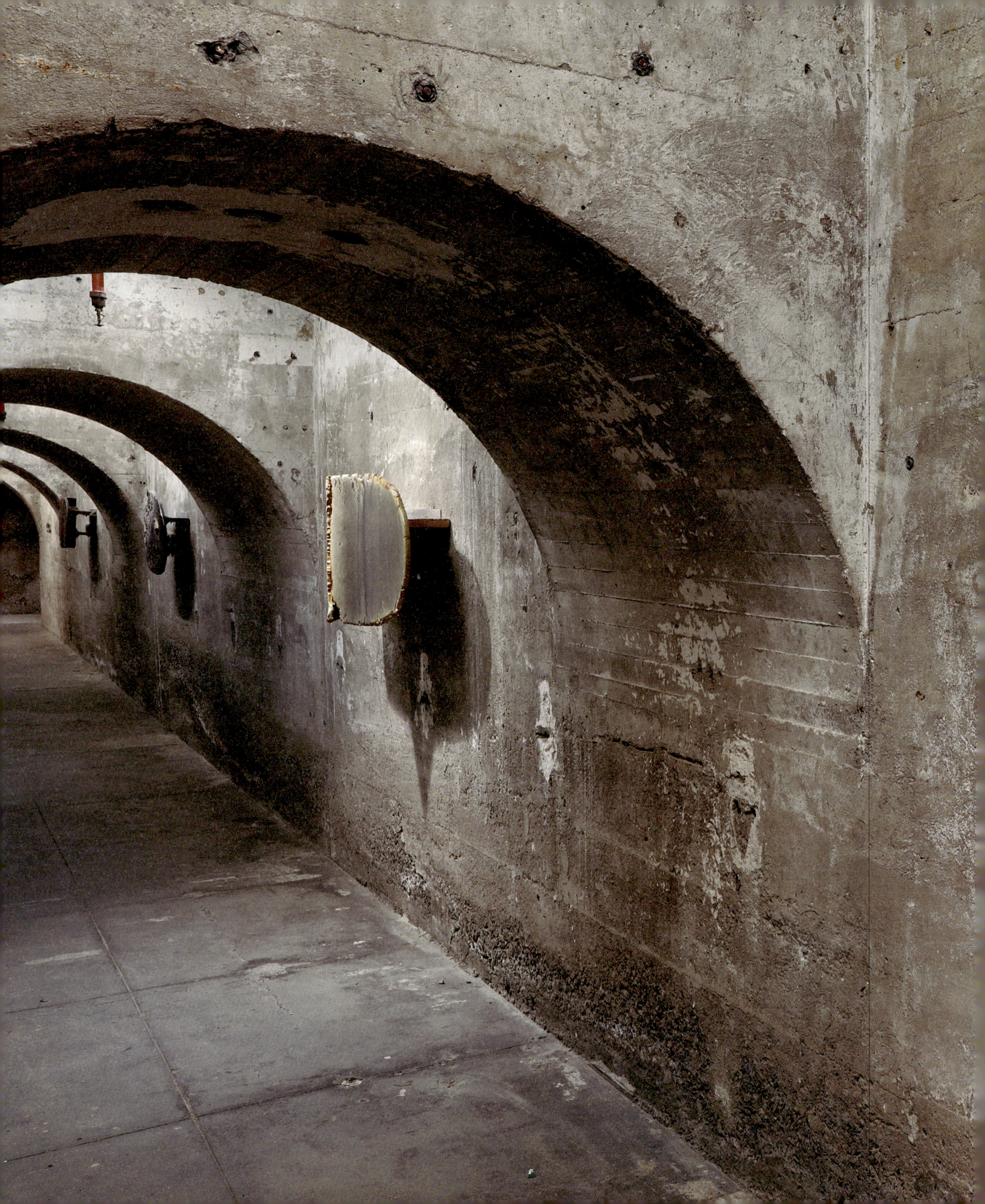

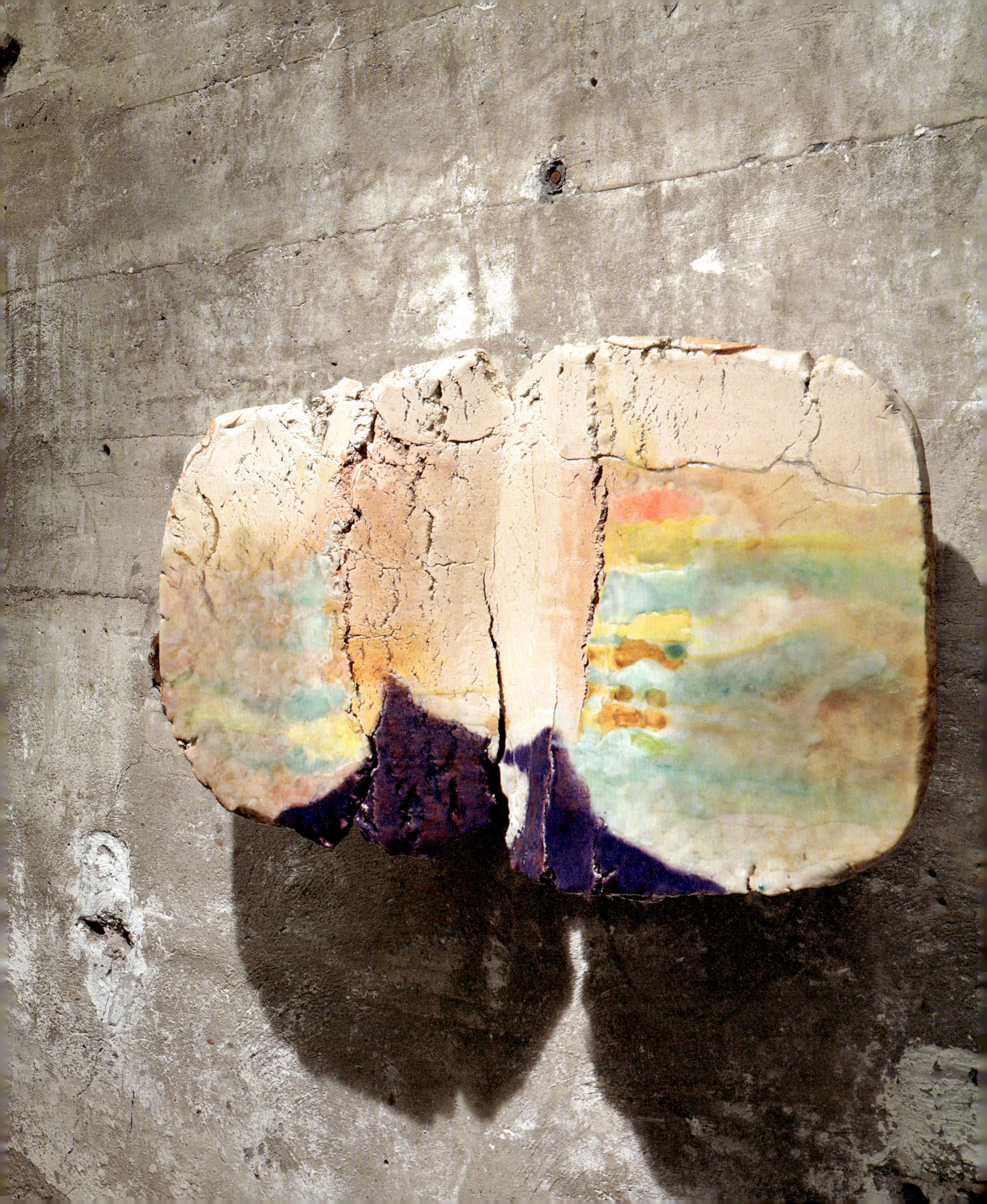

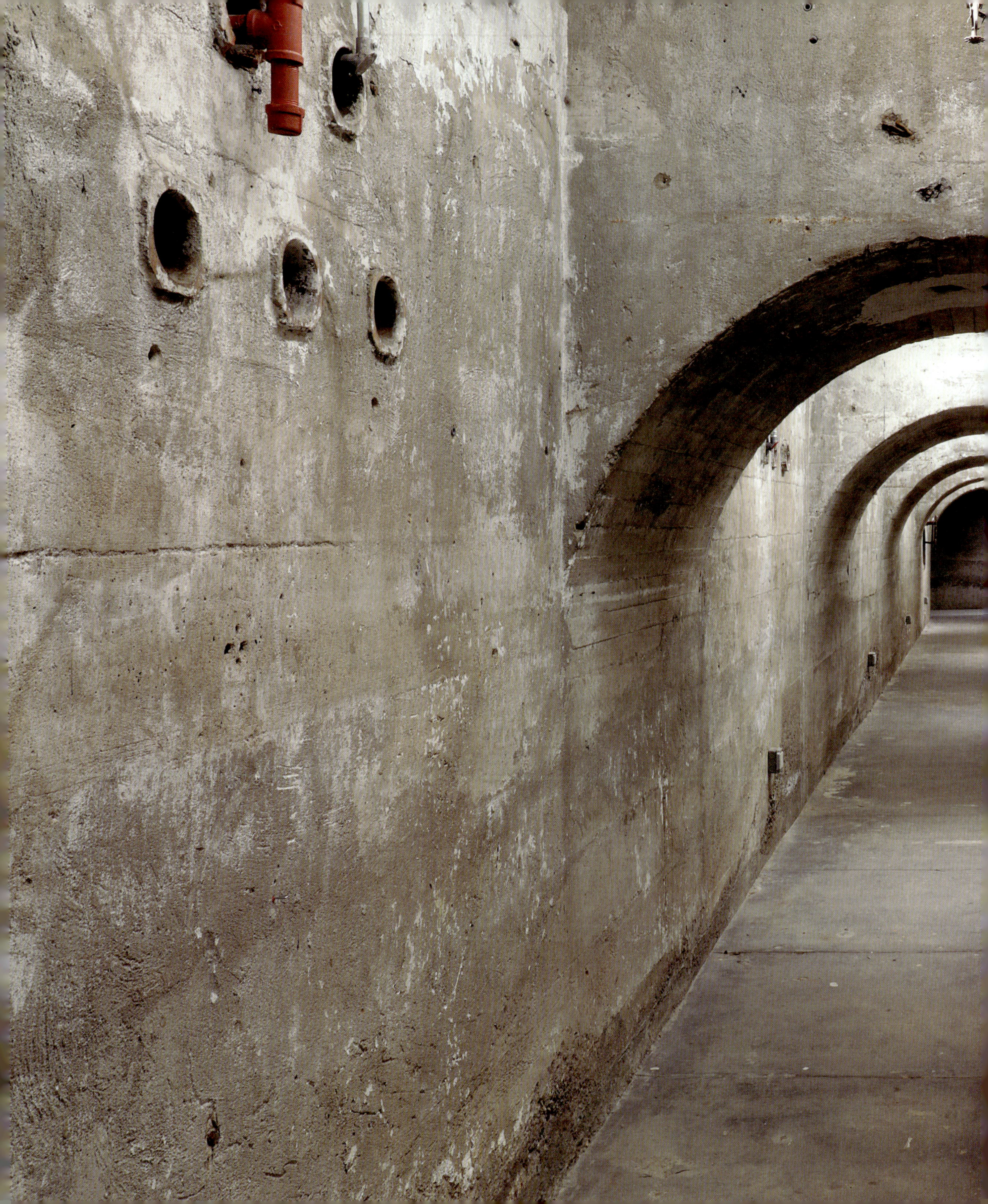

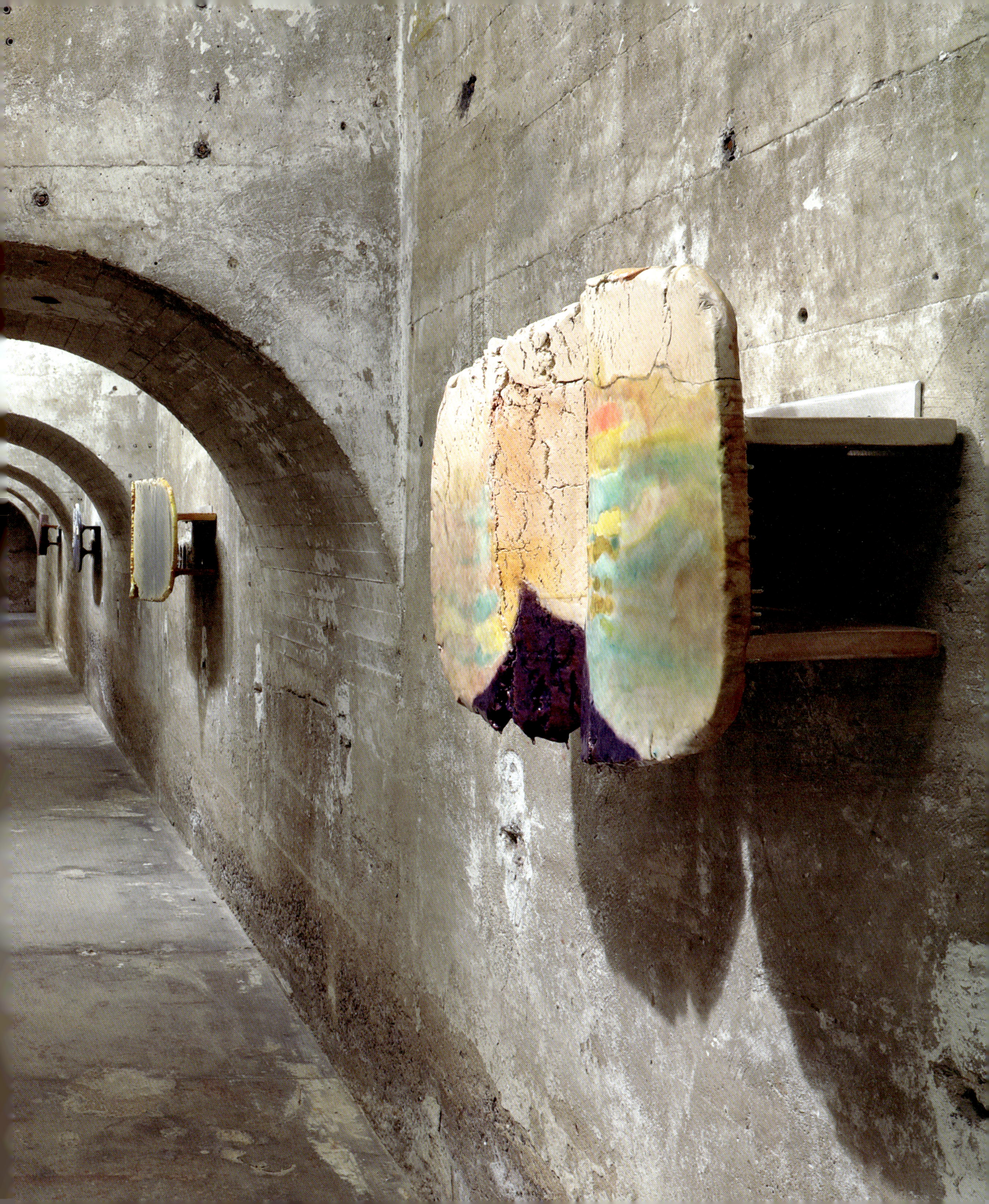

9 LLives: Some Notes on Liz Larner

ARIANA REINES

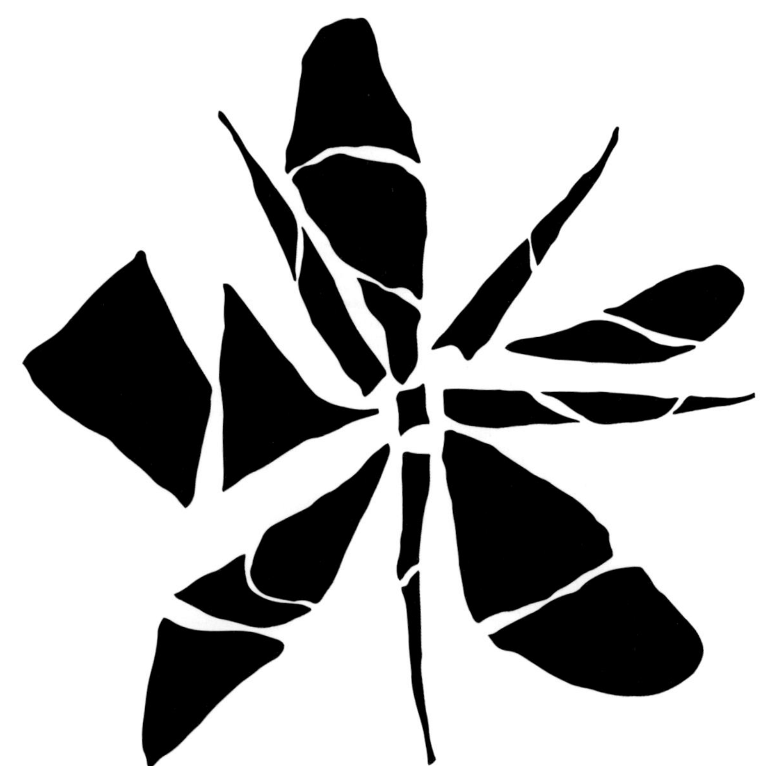

Between Loves Me and Not, 1992. Graphite on drafting film, 28 3/4 × 29 inches (73 × 73.7 cm)

I have resentments against sculpture. What I should have said is I envy it, I think. It tends to be mute, it isn't alive, it insinuates a claim on my attention I don't want to cow to, it gathers dust. It can be so beautiful.

I am tempted to explain what I see; I likewise resent the expectation that I explain what will not speak for itself, and I am slightly bothered by the verbiage my perceptions stimulate. Probably the reasons for this are fundamentally economic. In any case.

What I would like to write for you, here, is Rilke's "Archaic Torso of Apollo," because its final line, *You must change your life*, is the essential statement of any true encounter and is fundamental, I believe, to what sculpture does—and here I mark with an X the spot of my deepmost envy—an eloquence beyond words, the alchemical retort of a true encounter, after which you will never, ever be the same.

It seems to me that what Liz Larner makes is forged on the paradox of a "true encounter." Hers is an alchemy that declines to go mad. Instead, it plays.

I believe her to be an artist concerned with transformation, who is changed by what she makes, and who intends change for those who really relate, actually relate, in the room, on the sidewalk, to what she has put there.

My eyes aren't good at perceiving three-dimensional reality. There are physical reasons for this (astigmatism, etc.), but also, I think, the seeing I do is sluggish with a kind of kinesthetic and perceptual laziness that feels cultural, atmospheric. I'd like to blame it on my smartphone.

The above paragraph is meant to qualify some of the resentment against sculpture I admitted at the outset. It may simply be that I do not know how to see. What intrigues me most about this fact, at this point, is that—my birth defect aside—I am not alone.

Sculpture interposes itself uncannily into three-dimensional space. This is what is annoying about it: it is of the Earth; its assertions and pretensions to the beyond must eventually come down. It deals in gravity. It deals in solidity. It has a body.

Perhaps most peculiar of all: getting at the strangeness of the fact that it is not merely a matter of sight and seeing that ordinarily perceptible reality is three-dimensional. It has to do with the way we feel. It has to do with how we live and move. It has to do with things we can't express.

Culture, in Larner's body of work, does not signify the mass psychosis in which we all participate, or the chronology of high deeds and monumental catastrophes against which we estimate the present, but the agar upon and in which a substance ferments: the perfect, succinct parody of what our broader togetherness amounts to. Encounter produces strange chemical reactions; decay can resemble blooming. That which we would purport to preserve, we distort. The medium becomes the message.

Corners, likewise, are not where wallflowers hang around but the kinkiest, most heavy-metal parts of any room, where the punished go surlily to sulk, where two roads diverge in a yellow wood. Intersections are of course fragile; places of encounter, at times, require their chains and visors, their protectors. Larner's corners are like neglected Joans of Arc on horseback, sly, dreamy girls reemerging in armor as almost-unnoticed dominatrixes making bank off the guardians of the era . . . How do you build a monument to some of the less-celebrated streams and currents of the real without submitting to the lie of monumentality?

Substance meets agar, miles and miles of gauze metastasize and go solid, metal is woven like straw into a cube of Rumpelstiltskian transformation in reverse, a heavy Brancusi is launched into space, the weakest part of a room is bashed in here, girded up in metal there, disused armaments like stacks of old canonballs and old footballs, but also old alembics huddle together affectionately on the floor, a smile like a shattered ship that launched a thousand ships feels somehow like a nod to sculpture's archaic mode. . . . Open air enclosed by lines of paper and steel or metal implies chain mail, my mother's chore boys, dust bunnies, pubes, and the enervated legs of dead spiders.

Glazed ceramics like oblong gems, now fissured, now cracked into even more beauty, hang on the wall like the television screens and scrying mirrors of advanced life-forms: you have the feeling, looking at them, that the colors and innuendos upon them are moving, or that, if you were only slightly diviner, they would be. What is it, anyway, that gems, even the mere idea of them, do to the mind? A flat plane is twisted into the standing shadow of a dancer without a body; a bone, a joint, is stood for by its ceramic idea, which just sits there like a fossil or a bench. A cave has no opening; its inside is its outside. It almost beckons you to sit on it, but you can't, because it's art. Who reclines?

A few days ago, I received an exuberant email from my mother with a document attached. The buoyancy her note radiated was worth my attention, as she has been homeless for several months and the weather in New York has been bad, and really, she had no reason that I could see to be in a good mood. She had written an essay, clearly in an inspired or manic state, on the origin of the Sphinx at Giza and the formation of sphinxes, in general. My mother does not believe they were built by human beings. But her theory goes far beyond the kind of thing they talk about on *Ancient Aliens*.

According to my mother, when a deceased dignitary is lying in state and a celestial object passes by at a particular angle, a strobing effect between the decomposing face of the dignitary and the light emanated by the passing celestial object is produced. This strobing, as she calls it, causes strata of solid matter to accrete, like the layered quality of tourmaline or the sedimentary ridges we see in the Great Sphinx.

My mother finds it more compelling and more, perhaps, satisfying to imagine the Great Sphinx having somehow accumulated into its present form by virtue of this phenomenon—the mystical and mysterious encounter of the decomposing face of a deceased dignitary and a flash of light from a passing celestial object—than having been planned in a human mind and sculpted by human hands. Is it such a different idea than astrological principles prepare us for? The notion that the passing energies of planets interact with us somehow, and that when this celestial light meets our face, whether we are youthful and developing or dead and decomposing, a mystery, an unhoped-for beauty, cannot help but issue?

There is something in the way Larner plays that makes me feel she'd appreciate my mother's imagination, appreciate not only its sickness but also its health. I feel that part of the way Larner's sculpture occupies space—and one feels this in the sculpture of several seminal woman artists—is that it would wish to signal to such a woman, a woman like my mother, that Larner understands, just as her creations understand, that no matter how well and how fully we come into being and let our creations flower that there is more, and much more that's strange, to what we hunger to know and to all we cannot know, and to what we sense ourselves to be, and all the ways this being exceeds us.

Liz Larner pays attention to both cosmology and to geology, triangulating her own consciousness and the intentions of her making with and to these. I relate to this, though it's a difficult dynamic to put into words. I would hesitate to call it feminine, though feminine may be its true name. It has to do with the sense of felicity and mutual trust one feels when one is in the presence of a person who does not need every little thing explained to her, who simply understands. Larner's sculpture acts on the viewer with a sense of knowing complicity, whether in its gemlike beauty or its sly wit, and somehow they are resurrectionary experiences, making me feel not so much that I *must* change my life as Apollo's torso goaded Rilke to, but that, thank the goddess, I *can*. And that is why when I go to her I live again.

Bibliography

Compiled by the collaborators on this book—artist, curators, contributors, editors, and designers—this bibliography is a list of readings that may resonate with or provide entry points to the work of Liz Larner.

Alaimo, Stacy, and Susan Hekman, eds. *Material Feminisms*. Bloomington: Indiana University Press, 2008.

Barad, Karen. "Matter Feels, Converses, Suffers, Desires, Yearns and Remembers: Interview with Karen Barad." In *New Materialism: Interviews & Cartographies*, ed. Rick Dolphijn and Iris van der Tuin. Ann Arbor, MI: Open Humanities Press, 2012.

Bataille, Georges. *The Accursed Share: An Essay on General Economy*. 3 vols. Trans. Robert Hurley. New York: Zone Books, 1988–1991.

Batchelor, David. *Chromophobia*. London: Reaktion Books, 2000.

Baudrillard, Jean. *Simulations*. Trans. Paul Foss, Paul Patton, and Philip Beitchman. New York: Semiotext(e), 1983.

Bellamy, Dodie. *Cunt Norton*. Los Angeles: Les Figues Press, 2013.

The Bijak of Kabir. Trans. Linda Hess and Sukhdev Singh. 1986; New Delhi: Motilal Banarsidass, 2001.

Boyer, Anne. *A Handbook of Disappointed Fate*. New York: Ugly Duckling Presse, 2018.

Braidotti, Rosi. *Metamorphoses: Towards a Materialist Theory of Becoming*. Cambridge, UK: Polity Press, 2002.

——. *Nomadic Subjects: Embodiment and Sexual Difference in Contemporary Feminist Theory*. New York: Columbia University Press, 2011.

——. *Nomadic Theory: The Portable Rosi Braidotti*. New York: Columbia University Press, 2011.

——. *The Posthuman*. Cambridge, UK: Polity Press, 2013.

——. *Posthuman Knowledge*. Cambridge, UK: Polity Press, 2019.

Braidotti, Rosi, and Rick Dolphijn, ed. *Philosophy after Nature*. New York; Rowman & Littlefield, 2017.

Braidotti, Rosi, and Maria Hlavajova, ed. *Posthuman Glossary*. London: Bloomsbury, 2018.

Butler, Connie. *WACK! Art and the Feminist Revolution*. Los Angeles: Museum of Contemporary Art; Cambridge, MA: MIT Press, 2007.

Butler, Judith. *Gender Trouble: Feminism and the Subversion of Identity*. New York: Routledge, 1990.

——. *Notes toward a Performative Theory of Assembly*. Cambridge, MA: Harvard University Press, 2018.

Butler, Octavia E. *Adulthood Rites*. New York: Warner Books, 1988.

——. *Kindred*. New York: Doubleday, 1979.

Campbell, June. *Traveller in Space: Gender, Identity, and Tibetan Buddhism*. Rev. ed. 1996; London: Continuum, 2002.

Carson, Anne. *Glass, Irony, and God*. New York : New Directions, 1995.

Casid, Jill H. "Doing Things with Being Undone." *Journal of Visual Culture* 18, no. 1 (2019): 30–52.

Christensen, Inger. *Alphabet*. New York: New Directions, 2001.

Christensen, Julia. *Upgrade Available*. New York: Dancing Foxes Press, 2020.

Cleaver, Eldridge. *Soul on Ice*. New York: McGraw-Hill, 1967.

Colomina, Beatriz, ed. *Sexuality and Space*. New York: Princeton Architectural Press, 1992.

Debord, Guy. *Society of the Spectacle*. 1967; Detroit, MI: Black & Red, 1983.

Deleuze, Gilles. *Spinoza: Practical Philosophy*. Trans. Robert Hurley. San Francisco: City Lights Books, 1988.

Deleuze, Gilles, and Félix Guattari. *Anti-Oedipus: Capitalism and Schizophrenia*. Trans. Robert Hurley, Mark Seem, and Helen R. Lane. New York: Penguin, 1977.

Derrida, Jacques. *The Post Card: From Socrates to Freud and Beyond*. Trans. Alan Bass Chicago: University of Chicago Press, 1987.

Dickenson, Emily. *The Gorgeous Nothings*. New York: Christine Burgin and New Directions Press, in association with Granary Press, 2013.

Didion, Joan. *A Book of Common Prayer*. New York: Simon and Schuster, 1977.

——. *South and West: From a Notebook*. New York: Knopf, 2017.

——. *Where I Was From*. New York: Knopf, 2003.

Duras, Marguerite. *L'amant de la Chine du Nord*. Paris: Gallimard, 1991.

Firestone, Shulamuth. *The Dialectic of Sex: The Case for a Feminist Revolution*. New York: Morrow, 1970.

Francis, Conseula, ed. *Conversations with Octavia Butler*. Jackson: University Press of Mississippi, 2010.

George, Demetra. *Mysteries of the Dark Moon: The Healing Power of the Dark Goddess*. San Francisco: Harper San Francisco, 1992.

Grosz, Elizabeth A. *Time Travels: Feminism, Nature, Power*. Durham: Duke University Press, 2005.

——. *Volatile Bodies: Toward a Corporeal Feminism*. Bloomington: Indiana University Press, 1994.

Haraway, Donna J. *Staying with the Trouble: Making Kin in the Chthulucene*. Durham, NC: Duke University Press, 2016.

Howe, Fanny. *Radical Love: Five Novels*. Brooklyn, NY: Nightboat, 2006.

Irigaray, Luce. *This Sex Which Is Not One*. Trans. Catherine Porter with Carolyn Burk. Ithaca, NY: Cornell University Press, 1985.

Jess, Tyehimba. *Olio*. Seattle: Wave Books, 2016.

Kimmerer, Robin Wall. *Braiding Sweetgrass: Indigenous Wisdom, Scientific Knowledge and the Teaching of Plants*. Minneapolis: Milkweed Editions, 2013.

Kraus, Chris. *I Love Dick*. New York: Semiotext(e), 1997.

LaValle, Victor. *The Changeling: A Novel*. New York: Spiegel & Grau, 2017.

Le Guin, Ursula K. *The Found and the Lost: The Collected Novellas of Ursula K. Le Guin*. New York: Saga Press, 2016.

——. *The Lathe of Heaven*. New York: Scribner, 1971.

——. *The Unreal and the Real: The Selected Short Stories of Ursula K. Le Guin*. New York: Saga Press, 2017.

——. *The Word for World Is Forest*. New York: Berkley/Putnam, 1976.

Lee, Li-Young. *The City in Which I Love You*. Rochester, NY: BOA Editions, 1990.

Lemmey, Huw, and Hildegard von Bingen. *Unknown Language*. London: Ignota Books, 2020.

Lichtenstein, Jacqueline. *The Eloquence of Color: Rhetoric and Painting in the French Classical Age*. Trans. Emily McVarish. Berkeley: University of California Press, 1993.

Liu, Catherine. *American Idyll: Academic Antieletism as Cultural Critique*. Iowa City: University of Iowa Press, 2011.

——. *Virtue Hoarders: The Case against the Professional Managerial Class*. Minneapolis: Minnesota University Press, 2021.

Nelson, Maggie. *On Freedom: Four Songs on Care and Constraint*. Minneapolis: Graywolf Press, 2021.

Nietzsche, Friedrich. *Human, All Too Human: A Book for Free Spirits*. Trans. Marion Faber and Stephen Lehmann. Rev. ed. Lincoln: University of Nebraska Press, 1996.

Notley, Alice, *Descent of Alette*. New York: Penguin, 1996.

Porter, Jenelle, and Ingrid Schaffner. *Dirt on Delight: Impulses that Form Clay*. Philadelphia: Institute of Contemporary Art, University of Pennsylvania, 2009.

Potter, Norman. *Models & Constructs: Margin Notes to a Design Culture*. London: Hyphen Press, 1990.

Purdy, Jedediah. *After Nature: A Politics for the Anthropocene*. Cambridge, MA: Harvard University Press, 2015.

Rankine, Claudia. *Don't Let Me Be Lonely: An American Lyric*. Minneapolis: Graywolf Press, 2004.

Rattray, David. *Opening the Eyelid*. Brooklyn, NY: Diwan, 1990.

Rayner, Richard. *The Associates: Four Capitalists Who Created California*. New York: Norton, 2008.

Reines, Ariana. *The Cow*. Albany, NY: Fence Books, 2006.

——. *Mercury*. Albany, NY: Fence Books, 2011.

——. *A Sand Book*. Portland, OR: Tin House Books, 2019.

Rilke, Rainer Maria. *Duino Elegies*. Trans. J. B. Leishman and Stephen Spender. New York: Norton, 1939.

Robinson, James M., ed. *The Nag Hammadi Library in English*. New York: Harper & Row, 1977.

Sanders, Joel, ed. *Stud: Architectures of Masculinity*. New York: Princeton Architectural Press, 1996.

Shiva, Vandana. *Water Wars: Privatization, Pollution, and Profit*. Cambridge, MA: South End Press, 2002.

Simard, Suzanne. *Finding the Mother Tree: Discovering the Wisdom of the Forest*. New York: Knopf, 2021.

Skott-Myhre, Kathleen. *Feminist Spirituality under Capitalism: Witches, Fairies, and Nomads*. New York: Routledge, 2017.

Solnit, Rebecca. *As Eve Said to the Serpent: On Landscape, Gender, and Art*. Athens: University of Georgia Press, 2001.

Stanford, Frank. *The Battlefield Where the Moon Says I Love You*. Barrington, RI: Lost Roads Publishers, 2000.

Trismegistus, Hermes. *The Emerald Tablet of Hermes*. Dublin: Merchant Books, 2013.

Tsing, Anna Lowenhaupt. *The Mushroom at the End of the World: On the Possibility of Life in Capitalist Ruins*. Princeton, NJ: Princeton University Press, 2015.

Weber, Samuel. *Mass Mediauras: Form, Technics, Media*. Stanford, CA: Stanford University Press, 1996.

Wex, Marianne. *Let's Take Back Our Space: "Female" and "Male" Body Language as a Result of Patriarchal Structures*. Trans. Johanna Albert. Berlin: Frauenliteraturverlag Hermine Fees, 1979.

Wojnarowicz, David. *In the Shadow of the American Dream: The Diaries of David Wojnarowicz*. New York: Grove, 1999.

Wolkstein, Diane, and Samuel Noah Kramer. *Ianna Queen of Earth and Heaven: Her Stories and Hymns from Sumer*. New York: Harper & Row, 1983.

Yourcenar, Marguerite. *Memoirs of Hadrian*, trans. Grace Frick. New York: Farrar, Straus and Young, 1954.

Liz Larner   *Don't put it*
back like it was

SculptureCenter, New York
January 20–March 28, 2022

Walker Art Center, Minneapolis
April 30–September 4, 2022

** Walker Art Center only*

pp. 15 (bottom), 46
Orchid, Buttermilk, Penny, 1987
Orchid, buttermilk, penny, glass
Base: plywood, wood filler, latex paint
43 $^{7}/_{16}$ × 17 $^{1}/_{2}$ × 10 $^{1}/_{8}$ inches
(110.2 × 44.5 × 25.7 cm)
Private collection

pp. 57, 58, 59, 63
Out of Touch, 1987
Sixteen miles of surgical gauze
48 × 48 × 48 inches (121.9 × 121.9 × 121.9 cm)
Collection Peter Pakesch, Vienna

Used to do the job, 1987 *
Steel, aluminum, coal, copper, iron, zinc, copper
carbonate, brass, bronze, saltpeter, bursera
gummifera, glass, iron oxide, santalum album,
bluestone, sulfur, tar, rubber, volcanic ash,
lodestones, trinitrotoluene (TNT), ammonium
nitrate and other natura
48 $^{1}/_{2}$ × 25 $^{3}/_{4}$ × 24 $^{3}/_{4}$ inches (123.2 × 65.4 × 62.9 cm)
The Museum of Contemporary Art, Los Angeles;
Gift of Alan Dinsfriend and Matthew Ruble, M.D.

p. 71
Copper cube, woven, 1988
Copper
12 $^{7}/_{8}$ × 12 $^{15}/_{16}$ × 12 $^{7}/_{8}$ inches
(32.4 × 32.4 × 32.4 cm)
Private collection. Courtesy Galerie Max Hetzler,
Berlin, Paris, and London

pp. 30, 44, 45
Corner Basher, 1988
Steel, stainless steel, electric motor, speed control
106 × 36 × 36 inches (269.2 × 91.4 × 91.4 cm)
Gaby and Wilhelm Schürmann Collection,
Herzogenrath and Berlin

pp. 38 (bottom), 46, 47
Primary, Secondary: Culture of Empire
State Building and Twin Towers, 1988
Bacteria, nutrient agar, food coloring,
glass, aluminum
42 × 12 × 14 $^{1}/_{2}$ inches (106.7 × 30.5 × 36.8)
Courtesy of the artist

pp. 4, 28, 57, 59, 60–61, 100
Bird in Space, 1989
Nylon, silk, stainless steel
Dimensions variable
Smithsonian American Art Museum; Gift
of Susan and Leonard Nimoy and museum
purchase in part through the Gene Davis
Memorial Fund

pp. 17 (top), 48, 49, 56
Lash Mat, 1989
Leather, false eyelashes made from
human hair, glue
122 $^{1}/_{2}$ × 11 $^{1}/_{2}$ × $^{3}/_{8}$ inches (311.1 × 29.2 × 1 cm)
Museum of Contemporary Art, Los Angeles;
Gift of Kourosh Larizadeh and Luis Pardo

p. 13 (bottom)
Rubber Divider, 1989 *
Torch-cut steel, pure gum rubber sheeting
116 $^{1}/_{8}$ × 109 × 10 $^{1}/_{4}$ inches (295 × 276.9 × 26 cm)
Gaby and Wilhelm Schürmann Collection,
Herzogenrath and Berlin

p. 19
Verwoben (Head, Torso, Foot), 1989 *
Head: Newspaper, gauze, rubber, wire
Torso: Fabric, fur, canvas, plastic, paper
Foot: Fabric, silver, leather, cotton, nylon, rubber
Dimensions variable
Courtesy Galerie Max Hetzler, Berlin, Paris,
and London

pp. 17 (bottom), 50, 51
No M, No D, Only S & B, 1990
Leather, sand, brass zipper, bark, waxed
cotton thread
36 × 48 × 60 inches (91.4 × 121.9 × 152.4 cm),
height variable on installation
Walker Art Center, Minneapolis; T.B. Walker
Acquisition Fund, 2020

pp. 4, 13 (top), 56, 59, 62, 64
Too the Wall, 1990
Anealed steel, silver, leather
42 × 66 × 48 inches (106.7 × 167.6 × 121.9 cm)
Centre national des arts plastiques, Paris

pp. 4, 12, 49, 50, 59
Wrapped Corner, 1991
Chain, turnbuckles, steel brackets
49 × 90 inches (124.46 × 228.6 cm)
San Francisco Museum of Modern Art;
Gift of Norah and Norman Stone

pp. 2, 35 (top), 65
Hands, 1993
Hollow-cast pewter, chain
Ten parts: dimensions variable
Courtesy the artist and Regen Projects,
Los Angeles

pp. 4, 23, 52, 54–55, 56, 57, 59
2 as 3 and Some, Too, 1997–98
Mulberry paper, steel, watercolor
112 × 137 × 95 inches (284.5 × 348 × 241.3 cm)
Museum of Contemporary Art, Los Angeles;
Purchase in memory of Stuart Regen with funds
provided by Thea Westreich and Ethan Wagner,
Pam and Dick Kramlich, Norman and Norah
Stone, and Chara Schreyer

p. 31
Reticule, 1999 *
Cast polyurethane
74 × 112 × 80 inches (188 × 284.5 × 203.2 cm)
Blanton Museum of Art, the University of
Texas at Austin; Gift of Jeanne and Michael
Klein, 2007

p. 53
Untitled, 2000
Stainless steel, mulberry paper, watercolor
30 × 25 × 13 inches (76.2 × 63.5 × 33 cm)
Collection of Deedie Rose; Promised Gift
to Dallas Museum of Art

pp. 29, 70, 71
Guest, 2004
Gold-plated bronze, square section
Dimensions variable
Collection of Rosette Delug

pp. 72, 73
Guest, 2005
Silver-plated stainless steel, round section
Dimensions variable
Courtesy the artist and Regen Projects,
Los Angeles

pp. 74, 75
Guest, 2005
Blackened silver-plated stainless steel,
round section
Dimensions variable
Courtesy the artist and Regen Projects,
Los Angeles

pp. 10, 11
RWBs, 2005 *
Aluminum tubes, steel-and-nylon aircraft
cable, brass-and-chrome-plated steel padlocks,
natural and synthetic fabrics
82 × 117 × 117 inches (208.3 × 297.2 × 297 × cm)
San Francisco Museum of Modern Art;
Accessions Committee Fund purchase

pp. 66–67, 68–69
smile (after dark), 1996–2009
Porcelain, epoxy, ink
Smile: 16 $^{15}/_{16}$ × 37 $^{1}/_{8}$ × 7 $^{15}/_{16}$ inches
(42.9 × 94.3 × 20 cm)
Base: 30 × 38 × 38 inches (76.2 × 96.5 × 96.5 cm)
Private collection, New York

pp. 4, 25, 59, 60, 62
V (planchette), 2013
Mulberry paper, aluminum, pigmented
egg tempera
98 × 88 × 68 inches (248.9 × 223.5 × 172.7 cm)
Courtesy the artist and Regen Projects,
Los Angeles

pp. 80, 82, 88, 91
inflexion, 2013
Ceramic, epoxy, pigment
18 $^{1}/_{2}$ × 36 $^{3}/_{4}$ × 10 $^{1}/_{2}$ inches (47 × 93.3 × 26.7 cm)
Hammer Museum, Los Angeles; Purchase

p. 81
subduction, 2013
Ceramic, epoxy, pigment
20 $^{1}/_{2}$ × 34 $^{1}/_{2}$ × 7 $^{1}/_{2}$ inches (52.1 × 87.6 × 19.1 cm)
Private collection

pp. 80, 85, 86–87, 88, 91
xiii (caesura), 2014–15
Ceramic, epoxy, pigment
19 $^{1}/_{2}$ × 39 $^{1}/_{2}$ × 11 $^{1}/_{4}$ inches (49.5 × 100.3 × 28.6 cm)
Collection of Sonia Fernandes, Miami

pp. 80, 83, 84, 88, 91
vi (calefaction), 2015
Ceramic, glaze, stones, minerals
57 × 31 × 23 $^{1}/_{2}$ inches (144.8 × 78.7 × 56.7 cm)
Collection of Beth Rudin DeWoody

p. 39
x (calefaction), 2016 *
Ceramic, glaze, stones, minerals
21 $^{3}/_{4}$ × 32 $^{1}/_{2}$ × 8 $^{1}/_{2}$ inches (55.2 × 82.6 × 21.6 cm)
Courtesy the artist and Regen Projects,
Los Angeles

pp. 75, 76
boney ridge, 2016
Ceramic, glaze
30 × 19 × 23 inches (76.2 × 48.3 × 58.4 cm)
Courtesy the artist and Regen Projects,
Los Angeles

pp. 75, 77
cave, 2016
Ceramic, glaze
19 $^{5}/_{8}$ × 29 $^{1}/_{4}$ × 16 $^{1}/_{8}$ inches (49.8 × 74.3 × 41 cm)
Courtesy the artist and Regen Projects,
Los Angeles

pp. 80, 89, 91
Marthe, 2019
Ceramic, epoxy
22 × 35 × 11 inches (55.9 × 88.9 × 27.9 cm)
Courtesy the artist and Regen Projects,
Los Angeles

pp. 78, 79
xviii (caesura), 2019
Ceramic, glaze
21 $^{1}/_{2}$ × 37 × 11 $^{1}/_{2}$ inches (54.6 × 94 × 29.2 cm)
Courtesy the artist and Regen Projects,
Los Angeles

pp. 34, 67
You might have to live like a refugee, 2019
Patinated bronze
11 × 4 $^{1}/_{2}$ × 6 inches (27.94 × 11.43 × 15.24 cm)
Museum of Contemporary Art, Los Angeles;
Purchase with funds provided by the
Acquisition and Collection Committee

p. 45
Firestone, 2021
Ceramic, glaze
21 × 42 × 30 inches (53.4 × 106.7 × 76.2 cm)
Courtesy the artist and Regen Projects,
Los Angeles

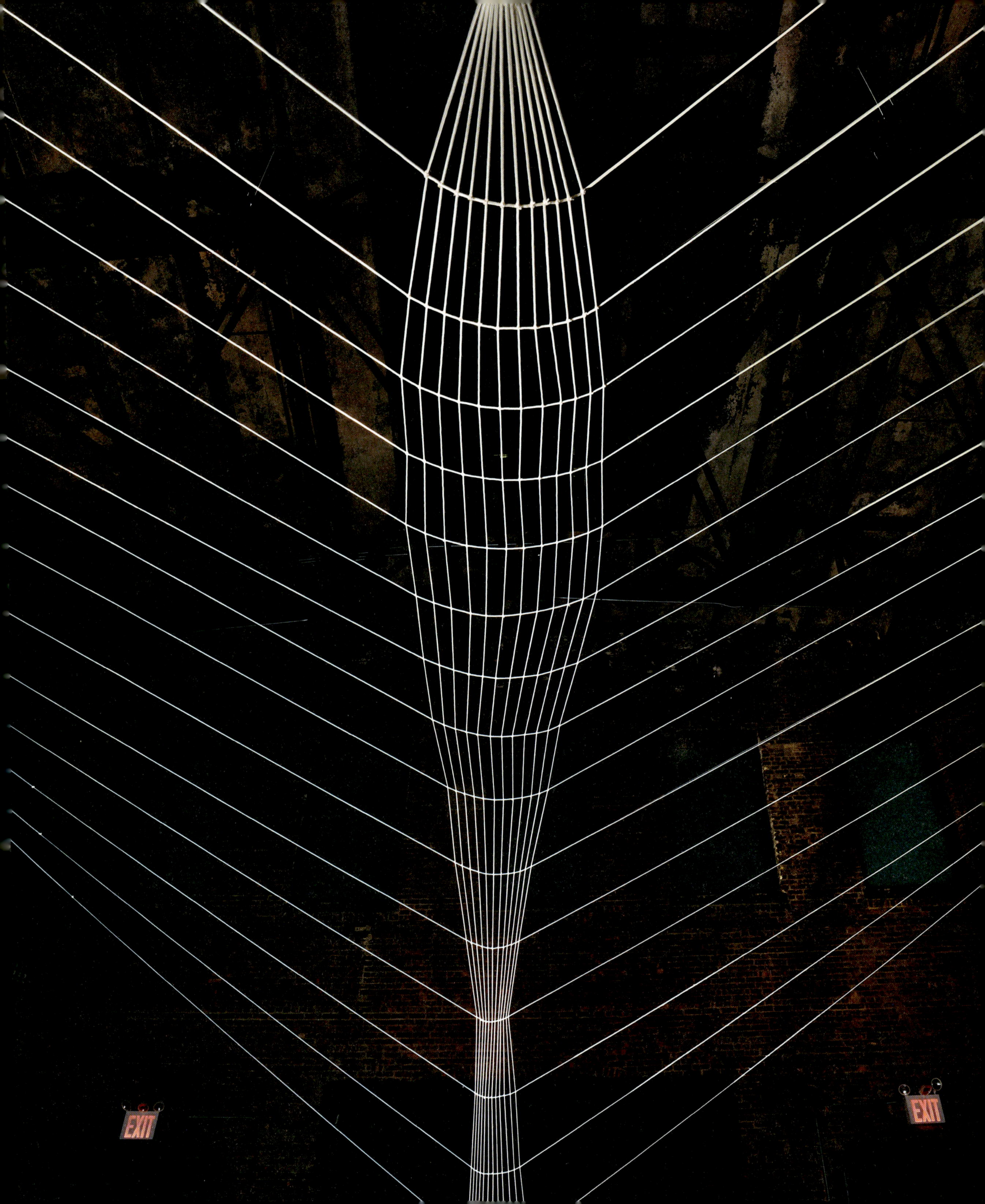
EXIT
EXIT

Contributors

CONNIE BUTLER is chief curator at the Hammer Museum at University of California, Los Angeles, where she has organized numerous exhibitions, including *Mark Bradford: Scorched Earth* (2015), *Marisa Merz: The Sky Is a Great Space* (2017), and, most recently, *Witch Hunt* (2021), in addition to the biennial of Los Angeles artists *Made in LA* (2014). She also cocurated *Adrian Piper: A Synthesis of Intuitions* (which opened at the Museum of Modern Art, New York, in April 2018, and at the Hammer in October 2018), *Andrea Fraser: Men on the Line* (2019), and *Lari Pittman: Declaration of Independence* (2019). From 2006 to 2013, she was the Robert Lehman Foundation Chief Curator of Drawings at the Museum of Modern Art, New York, where she cocurated the first major Lygia Clark retrospective in the United States, *Lygia Clark: The Abandonment of Art, 1948–1988* (2014), cocurated *On Line: Drawing through the Twentieth Century* (2010), and mounted *Marlene Dumas: Measuring Your Own Grave*, the first US retrospective of the artist's career. Butler also organized the groundbreaking survey *WACK! Art and the Feminist Revolution* (2007) at the Museum of Contemporary Art, Los Angeles, where she was curator from 1996 to 2006. Butler was the 2020 recipient of the CCS Bard College, Audrey Irmas Award for Curatorial Excellence.

MARY CERUTI is the executive director of the Walker Art Center in Minneapolis. Before joining the Walker in January 2019, she served for nineteen years as the executive director and chief curator of SculptureCenter in Long Island City, New York. Ceruti has organized dozens of solo and group exhibitions and curated special projects and commissions by more than fifty emerging and established artists, including Nairy Baghramian, Sanford Biggers, Monica Bonvicini, Alejandro Cesarco, Liz Glynn, Leslie Hewitt, Mike Kelley and Michael Smith, Katrín Sigurdardóttir, Xaviera Simmons, and Mika Tajima, among many others. Prior to joining SculptureCenter, Ceruti worked as an independent writer and curator with various arts institutions and agencies, including the San Francisco Arts Commission and Yerba Buena Center for the Arts. From 1992 to 1998, she served as the director of programs at San Francisco's Capp Street Project, an acclaimed international residency program, where she commissioned large-scale, site-specific installation projects by artists such as Janine Antoni, Mona Hatoum, Gary Hill, Cildo Meireles, and Fred Wilson.

LIZ LARNER is an artist who lives and works in Los Angeles. Larner's work has been the subject of numerous exhibitions throughout Europe and the United States. Survey exhibitions of her work have been held at the Kunsthaus Graz, Austria (2006); the Museum of Contemporary Art, Los Angeles (2001); the Museum of Applied Arts, Vienna (1998); and the Kunsthalle Basel, Switzerland (1997). In 2013, she created two versions of her sculpture *X* for the Edith O'Donnell Arts and Technology Building in Dallas. In 2016, the Aspen Art Museum, in Aspen, Colorado, hosted a solo exhibition of Larner's work, which surveyed her ceramics since 2011. Her work was included in the 2006 Whitney Biennial and *Helter Skelter: L.A. Art in the 1990s* (1992) at the Museum of Contemporary Art, Los Angeles. Organized by the Public Art Fund, Larner's sculpture *2001* was installed at Doris C. Freedman Plaza near the southeast entrance to Central Park in New York City in 2006.

CATHERINE LIU is professor of film and media studies at the University of California, Irvine, and is, most recently, the author of *Virtue Hoarders: The Case against the Professional Managerial Class* (University of Minnesota Press, 2021). She is also the author of two academic monographs, *Copying Machines: Taking Notes for the Automaton* (University of Minnesota Press, 2000) and *American Idyll: Academic Anti-Elitism as Cultural Critique* (University of Minnesota Press, 2000), as well as the novel *Oriental Girls Desire Romance* (Kaya Press, 1997). She is currently at work on a memoir called *Panda Gifts*. Liu contributed to Liza Featherstone's collection *False Choices: The Faux Feminism of Hillary Clinton* (Verso, 2016), and, as president of the Western Humanities Alliance, edited a special issue of the *Western Humanities Review* (2016) on the topic of prestige.

ARIANA REINES is a poet, an Obie-winning playwright, and a performing artist. Reines is the author of *A Sand Book* (Tin House, 2019), *The Origin of the World* (Semiotext[e] for the Whitney Biennial, 2014), *Mercury* (Fence, 2011), *Coeur de Lion* (Mal-o-mar, 2007; Fence, 2011), and *The Cow* (Alberta Prize, Fence, 2006). Her performance and theatrical works include *Mortal Kombat* (2015) and *Lorna* (2013), both in collaboration with Jim Fletcher; *The Origin of the World* (2013); and *Telephone* (2017). She has participated in such exhibitions as *Sperm Cult*, LAXART, Los Angeles (2018–19); *Pubic Space* (2016), a collaboration with Oscar Tuazon, Modern Art, London; and *Exhaust* (2016), Contemporary Art Tasmania, Australia. Reines is the translator of Charles Baudelaire's *My Heart Laid Bare* (Mal-o-mar, 2009), Jean-Luc Hennig's *The Little Black Book of Grisélidis Réal: Days and Nights of an Anarchist Whore* (Semiotext[e], 2009), and Tiqqun's *Preliminary Materials toward a Theory of the Young-Girl* (Semiotext[e], 2012). Reines has taught poetry at Columbia University, New York; New York University; Tufts University, Medford, Massachusetts; and Yale University, New Haven, Connecticut, among others. In 2009, she was named Roberta C. Holloway Lecturer in Poetry at the University of California, Berkeley. She is currently a student at Harvard Divinity School, Cambridge, Massachusetts. Her poetry, essays, and interviews have appeared in *Artforum*, *Art in America*, *The Believer*, *Bomb*, *Granta*, *Harper's*, *The Los Angeles Review of Books*, and *Poetry*, among other magazines and journals.

SCULPTURECENTER

44-19 Purves Street
Long Island City, NY 11101
+1 718 361 1750
www.sculpture-center.org

SculptureCenter leads the conversation on contemporary art by supporting artistic innovation and independent thought highlighting sculpture's specific potential to change the way we engage with the world. Positioning artists' work in larger cultural, historical, and aesthetic contexts, SculptureCenter discerns and interprets emerging ideas. Founded by artists in 1928, SculptureCenter provides an international forum that connects artists and audiences by presenting exhibitions, commissioning new work, and generating scholarship.

Generous support for *Liz Larner: Don't put it back like it was* at SculptureCenter is provided by the Girlfriend Fund, The Deborah Buck Foundation, Sarah Miller Meigs, and the Henry Moore Foundation.

Leadership support for SculptureCenter's exhibitions and programs is provided by Carol Bove, Jill and Peter Kraus, the Pollock-Krasner Foundation, Lee Elliott and Robert K. Elliott, Eleanor Heyman Propp, Jacques Louis Vidal, Miyoung Lee and Neil Simpkins, Robert Soros and Jamie Singer Soros, and Jane Hait and Justin Beal.

SculptureCenter's annual operating support is provided by the Elaine Graham Weitzen Foundation for Fine Arts; the Lambent Foundation Fund of Tides Foundation; the Anna-Maria and Stephen Kellen Foundation; A. Woodner Fund; Libby and Adrian Ellis; The Willem de Kooning Foundation; Teiger Foundation; Helen Frankenthaler Foundation; Cy Twombly Foundation; Arison Arts Foundation; public funds from the New York City Department of Cultural Affairs in partnership with the City Council; the New York State Council on the Arts with the support of the Office of the Governor and the New York State Legislature; and contributions from our Board of Trustees, Director's Circle, SC Ambassadors, and many generous individuals and friends.

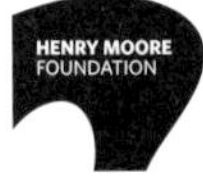
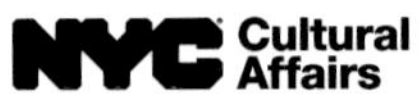
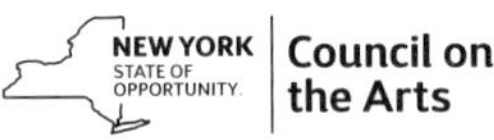